Decision Support for Crew Rostering in Public Transit

Lin Xie

Decision Support for Crew Rostering in Public Transit

Web-Based Optimization System for Cyclic and Non-Cyclic Rostering

Springer Gabler

Lin Xie
Paderborn, Germany

Dissertation University of Paderborn, Germany, 2014

ISBN 978-3-658-08166-9 ISBN 978-3-658-08167-6 (eBook)
DOI 10.1007/978-3-658-08167-6

Library of Congress Control Number: 2014955155

Springer Gabler

Printed on acid-free paper

Springer Gabler is a brand of Springer Fachmedien Wiesbaden
Springer Fachmedien Wiesbaden is part of Springer Science+Business Media
(www.springer.com)

The journey of a thousand miles
begins with one step.

Laozi

Acknowledgements

This thesis is a result of the research that I conducted as member of the *Graduate School on Applied Network Science* and the *Decision Support & Operations Research Lab (DS&OR Lab)* at the University of Paderborn. First, I am very grateful to my supervisor Prof. Dr. Leena Suhl for giving me the opportunity to work in her research group and for always being a positive advisor. Second, I would like to extend my grateful thanks to my co-supervisor Prof. Dr. Natalia Kliewer for her great advice and her insights. This PhD would definitely not have been possible without their valuable guidance and support.

I would like to thank the *Graduate School on Applied Network Science* for offering me a fellowship, and I would like to express my appreciation to the graduate school team, especially Prof. Dr. Michael Dellnitz and Dr. Mirko Hessel-von Molo.

Moreover, I would like to thank the Moveo Software GmbH, especially Martin Finker, Matthias Kramp, as well as Alvar Schulze of that company for the helpful comments and fruitful discussions. I want to thank Prof. Dr. Marco Dorigo for helping me to improve the writing about the implementation of the ant colony algorithms. Additionally, I would like to thank Jun. Prof. Dr. Kevin Tierney for his comments on this work.

Furthermore, I thoroughly enjoyed the friendly atmosphere and innumerable interesting discussions that I had with my colleagues at the working group. I would like to thank Stefan Kramkowski for great mentoring and continued encouragement, which gave me the knowledge that was necessary to complete this thesis. Moreover, I would like to thank Marc Naumann, Boris and Bastian Amberg, for their support and many fruitful discussions. Additionally, several students and student assistants made valuable contributions in the implementation of the optimization system. Among others I wish to thank Marius Merschformann, André Hottung, and Maxim Siemens.

Finally, I wish to sincerely thank my parents for their constant support and encouragement in everything I have done and I want to do in the future, even when moving halfway around the world. Most importantly, I thank my husband, Hanyi, for his constant support and patience throughout my PhD.

Lin Xię
Paderborn, March 2014

Contents

List of Figures

List of Tables

List of Algorithms

Part I.

Focus and Objectives

1. Introduction

The crew rostering problem is one of the main operational problems in public bus transit, and is being paid an increasing amount of attention in literature and in practice. There are several reasons for this. Firstly, there is increased competition in the public bus transit market due to deregulation. Secondly, the size of the problem has increased because of the fast growth of bus traffic; additionally, the complexity of labor rules has increased. Thirdly, crew costs mostly outweigh vehicle costs; moreover, it is important to consider the preferences of drivers when generating rosters. In this thesis, we do not minimize the number of drivers, but we do minimize the number of additional drivers as planned. Fourthly, the power of computers and algorithms has increased significantly.

The crew rostering problem involves defining a schedule for each driver for a planning period, such as two months. The objective is to reduce operational costs while maximizing the satisfaction of drivers. Traditionally, sequential approaches have been used to deal with this complex real-world problem. However, in this thesis we focus on several solution approaches to solve the crew rostering problem within one step, since sequential planning often produces some unassigned duties that require additional drivers to cover them, while some drivers do not get jobs on some days. The integrated approach reduces additional personnel/operational costs and improves the satisfaction of drivers compared with the sequential one.

Moreover, a web-based decision support system is developed in this thesis, which supports the planner in choosing a customized model as well as a suitable solution approach for solving the problem. Additionally, some functions are provided in that system to support drivers, controllers, and managers in bus companies.

The thesis comprises nine chapters within three parts, which are arranged as follows.

In the first part we present the background and scope of this thesis. The first chapter consists of this introduction. In Chapter 2 we outline both the practical and theoretical foundations of the thesis, while in Chapter 3 we review the existing models and solution approaches to cyclic and non-cyclic crew rostering problems. Based on this background of theory and literature, we define the scope and purpose of this thesis in Chapter 4.

The second part of this thesis includes the solution approaches we propose for solving the crew rostering problem. This includes Chapters 5, 6, and 7. Chapter 5 presents new exact approaches for cyclic and non-cyclic crew rostering problems in sequential and integrated manners. More specifically, we propose a novel multicommodity network flow model for both cyclic and non-cyclic crew rostering problems. In Chapter 6 a computational study using real-world instances is described in order to show that the integrated approach outperforms the sequential one. In Chapter 7 we compare different metaheuristics for solving the sub-problem to pick the best metaheuristic approach to tackle the integrated crew rostering problem. Furthermore, we propose a novel column generation approach to deal with sequential and integrated crew rostering problems (both cyclic and non-cyclic).

Moreover, we show how a multi-objective metaheuristic can be used to estimate the preferred weights of all objectives for a human planner. The chapter is concluded with a comparison of the solutions obtained by heuristics with the ones obtained by the exact optimization approach in Chapter 6.

In the third part of this thesis, we address the web-based decision support system in Chapter 8, which provides different functions for different users, i.e. planner, driver, manager, and controller. Finally, in Chapter 9 we conclude the thesis with a summary and some final remarks.

2. Background

In this chapter, we describe the planning process of a public transport company (Section 2.1) and, especially, the crew rostering problem in Section 2.2. In Section 2.3 we discuss some well-known optimization problems and techniques, which will be applied in the remainder of this thesis.

2.1. Planning Process of Public Bus Transport Companies

The complete planning process in public bus transit is very complex, therefore, it is traditionally divided into three phases: the strategic, tactical, and operational phases. Each phase can be further divided into several sub-problems, which are solved sequentially. The details about each phase can be found in Desaulniers & Hickman (2007). Figure 2.1, derived from Steinzen (2007), illustrates the relationship between the different problems in the planning process. In the *strategic planning* process, network design and line planning problems are solved based on a given original-destination (O-D) matrix. Each entry in the matrix represents the number of passengers travelling between any two points in the network by the time of day. The *network design* problem involves minimizing construction costs for determining the links in the network, while the line routes and their frequencies are determined in the *line planning* problem for the given transportation network. In both problems, the demand from passengers should be satisfied. The planning horizon of this stage is typically several years.

In the *tactical planning* process, line routes and their frequencies are given as input for the *timetabling* problem. In addition, the travel times along the lines and any potential layover times at stations are assumed to be known. The planning horizon for this problem is normally seasonal. In timetabling, timetables are determined, and a set of service trips with start and end locations and times are given for the next step: *operational planning.*

In *vehicle scheduling*, vehicles are assigned to service trips, resulting in vehicle blocks. After defining a sequence of tasks in each vehicle block, each task must be assigned to one duty that can be performed by a single anonymous crew (driver) for one day. This process is defined as *crew scheduling.* The planning horizon for both vehicle and crew scheduling is usually one day. Each generated duty must satisfy some work regulations. Examples of work regulations are maximum length of a duty, maximum driving time without a break in a duty, minimum break time during a duty, etc. Each generated duty has the following properties:

- a start time, when it begins,
- an end time, when it ends,
- the duration, which is equal to end time minus start time,

- a depot, where it begins and ends,
- a vehicle type it belongs to,
- the paid time, which is possibly not equal to the duration — this is calculated depending on the duty type,
- a shift type, which depends on its start and end time; for example, one duty beginning between 3 am and 6 am is an early shift, and
- the calendar date or day of the week that the duty belongs to.

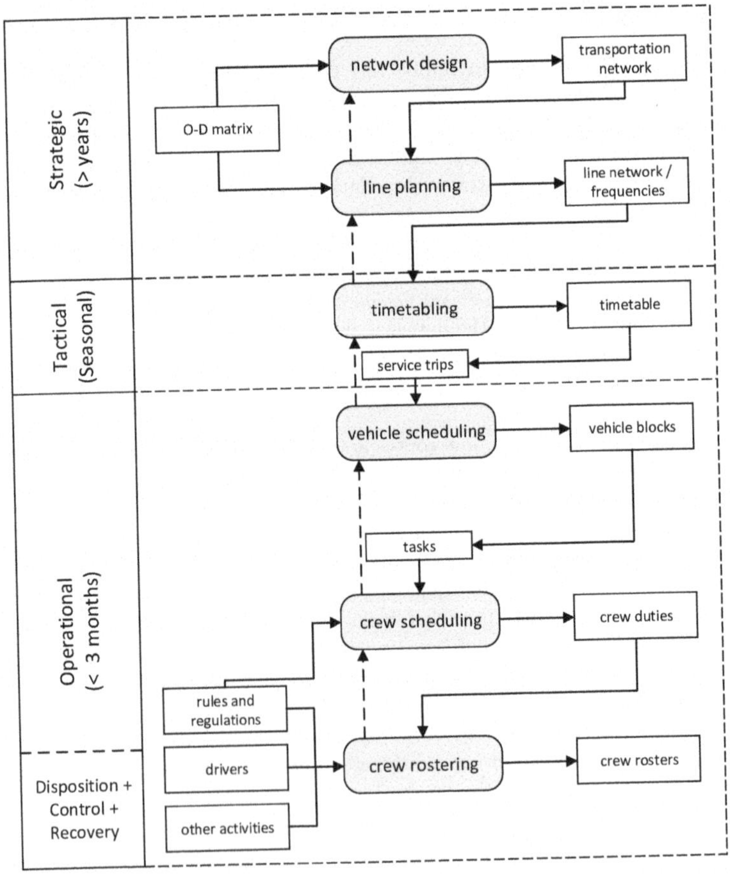

Figure 2.1. The sequential planning process in public bus transit.

The generated duties, as well as some other given activities, such as standbys, are required to be covered by drivers. Driver assignment occurs in the last step of the operational planning process in the *crew rostering problem*, which is solved on a monthly or semi-monthly basis. Law and labor union rules, as well as personal preferences of drivers, are considered during the assignment. The resulting schedule for each driver or group of drivers is called a *roster*. The details of the input information about activities and drivers, and the rules and regulations of the crew rostering problem, can be found in Section 2.2.1.

On the day of operations, the schedules generated in the operational planning process are seldom operated exactly as planned due to frequent disruptions, such as incidents, variations in traffic conditions, vehicle breakdowns, and absences of drivers. Therefore, operations control or recovery techniques should be applied for these problems.

Crew scheduling and rostering problems are becoming more and more important in the planning process at a public bus company since crew costs mostly outweigh vehicle costs (see Bodin et al. (1983) and Leuthardt (1998)). Compared with crew scheduling problems in the planning process, crew rostering has received much less attention in the academic literature. One reason is that most of the cost benefits can be achieved in crew scheduling for generating duties. However, the generation of duties in crew scheduling does not include any information about drivers (anonymous duties). The assumption made in solving this problem is that all crews are equal. Therefore, it causes difficulties generating schedules of drivers in the crew rostering problem, since the drivers are individual people with different qualifications and preferences. It is possible that some duties cannot be covered on some days, while some drivers do not get any jobs on some other days. In crew rostering, the minimization of operational costs is still important; moreover, drivers' preferences are considered as well. Rosters which are generated by considering the desires of drivers bring higher acceptance than rosters that ignore individual wishes (see Hanne et al. (2009)). That means fewer exchanges, and less absence in operational days. Therefore, fewer recovery activities are expected, which implies lower operational costs. Besides that, the even distribution of workload is considered an important objective, which induces fewer payments for overtimes. For these reasons, the crew rostering problem becomes very difficult to solve, and more complex when dealing with large real-world problems.

2.2. Crew Rostering Problem

In this section, we first give details about the input information for solving the crew rostering problem. After a definition of cyclic and non-cyclic crew rostering problems, a short description of sequential and integrated approaches follows.

2.2.1. Input Information

Different kinds of input information for solving the crew rostering problem, including information on duties, other activities, drivers, and rules and regulations, are shown below.

Activities

Not only must the duties and shifts, which are described in Section 2.1, be assigned to drivers, but also some other activities, such as standbys, days off, leaves, and training periods. *Days off* consist of a couple of rest days between working days. *Standby* activities are planned to cover the absences of drivers, while *leaves* are vacations. The training periods and leaves are preassigned and fixed for each driver and cannot be changed in the optimization. Their distribution is decided by bus companies and drivers.

Driver information

The data about drivers includes not only the depot (where a driver begins and ends) and vehicle types (depending on the capacity, speed, or equipment of each vehicle), but also the number of days off, the target working hours for the current planning period, the target number of standby activities, and the required training periods and leaves. All of these depend on the work contracts and the drivers' current work-accounts. The work-account of each driver includes their current overtime and their number of days off from previous periods. It describes the driver's credit, e.g. a driver with more overtime in previous periods can get more jobs with shorter working hours in order to reduce overtimes gradually. Additionally, the drivers can express their preferences, including their daily desired activities and their possible combination of activities. The daily desires of a driver mean that the driver wishes to get one activity on one day, while the possible combination of activities can be, for instance, similar shifts within a working week, and/or not to get an early shift after a day off. Hanne et al. (2009) explain the importance of considering employees' preferences in scheduling their working time; in particular, the advantages of assigning flexible working times to employees. They mention that the employees can better manage their work-life balances, which brings increased morale and reduced absenteeism. That means fewer exchanges and less absence in operational days, which implies lower operational costs, since fewer recovery activities are expected. Moreover, they assume that "happy staff means happy customers". Better services are expected.

Rules and regulations

The rules and regulations can be labor rules, some of which are imposed by the bus company, and others are due to the agreement between the bus company and employee unions. Every bus company can also define its own internal constraints that are stricter than those required by law. We consider three types of rules: horizontal rules, vertical rules, and quality rules. Horizontal rules are rules that depend only on one roster, while vertical rules combine the information among all rosters. Quality rules are horizontal rules — without these rules the generated rosters are still legal — but they affect the quality of the rosters. Compared with the rules in the airline sector discussed in Kohl & Karisch (2004), we have more complex horizontal rules to generate a feasible roster, but less complex vertical rules (since drivers work mostly alone).

Horizontal rules These rules consist of compatibility, working block, and days off block. The *incompatible* connections of activities are gathered in a list of forbidden sequences according to, for example, the working regulations. It is forbidden to follow an early shift with a late shift because of the short rest time between them. The forbidden sequences are provided by bus companies, and it is possible that a combination of activities that drivers find undesirable is regarded as forbidden as well. The length of forbidden sequences is not limited to two; for instance, a late shift one day before a standby and an early shift one day later may be forbidden if they appear simultaneously on three consecutive days. Additionally, two other situations are also considered: *double-off* is defined as at least two consecutive days off, while a *single-off* is a single day off between two work-related activities. Many of the restrictions in this class can be implicitly considered during the network generation (see Section 5.1). The maximum consecutive numbers of working days and days off (*working/days off block*) are restricted based on working regulations. For example, the number of consecutive working days is limited to five, while the number of consecutive days off is restricted to three.

Vertical rules These rules consider restricted resources among all rosters. Not only are the limits on the assignment of the amount of duty/shift during each day considered, but also the limits on the available numbers of days off and standbys. The limit depends on the number of drivers and duties available on that day. The upper bound can be easily computed before optimization.

The horizontal and vertical rules described above are formulated as hard constraints in Section 5.2, while the following quality rules are formulated as soft constraints. They can be suspended by applying specific penalty costs in the objective to restrict the number of violations.

Quality rules These rules include preferences of the bus company and drivers, real operational costs, fairness among all drivers, and the robustness of the rosters.

Preferences: In this category, the preferences of the bus company as well as of the drivers are considered. As mentioned before, the daily desired activities and the possible combination of activities are given by drivers. Some alternatives can be provided by the bus company if the primary desires of the drivers cannot be satisfied. The number of alternatives and the penalty costs resulting from them can vary from one bus company to another (see Example 1).

Example 1. Bus companies A and B have four types of shifts (early1, early2, midday, late shift). Early2 (ES2) begins later than early1 (ES1) but earlier than midday. In both bus companies, 50% of drivers want to get early shifts (regardless of early1 or early2) and 40% of them want to get midday shifts (MS). Late shifts are unpopular. However, some drivers are required to cover the late shifts. Company A wants to maximize the number of satisfied drivers, while company B wants to minimize the total distance between the desired and assigned shifts for all drivers. Figure 2.2 shows the different functions for selecting alternatives (i.e. ES1, ES2, and MS) to cover late shifts. Company A will select the function on the left to make sure most of the drivers desiring MS get their wish fulfilled, while company B will select the function on the right to guarantee that most of late shifts are carried by the drivers desiring MS.

Additionally, a linear function as shown in Day & Ryan (1997) is also possible for calculating the penalty costs of alternatives. Due to the limited number of drivers that may simultaneously take a day off, some desired days off (on weekends) can not be satisfied, but can be moved to within a couple of days earlier or later. These are called *moved days off* and *moved days off on weekends.* The numbers of these are limited due to their unpopularity. The number of single-off activities is often restricted due to drivers' preferences. The distance between two double-off activities is defined in the company rules to make sure, for example, that a driver gets at least two doubles-offs within 16 days.

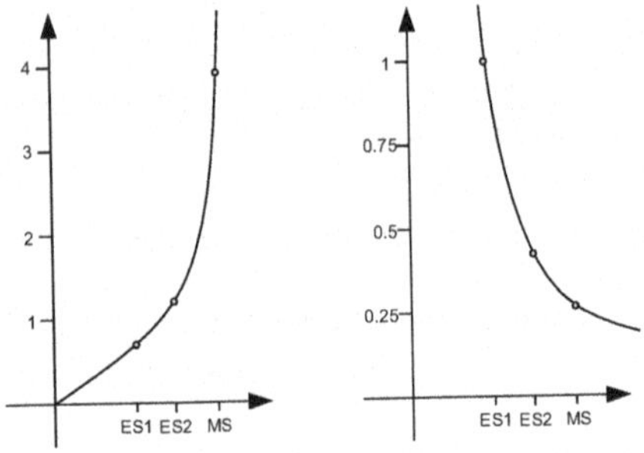

Figure 2.2. An example of different functions of the penalty costs for the alternatives of late shifts.

Real costs: The insufficient assignment of standbys and duties/shifts might cause additional personnel costs or additional costs for the overtimes of all planned drivers. The same is true for open days, on which drivers do not get any activities. Therefore, the number of open days should be minimized. An additional situation that should be avoided is one where, for example, some drivers work overtime while others work substantially less than the regular working time. This can be avoided by minimizing the maximum overtime for all drivers, which results in less payment for overtime.

Fairness: Besides the above mentioned fair distribution of working times, insufficient days off for each driver will impact the fairness of the days off distribution for all drivers. Moreover, the distribution of unpopular activities is embedded in the preferences of drivers (i.e. the desirability of an activity on one particular day).

Robustness: Sometimes in operational days disruptions occur, such as illness. Therefore, a set of standbys should be planned to cover for absences, but the number of these should be minimized to avoid unused standbys. In this work, the number of standbys per day is defined by the bus company, based on experience. The optimal planning of the assignment of standbys based on historical statistics of illness is discussed in Xie et al. (2012b).

Moreover, we need to consider the previous planning period, which is assumed to be fixed for the current planning period. Some other fixed activities are also considered in the current planning period, such as a training period and annual leave. We assume that all fixed activities comply with the horizontal and vertical rules. However, the horizontal rules should be checked between fixed and unfixed activities. The details will be shown in Section 5.1 together with the example shown in Figure 2.4 in the next sub-section.

2.2.2. Cyclic and Non-Cyclic Crew Rostering

There are several ways to generate a roster. A *cyclic roster* is generated for a group of drivers who have the same qualifications and similar preferences. Such a roster includes several rows of duties from Monday to Sunday. The number of rows is equal to the number of drivers in the group. All drivers within a group use the same roster but begin with different rows. An example is shown in Figure 2.3, in which different activities, ES (early shift), MS (midday shift), LS (late shift), and F (day off), are assigned to two drivers.

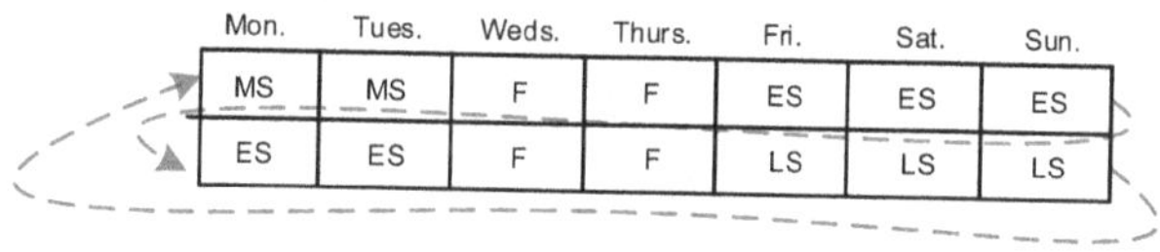

Figure 2.3. An example of a cyclic roster.

In cyclic rostering, the number of days in the planning period is equal to the number of drivers multiplied by seven. Each week is assigned to each driver in such a way that each weekly pattern is worked in parallel with a person. Cyclic rostering is a rather simple way to generate rosters, because instead of generating a roster for each driver a roster is generated for a group of drivers. Furthermore, the roster is fair since drivers within a group have the same duties, including unpopular duties, and the days off and weekends off are evenly distributed. However, this fairness is only achieved if absences and other occurrences do not arise in real life, otherwise the cycles are destroyed. Moreover, a cyclic roster considers duties from days of the week, not calendar dates. Therefore, it is not flexible enough to respond to changes in traffic, such as an increase in traffic on holidays. Moreover, a new employee can not be easily added to an existing group, since the planning horizon will be changed and one more week must be planned.

The shortcomings of cyclic rostering can be avoided if an individual roster is generated for each driver within a given time period (e.g. two months). Such a *non-cyclic roster* may consider wishes with respect to a special single day off or vacation periods. Non-cyclic rostering provides more freedom to take holidays and special events into account. Figure 2.4 shows an example of a two-week, non-cyclic roster for two drivers, in which the first five days are in the previous period. As mentioned before, the horizontal rules between fixed and unfixed activities must be enforced. We assume that the maximum consecutive number of working days is restricted to five. The five fixed activities in the last period for driver $d2$ are work-related activities. Therefore, a day off activity should be assigned to the first day of the planning period (day 6 in the example). Additionally, we assume the maximum length of a days-off period is three days. A working day is therefore required for $d1$ on day 6. We assume that the distance between two double-off activities from the previous period to the current one is defined to be seven. The last double-off in the previous period of $d1$ is on 5th day, and a double-off is required within the next seven days, such as on days 10 and 11. Such restrictions have been used to reduce the complexity of our network design introduced in Section 5.1. Note that the previous period is implicitly considered in the cyclic roster, if the roster is not disrupted.

	Day1	Day2	Day3	Day4	Day5	Day6	Day7	Day8	Day9.	Day10	Day11	Day12	Day13	Day14
d1	MS	MS	F	F	F	ES	ES	ES	ES	F	F	LS	LS	LS
d2	ES	ES	MS	MS	MS	F	F	MS	MS	MS	MS	ES	F	F

Figure 2.4. An example of a non-cyclic roster.

The non-cyclic rostering approach is widely used in the airline industry, especially in Europe (see Kohl & Karisch (2004), Cappanera & Gallo (2004) and Maenhout & Vanhoucke (2010)). In recent years, this way of generating rosters has also been investigated in railways (see De Pont (2006) and Hanne et al. (2009)). In *bidline rostering*, which is used mostly in North American airlines, a roster is generated subsequently for each individual crew member in decreasing order of seniority in the crew rank (see Kohl & Karisch (2004) for an overview). In the rest of this thesis, the cyclic crew rostering is called CCR and non-cyclic crew rostering NCCR.

The crew rostering problem in transportation is different from the ones in other applications, since it deals with trips/flights. The rostering of call centers, police services, or airport ground staffs deals with flexible demand, while the rostering of nurses and ambulance services deals with shift-based demand. More details can be found in Ernst et al. (2004).

2.2.3. Sequential vs. Integrated Approach

The crew rostering problem is usually divided into several sequential sub-problems due to its high complexity (see Moz & Pato (2007) for the nurse rostering problem). A roster is considered as a schedule of combinations of work-related activities (standby, shift/duty) and day off activities (single-off, double-off). The sub-problems are *days off scheduling* (the optimal distribution of days off by considering fair distribution of days off), *shift assignment* (the allocation of shifts to drivers), and *duty sequencing* (according to the result of shift assignment, duties are assigned to drivers). The problem of integrated days off scheduling and shift assignment is named *rota scheduling* in Emden-Weinert et al. (2000) and Xie et al. (2012b). In this thesis, the integrated shift assignment and duty sequencing problem is called *shift-duty assignment*.

In order to understand the drawbacks of the sequential crew rostering problems, for example the approach we use in this thesis, with rota scheduling first and duty sequencing second, two examples will be shown below. An *early shift* (ES) means a duty begins between 0:01 am and 11:59 am, while a duty with the *midday shift* (MS) begins between 12:00 noon and 8:59 pm. Each *late shift* (LS) duty begins between 9:00 pm and 12:00 midnight. The minimum rest period is defined as 12 hours.

Example 2. We assume that the sequence (MS, ES) is selected in the rota scheduling problem. The rush hours in the morning are, for example, between 6:00 and 8:00 am, and in the evening between 4:00 and 7:00 pm. However, a duty with MS that begins at 3:00 pm (shortly before rush hour in the evening) and ends at 10:00 pm cannot be followed by any duties in the next day with ES, which begins before 10:00 am. That means, if we allow the sequence (MS, ES) in the rota scheduling problem, however, many MS duties that begin after the rush hour in the evening can not be followed by any ES during the rush hour in the morning. Therefore, the selected sequences (MS, ES) in the rota scheduling can not be assigned by most duties in duty sequencing. This results in many empty days for the employees, and more duties remain unassigned. However, some of them could be assigned, if we consider the duties in rota scheduling. Such an approach is called *integrated crew rostering.*

Example 3. We assume that the sequence (LS, MS) is forbidden in the rota scheduling problem, due to violating overnight rest time. However, some duties of LS, such as ending after 4:00 am, can take the duties of MS on the day beginning after 4:00 pm. Therefore, they are not needed in the list of forbidden sequences of shifts. The check for a violation can occur directly with the duties in the integrated crew rostering.

In order to avoid the drawbacks of the sequential approach in practice, it is standard practice to define more and more shift types, such as defining 14 shift types instead of 4. However, this brings more complexity, and some duties are still left unassigned. Details will be shown in the results chapter (see Chapter 6).

2.3. Mathematical Background

The crew rostering problem addressed in this thesis is often formulated using mathematical optimization models. In this work the crew rostering problem is formulated as a mixed-integer problem and a network flow problem. Therefore, the necessary background of the both problems is provided, including the relevant combinatorial optimization techniques.

2.3.1. Linear and Mixed-Integer Programming

A *mixed-integer program* (MIP) is formulated as follows.

$$\min \quad c^T x \tag{2.1}$$
$$s.t. \quad Ax \geq b \tag{2.2}$$
$$x_i \in \mathbb{Z}, \forall i \in \mathcal{I} \tag{2.3}$$
$$x_j \in \mathbb{R}, \forall j \notin \mathcal{I} \tag{2.4}$$

where x is a vector of n decision variables, while $c \in \mathbb{R}^n$ is a vector of objective coefficients. Let $b \in \mathbb{R}^m$ be a vector of upper bounds on constraints. A is defined as an $m \times n$ matrix of constraint coefficients. The set $\mathcal{I}$ defines the set of variables that take integer values. If $\mathcal{I} = \emptyset$, then the problem is a *linear program* (LP). However, if $\mathcal{I} = \{1, 2, ..., n\}$, then the problem is an *integer program* (IP). A special case, a 0-1 integer program, is called a *binary program.* Unlike LPs, which can be solved in polynomial time, MIPs and IPs are

NP-hard (see Wolsey (1998)). There are several efficient algorithms to solve LP problems, such as the interior point method described in Karmarkar (1984), and the simplex method described in Dantzig et al. (1955).

The crew rostering problem in this thesis is formulated as an MIP problem (see Section 5). Solution approaches for MIPs are well studied; a number of solvers are commercially available to solve MIPs, such as the ones used in this thesis, the CPLEX and Guorbi solvers (see IBM Corporation (2014) and Gurobi Optimization (2014)).

2.3.2. Network Flow Problem

A network is defined as an acyclic graph with only one source and sink. Network flow problems are widely used in operations research, which use the models and methods of optimization together with graph theory. In this section two related network flow problems are described, which will be used in the remainder of the thesis, namely the minimum cost flow, and multicommodity cost flow problems.

Minimum cost flow problem The *minimum cost flow problem* (MCFP) is a very fundamental network flow problem, since many other well-known network problems are special cases of this problem, such as the multicommodity flow problem, which will be described later in this subsection. The MCFP is also known as the transshipment problem. The goal of this problem is to find a minimum cost shipment of one commodity through a network, such that the demands at certain nodes are satisfied from available supplies at other nodes (see Ahuja et al. (1993)).

Define $\mathcal{G}$=($\mathcal{N}$,$\mathcal{A}$) as a directed graph with $\mathcal{N}$ as the set of nodes and $\mathcal{A}$ as the set of directed arcs. Let c_{ij} be the cost per unit flow on the arc $(i,j) \in \mathcal{A}$. Moreover, the cost varies linearly with the amount of flow. Besides that, an integer upper and lower bound u_{ij} and l_{ij} on the amount of flow are defined for each arc $(i,j) \in \mathcal{A}$. For each node $i \in \mathcal{N}$ an integer b_i is referred to as the property of this node; if b_i is positive or negative, then node i is a supply or demand node, respectively. Otherwise, node i is a transshipment node. Let a decision variable x_{ij} be the amount of flow on arc $(i,j) \in \mathcal{A}$. The mathematical model is formulated as follows.

$$\min \sum_{(i,j)\in\mathcal{A}} c_{ij}x_{ij} \tag{2.5}$$

$$s.t. \quad \sum_{j:(i,j)\in\mathcal{A}} x_{ij} - \sum_{j:(j,i)\in\mathcal{A}} x_{ji} = b_i \quad \forall i \in \mathcal{N} \tag{2.6}$$

$$l_{ij} \leq x_{ij} \leq u_{ij} \quad \forall (i,j) \in \mathcal{A} \tag{2.7}$$

The objective function (2.5) minimizes the total costs such that the total outflow minus the total inflow in each node is equal to its demand/supply (see constraints (2.6)). Furthermore, the constraint set (2.7) indicates that the flow on each arc is between the lower and upper bounds of that arc. The constraint set (2.6) is also called the *flow conservation/required flow* constraint while the constraint set (2.7) is a *flow capacity* constraint.

Note that supplies, demands and bounds are integral; each solution is therefore integral, although the decision variables are not defined as integral. Since the constraint matrix is totally unimodular (see Nemhauser & Wolsey (1988)), solving MCFPs as linear programs always results in an integral solution. Therefore, this problem can be solved with efficient LP-methods in polynomial time.

The *shortest path problem* is a special case of MCFP — the goal of this problem is to find a path with minimum cost from a source s to a sink t in the network. The objective function of MCFP (2.5) remains for the shortest path problem. The constraints (2.6) and (2.7) change to (2.8) and (2.9), such that the shortest path problem sends the unit flow from s to t.

$$\sum_{j:(i,j)\in\mathcal{A}} x_{ij} - \sum_{j:(j,i)\in\mathcal{A}} x_{ji} = 0 \quad \forall i \in \mathcal{N} \setminus \{s,t\} \tag{2.8}$$

$$\sum_{j:(s,j)\in\mathcal{A}} x_{sj} = 1$$

$$\sum_{j:(j,t)\in\mathcal{A}} x_{jt} = 1$$

$$x_{ij} \in \{0,1\} \quad \forall (i,j) \in \mathcal{A} \tag{2.9}$$

The *resource constrained shortest path problem* is an extension of the shortest path problem. It aims to find the minimum cost path from a source s to a sink t while constraints on resource consumption are considered. Therefore, the objective function of this problem remains the same as for the shortest path problem. The model of the shortest path problem is extended with the set of resources $\mathcal{R}$. Additionally, let d_{ij}^r denote the positive resource consumption for each resource $r \in \mathcal{R}$ of each arc $(i,j) \in \mathcal{A}$. The consumption of resource $r \in \mathcal{R}$ along a path p is represented as the sum of the consumptions of all arcs in this path. Besides the constraints for the shortest path problem, an additional constraint (2.10) should be held for all resources $r \in \mathcal{R}$ to make sure that the found path is resource-feasible.

$$l_{ij} \leq d_{ij}^r x_{ij} \leq u_{ij} \quad \forall (i,j) \in \mathcal{A} \tag{2.10}$$

Irnich & Desaulniers (2005) show an extensive survey on shortest path problems with resource constraints. This problem is NP-complete even for the case of one resource (see Handler & Zang (1980)). Dynamic programming (see Ahuja et al. (1993)), Lagrangian relaxation (see Irnich & Desaulniers (2005)), and constraint programming (see Marriott & Stuckey (1998)) are the well-known methods for solving this problem.

In this thesis, a resource constrained shortest path problem is formulated to solve a pricing problem in column generation, which will be described later in this section. The resources in our problem represent, for example, a restricted number of consecutive work-related days.

Multicommodity flow problem The *multicommodity flow problem* is not composed of a single commodity as is the case with MCFP, but several commodities instead. Therefore, it is seen as an extension of MCFP. Each commodity has its own origin and destination, and it has a separate flow conservation constraint at each node, whereas all commodities share the same flow capacity constraint at each arc.

The mathematical model of MCFP can be extended with $\mathcal{K}$ as the set of commodities and the flow variables x_{ij}^k of all arcs $(i,j) \in \mathcal{A}$, supply/demand b_i^k of all $i \in \mathcal{N}$, costs c_{ij}^k and flow capacities l_{ij}^k and u_{ij}^k of all arcs $(i,j) \in \mathcal{A}$ are separated for each commodity $k \in \mathcal{K}$. Additionally, let U_{ij} be the upper bound for all commodities at arc $(i,j) \in \mathcal{A}$. The constraint set (2.11) indicates the limited capacity of each arc through different commodities. Unlike the minimum cost flow problem, the constraint set (2.12) should be added to obtain an integral solution.

$$\min \sum_{k \in \mathcal{K},(i,j) \in \mathcal{A}} c_{ij}^k x_{ij}^k \tag{2.5a}$$

$$s.t. \quad \sum_{j:(i,j) \in \mathcal{A}} x_{ij}^k - \sum_{j:(j,i) \in \mathcal{A}} x_{ji}^k = b_i^k \quad \forall i \in \mathcal{N}, k \in \mathcal{K} \tag{2.6a}$$

$$l_{ij}^k \leq x_{ij}^k \leq u_{ij}^k \quad \forall (i,j) \in \mathcal{A}, k \in \mathcal{K} \tag{2.7a}$$

$$\sum_{k \in \mathcal{K}} x_{ij}^k \leq U_{ij} \quad \forall (i,j) \in \mathcal{A} \tag{2.11}$$

$$x_{ij}^k \in \mathbb{N} \quad \forall (i,j) \in \mathcal{A}, k \in \mathcal{K} \tag{2.12}$$

The integral multicommodity flow problem is NP-hard if there are at least two commodities (see Garey & Johnson (1979)), while the single commodity flow (minimum cost flow) problem can be solved in polynomial time.

In this thesis, the crew rostering problem is formulated as a multicommodity flow MIP problem, where each network layer (commodity) represents the feasible activities (nodes) and combinations of them (arcs) for a driver.

2.3.3. Dantzig-Wolfe Decomposition and Column Generation

We restate the MIP problem in Section 2.3.1 as the following LP problem, where the integer restrictions on variables are relaxed (LP relaxation). The obtained solution is considered as a lower bound of the original MIP problem. Moreover, the matrix A is split into two matrices B and D, which are defined as an $m1 \times n$ matrix and an $m2 \times n$ matrix of constraint coefficients, where $m = m1 + m2$. The main idea of the Dantzig-Wolfe decomposition is to decompose the constraint set (2.2) into two sets of constraints, i.e. $Bx \geq d$ and $Dx \geq e$, where the LP over the $Dx \geq e$ can be easier to optimize than the original problem.

$$\min \quad c^T x \tag{2.1}$$

$$s.t. \quad Bx \geq d \tag{2.2a}$$

$$Dx \geq e \tag{2.2b}$$

$$x \geq 0 \tag{2.13}$$

where x is a vector of n decision variables, while $c \in \mathbb{R}^n$ is a vector of objective coefficients. Let $d \in \mathbb{R}^{m1}$ and $e \in \mathbb{R}^{m2}$ be a vector of upper bounds on constraints. Moreover, the constraints $Dx \geq e$ are replaced with variables in the polyhedron X.

$$\min \quad c^T x \tag{2.1}$$

$$s.t. \quad Bx \geq d \tag{2.2a}$$

$$x \in X \tag{2.14}$$

where $X = \{x \in \mathbb{R}^n | Dx \geq e, x \geq 0\}$, and the polyhedron X is non-empty and contains a finite number of elements. We assume that X is bounded. Therefore, as the simplified case of the Minkowski theorem shows (see Nemhauser and Wolsey, 1998), each point $x \in X$ can be written as a convex combination of the extreme points in X. Let $x^1, ..., x^t$ be the extreme points of X. The convex hull $conv(X)$ is defined as follows.

$$conv(X) := \{x | x = \sum_{i=1}^{t} \lambda_i x^i, \ \sum_{i=1}^{t} \lambda_i = 1, \ \ \lambda_i \geq 0, i = 1, ..., t\} \tag{2.15}$$

It is well known that the optimal objective value remains if X is replaced with the convex hull $conv(X)$. Therefore, our LP can be replaced with the following formulation, which is called the *master problem* (MP). We define $c_i := c^T x^i$ and $b^i := Bx^i$.

$$\min \quad \sum_{i=1}^{t} c_i \lambda_i \tag{2.16}$$

$$s.t. \quad \sum_{i=1}^{t} b^i \lambda_i \geq d \tag{2.17}$$

$$\sum_{i=1}^{t} \lambda_i = 1 \tag{2.18}$$

$$\lambda_i \geq 0 \ \ \forall i \in \{1, ..., t\} \tag{2.19}$$

Recall that B and D in the original LP have $m1$ and $m2$ rows, respectively. Instead of generating $m1 + m2$ rows, the MP of Danzig-Wolfe decomposition generates $m1 + 1$ rows. However, the MP considers each extreme point as a variable. This may result in too many variables to solve the LP, even more than in the original problem. It is worth noting that as most of the variables will be non-basic and assumed to have a value of zero in the optimal solution, only a subset of variables need to be considered while solving the problem. Therefore, only the variables that have the potential to improve the objective function are generated on the fly. This efficient algorithm for solving large LPs is called *column generation* (CG). The set τ is defined as a small subset of $\{1, ..., t\}$ and only the variables of this set are considered in the master problem (see constraint set (2.19a)), this is called the *restricted master problem* (RMP).

$$\min \quad \sum_{i \in \tau} c_i \lambda_i \tag{2.16}$$

$$s.t. \quad \sum_{i \in \tau} b^i \lambda_i \geq d \tag{2.17}$$

$$\sum_{i \in \tau} \lambda_i = 1 \tag{2.18}$$

$$\lambda_i \geq 0 \quad \forall i \in \tau \tag{2.19a}$$

The reduced cost of λ_i is calculated as $c_i - u_1^T b^i - u_2$, where (u_1, u_2) is the set of optimal dual multipliers related to the constraints (2.17) and (2.18), respectively. If there is no variable in the RMP with the negative reduced cost, then the CG terminates, and the optimal solution to the RMP is found. Algorithm 2.1 shows the process used in this method.

Another sub-problem of column generation is the pricing problem, which is used to identify a new variable, based on the reduced costs of the potential new variables calculated in the RMP. The variable with the smallest negative reduced cost will be priced out and added to the RMP. The objective coefficients of the pricing problem are the reduced costs of the potential new variables with respect to the current dual variables. The pricing problem here is a single pricing, which produces one variable with least negative reduced cost per iteration. Desrochers & Soumis (1989) propose multiple pricing, which produces several variables with negative reduced costs per iteration. This multiple pricing was shown to accelerate the convergence of the column generation method.

Algorithm 2.1: Column Generation

Step 1: **Initialization**
Choose a feabile initial set of columns τ
Step 2: **Solve RMP**
Solve RMP and get an optimal set of dual multipliers (u_1, u_2)
Step 3: **Solve pricing problem**
Solve pricing problem and get the $c_j = min\{c_i - u_1^T b^i - u_2 : i \in \tau\}$
The CG terminates if $c_j \geq 0$
Step 4: **Add column to RMP**
Add the column $\begin{bmatrix} c_j \\ 1 \end{bmatrix}$ to the RMP, update $\tau := \tau \cup \{j\}$
Goto Step 2

In the process of column generation, the solution to the RMP does not satisfy the integrality constraints. Integer solutions can be obtained by integrating the column generation algorithm with the branch-and-bound method (see Section 2.3.4). If the column generation algorithm is used to solve the LP relaxation of problems during branch-and-bound, the algorithm is called *branch-and-price.* More discussion on IP column generation can be found in Barnhart et al. (1998).

In many cases, the master problem is formulated as a set partitioning, covering or packing problem. Instead of that, we formulate the master problem as a multicommodity network flow problem. The reasons for that can be found in Sections 3 and 7. Moreover, as mentioned before, the pricing problem is formulated as a resource constrained shortest path problem.

2.3.4. Branch-and-Bound

Branch-and-bound is an exact solution method for MIPs. This approach is based on the divide-and-conquer principle (see Wolsey (1998)). The basic idea is to divide the problem into some smaller problems which are easier to solve rather than solving the original problem directly. After the smaller problems have been solved, information about their solutions is put together to solve the original problem. The method begins with solving a relaxation of the original MIP, usually an *LP relaxation*, i.e. the integer restrictions on decision variables are relaxed. If the solution to the relaxed problem is not feasible in the original problem, the relaxed problem is divided into two or more parts. This process is called *branching.* A search tree is obtained to represent each part as a node. The root of the tree is the original solution space. The lower bound for a minimization problem is obtained by the relaxation of each node. Algorithm 2.2 shows the outline of the method. The next node in the search tree is selected based on some fundamental search strategies, such as depth-first search, breadth-first search and best-first search (see Wolsey (1998)). After that the node n is removed from $\mathcal{N}$. After the LP relaxation of the problem has been solved, the bounding is evaluated.

Bounding differentiates the branch-and-bound approach from the complete enumeration approach, which enumerates all feasible solutions and then finds the optimal solution. But this complete enumeration approach is impractical for most real-life problems, because of their size. Bounding is used to prune nodes of the search that cannot contain a solution better than the best solution found so far. This prevents unnecessary exploration of the solution space, through eliminating nodes. Bounding includes three steps. First, if no solution can be found, the node is pruned by infeasibility. Second, if the dual value is better than the existing best one, then it is stored for bounding. Furthermore, if the solution to the relaxed problem is feasible, then the corresponding node is pruned due to optimality.

2.3.5. Metaheuristics

The following definition of "metaheuristic" is referred to in Glover & Laguna (1997).

> A metaheuristic is a master strategy that guides and modifies other heuristics to produce solutions beyond those that are normally generated in a quest for local optimality. The heuristics guided by such a meta-strategy may be high level procedures, or may embody nothing more than a description of available moves for transforming one solution into another, together with an associated evaluating rule.

Algorithm 2.2: Branch-and-Bound

Initialization
$\mathcal{N} :=$ set of unprocessed nodes of the original problem
Upper bound $Z^* \leftarrow \infty$
while $\mathcal{N} \neq \emptyset$ **do**
    Select next node: $n \in \mathcal{N}$, $\mathcal{N} \leftarrow \mathcal{N} \backslash \{n\}$
    Calculate bound: Solve LP relaxation of the problem in node n with dual bound Z' and solution x'
    Bounding:
    if x' *is empty* **then**
        Prune by infeasibility
    else
        if $Z' \geq Z^*$ **then**
            Prune by bound
        else
            if $x' \in \mathbb{Z}$ *and* $Z' \leq Z^*$ **then**
                Prune by optimality
                Return x'
            else
                Branching:
                Create two sub-problems $n1$ and $n2$, which split the current LP solution
                $\mathcal{N} \leftarrow \mathcal{N} \cup \{n1, n2\}$

In this thesis, three metaheuristics are applied to solve the sub-problem and/or the integrated problem: ant colony optimization, simulated annealing, and tabu search.

Ant Colony Optimization

Ant colony optimization (ACO) is a technique for optimization introduced in the early 1990s by Dorigo and his colleagues (see Dorigo (1992), Dorigo et al. (1996)). It is based on the principles of the swarm intelligence, which applies the behavior of real swarms or insect colonies to efficient computational methods (see Burke & Kendall (2005) for an overview). The ACO technique was inspired by the foraging behavior of real ant colonies, where ants can find the shortest paths between their nest and food sources (see an example shown in Figure 2.5a). Initially, ants search randomly near their nest to find food (Figure 2.5b). While searching, they leave a chemical pheromone trail on the ground. Ants which choose the shorter path arrive earlier at the food source (Figure 2.5c). When they go back to the nest, they smell some pheromone on the shorter path and therefore prefer this path (Figure 2.5d). The other ants will choose the path with the stronger pheromone concentration to find the food source. The pheromone will accumulate faster on the shorter path than on the others, therefore, after some time, nearly all ants will take the shorter path.

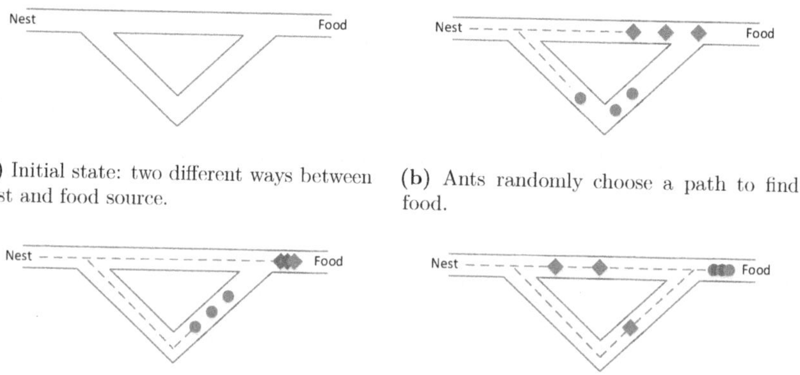

(a) Initial state: two different ways between nest and food source.

(b) Ants randomly choose a path to find food.

(c) Ants which choose the shorter path arrive earlier at the food source.

(d) When they go back they smell some pheromone on the shorter path and therefore prefer this path.

Figure 2.5. Illustration of the foraging behavior of real ant colonies.

The basic ACO algorithm for combinatorial optimization problems is shown in Algorithm 2.3 (from Dorigo & Stützle (2010)). After the parameters are initialized, a main loop including three steps is repeated until a termination condition is met. First, feasible solutions are constructed by ants, then they are improved by using a local search (optional), and finally the pheromones are updated. During the update all pheromone values are decreased by a certain percentage (evaporation), while the pheromone values corresponding to good solutions are increased (intensification). The most commonly used stopping criteria (possibly used in combination) are that a predefined maximum number of iterations has been reached, a time limit has been exceeded, or the best solution has not changed over a certain number of iterations.

Algorithm 2.3: ACO algorithm for combinatorial optimization problems

```
Initialization
while termination condition not met do
    ConstructAntSolutions
    ApplyLocalSearch    %optional
    UpdatePheromones
```

Simulated Annealing

Simulated annealing (SA) was inspired by cooling in metallurgy. This algorithm is independently described by Kirkpatrick et al. (1983) and Černý (1985), who have developed an algorithm based on the physical process described in Metropolis et al. (1953). Algorithm 2.4 describes the basic simulated annealing algorithm for combinatorial optimization problems. In the function Initialize(), an initial solution $i_{initial}$ is found, as well as an initial temperature t_0 and L, which is defined as the number of iterations within a temperature level. The function Generate() selects a solution j from the neighborhood S_i of the current solution i, while the function Update() calculates a new reduced value of the temperature t.

Algorithm 2.4: SA algorithm for combinatorial optimization problems

Initialize($i_{initial}, t_0, L$)
$i \leftarrow i_{initial}$, $t \leftarrow t_0$
while *termination condition not met* **do**
    for $l = 1...L$ **do**
        Generate(j from S_i)
        if $f(j) \leq f(i)$ **then**
            $i \leftarrow j$
        else
            if $e^{\frac{f(i)-f(j)}{t}} > random(0,1)$ **then**
                $i \leftarrow j$
    $t \leftarrow$ Update(t)

In order to overcome local optima shown in Figure 2.6, a limited probability of accepting deteriorations is possible; this is implemented by comparing the value of $e^{\frac{f(i)-f(j)}{t}}$ with a random number generated from a uniform distribution on the interval $(0, 1)$. At the beginning of the simulated annealing, we have large value of t, therefore large deteriorations will be accepted. However, as we decrease the temperature t gradually, only smaller deteriorations will be accepted.

The algorithm terminates if the temperature t is reduced to near 0 or the given time limit is reached.

Tabu Search

Another local search method we use in this thesis is Tabu Search (TS), which was proposed in Glover (1986). The basic idea is to collect the subset of the moves in a forbidden neighborhood (tabu), which prevents cycling when moving away from local optima through non-improving moves. The search space is the set of all feasible solutions that can be visited during the search. Algorithm 2.5 shows the basic tabu search algorithm, which begins with an initial solution $i_{initial}$ and a empty set of tabu list T. All solutions j in the neighborhood S_i of current solution i, which are not included in the tabu list T, are searched. The value

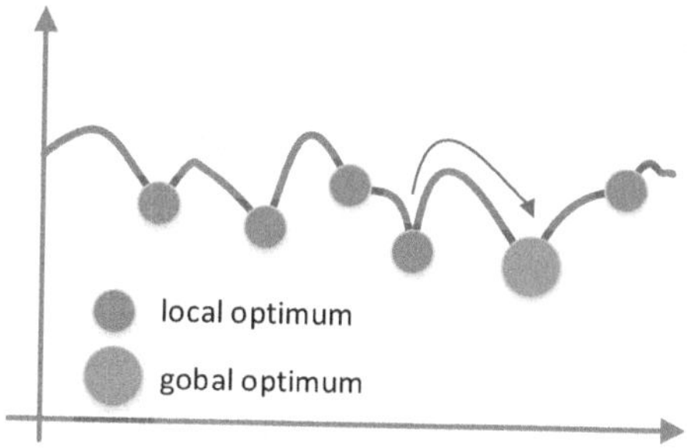

Figure 2.6. Illustration of the search in SA.

of the best one $f(j)$ is selected and is compared with the value of the current solution $f(i)$. Only the improvement is accepted. After that, T is recorded. The decision about whether a move is defined as a tabu is made according to memory, including short-term memory to prevent the reversal of recent moves (in short: recency), and longer-term memory to reinforce attractive components (in short: frequency). The most commonly used stopping criteria are after a fixed number of iterations (or a fixed amount of CPU time), after some number of consecutive iterations without an improvement in the objective function value, or when the objective function reaches a pre-specified threshold value. More details can be found in Glover (1989), Glover (1990b), and Glover (1990a).

Algorithm 2.5: TS algorithm for combinatorial optimization problems

Initialize($i_{initial}, T$)
$i \leftarrow i_{initial}$, $T \leftarrow \emptyset$
while *termination condition not satisfied* **do**
    $j \leftarrow \underset{j \in S_i \text{ and } j \notin T}{\arg\min} f(j)$
    if $j \neq \emptyset$ *and* $f(j) < f(i)$ **then**
        $i \leftarrow j$
    Record tabu for the current moves in T

2.3.6. Multi-Objective Optimization

As described in Section 2.2.1, the preferences of the bus company as well as the drivers are considered in the optimization. From the company's point of view it is important to minimize operational costs. However, from the point of view of drivers their preferences should be satisfied as far as possible. Therefore, some objectives conflict with each other, such as covering all activities and minimizing overtimes for all drivers. Therefore, the crew rostering problem is formulated as a multi-objective optimization problem. The detailed explanations of multi-objective optimization, and the current techniques, are shown in Deb (2001) and Ehrgott (2005). Due to the simple implementation, the multi-objective problem is widely solved using the sum of weighted objectives. We adopt the same approach to solve the crew rostering problem with different solution approaches (see Sections 5 and 7). Additionally, we choose an appropriate solution approach to solve our multi-objective crew rostering problem in Section 7.5.

3. Crew Rostering: State of the Art

The purpose of this chapter is to review state-of-the-art models and solution approaches for solving cyclic and non-cyclic crew rostering problems, including sequential as well as integrated approaches for both types of problem.

As described in Barnhart & Laporte (2006), the sizes of real-world instances of the crew rostering problem in public bus transit are larger than those for the air/rail rostering problem. A duty (known as pairing) in air/rail rostering can span up to several days, while a duty in public bus transit is a daily job for a driver. This creates a large number of duties to be considered in rosters in public bus transit. Moreover, it is common that a driver can drive different types of vehicles, therefore many drivers are capable of carrying out the same duty, which increases the complexity of the assignment problem.

Therefore, we will not only review literature regarding public bus transport in this chapter — we will also include some results from airline and rail crew rostering, since most methodological advances there are relevant for crew rostering in public bus transit, at least for small and medium-sized problems.

This chapter is organized as follows. In Sections 3.1 and 3.2, we discuss the state of the art for the cyclic and non-cyclic crew rostering problems respectively. In the next section, we summarize the solution approaches for multi-objective cyclic and non-cyclic crew rostering problems. Finally, in Section 3.4 we describe briefly the purpose of a decision support system and the existing ones applied for solving crew rostering problems.

3.1. Cyclic Crew Rostering (CCR)

As described in Section 2.2.2, the CCR problem aims at generating for each driver group, a roster based on a weekly pattern. This method of generation is widely used in the public bus transit and railway sectors, since there are many regular trips from Monday to Friday in both sectors. However, airline crew rosters are non-cyclic, due to the irregularity of trips. There are also some applications of CCR in the airline sector, but mostly for airport ground staffs or apron services (see Hao et al. (2004) and Chew (1991)). We classify the papers about CCR according to which (sub-)problems they consider, as well as the corresponding solution approaches.

Days off scheduling

Prakash et al. (1984) use goal programming to solve the multi-objective days off scheduling problem. The goals are to limit the total number of crews having non-consecutive and consecutive days off, and to minimize the number of crews having non-consecutive days off. Two days off for each driver per week are guaranteed. In order to get an integer solution, a modified simplex algorithm is used to solve the problem. Pedrosa & Constantino (2001) present a set covering model for the days off scheduling problem to minimize the total number of workers. Column generation is used in which the master problem is a set covering model, while the pricing problem is solved by using the resource constrained shortest path problem of a designed network. The LP solution is rounded, or branch-and-bound is used, to get an integer solution.

Rota scheduling

Xie et al. (2012b) propose a stochastic model for the rota scheduling problem in public bus transit in order to reduce the discrepancy between a planned roster and the actual one. Standbys are normally evenly planned for all drivers (e.g. in Lezaun et al. (2006)) without considering more detailed information such as historical or day-depended sickness absence rates. In case where the absence rate exceeds the available standbys, additional drivers are called in manually. This causes discontent for the drivers as well as continuous organizational effort for the bus company.

Duty sequencing

Jachnik (1981) advocates solving the duty sequencing problem by using a constructive heuristic that minimizes roster costs while considering planned leaves. After that, the solution is improved through swaps. Townsend (1988) aims at producing an even spread of work at weekends through the roster, so a method is developed to produce the roster skeleton, which includes standard units containing fixed patterns of working (similar to duty sequencing based on the skeleton). In Ferreira & Guimarães (1995), the duty sequencing problem is modeled as an asymmetric traveling salesman model and solved using a 3-opt based heuristic. The goal is to minimize the variance in rest periods between successive duties.

Shift-duty assignment

The objective of Townsend (1986) (a simplified shift-duty assignment problem) is to produce a good match of weekday with weekend duties, and the weekday duties are considered to be identical. The three basic building units (1-week, 4-week and 5-week designs) are used. The problem is formulated as a 3-dimensional assignment problem by considering minimum breaks between consecutive duties. A 2-dimensional assignment problem is then solved, and alternatively a heuristic is used to reduce the computational effort with a small loss in optimality. Xie et al. (2012a) propose a duty-block network for solving the shift-duty assignment problem. Optimal rosters are characterized by the maximal satisfaction of drivers, the minimal difference in overtime among all drivers, and the minimal number of unassigned duties. The model aims at minimizing the punishment costs for undesired jobs for each driver while minimizing the maximum overtime for all drivers. Unassigned duties are also described as undesired duties with high punishment cost. In order to deal with multiple objectives, the former objective is included in the model of the duty-block network, and improved using simulated annealing that considers the latter objective. The generated solution is shown to outperform the sequential approach to crew rostering, i.e. first shift assignment, followed by duty sequencing.

Sequential approach

Lezaun et al. (2006) propose a practical model at Metro Bilbao in Spain, which is solved as a sequence of four types of integer programming problems. It is planned for the whole year, i.e. different periods of the year are planned and vacations and standby days are allocated by calendar weeks. First of all, standby days are grouped into weeks, and standby weeks should, when possible, immediately precede or follow vacations. After that, multi-shift weekly patterns are determined for all combinations of shifts, and the most attractive patterns are generated and assigned to drivers. Finally, the annual assignment of weekly work patterns to drivers, i.e. the compatibility of the last week of the last period with the first week of the actual period, should be checked. The obtained solution is quasi-optimal because all drivers do the same job.

Emden-Weinert et al. (2000) solve the CCR problem sequentially, as rota scheduling and duty sequencing problems, at the Bremer Strassenbahn AG in Bremen, Germany. The former problem is modeled as a 0-1-MIP and solved with a standard solver, while the latter ones use simulated annealing with pre- and post-processing to modify infeasible solutions. Multiple objectives are considered in the rota scheduling problem, such as even distribution of weekends off, preferred shift distribution, etc. A weight for each objective defines its importance. The objectives considered in the duty sequencing problem include even distribution of work over the duty blocks in the roster, meeting the predefined average working time, etc. Sodhi & Norris (2004) decompose the CCR problem into two steps: first, shift pattern generation for the entire roster (rota scheduling) and, second, assigning duties to the resulting patterns (duty sequencing). Rota scheduling aims at maximizing crew satisfaction by the weighted sum of regular weekends, pairs of consecutive days off not including weekends, and long weekends. A network MIP model is used to find an optimal cyclic path to cover the roster. The objective of duty sequencing is to minimize the violation of soft constraints. Both steps are solved with a standard commericial MILP solver. This is applied on the London Underground.

In 2007, an applied study commissioned by EuskoTren was presented in Lezaun et al. (2007), which solves the train CCR in four sequencing steps. Each of them is formulated as a binary programming problem. They aim for an equal annual distribution of workload not only in the number of worked/rest days, but also the working hours. First of all drivers' vacations are fixed, and follow the annual assignment of the weekly patterns to drivers for different periods, such as winter and summer periods. In the third step, the annual assigned weekly patterns are deployed in days to get an annual assignment of shifts. Public holidays are considered in this step. Finally, the duty sequencing is carried out. Unlike standard CCR, different periods are considered in the paper, and periodically-based rosters are generated. Another decomposition approach, proposed in Hartog et al. (2009), decomposes the whole problem into three steps. First of all, the duties are assigned to the different groups so that the popular and unpopular duties are evenly distributed. The second and third steps are similar to rota scheduling and duty sequencing in Sodhi & Norris (2004), respectively. Both problems can be formulated as an assignment problem with additional constraints, which aims at minimizing the total number of undesired assignments. Seven groups of train drivers are tested for the crew based in Utrecht of NS. However, the first step causes a loss in flexibility due to the assignment of duties to groups.

Integrated approach

The integrated approach for CCR is mostly applied in the railway transport sector by applying different heuristics including metaheuristics. Monfroglio (1996) describes the combination of a greedy algorithm with two genetic algorithms (one using an order-based representation similar to Tadei et al. (1995) and the other using a traditional chromosome scheme) for solving a large-sized real life CCR problem in Italian Railways, which includes 1000 duties as input during 125 days in the summer. The objective is to minimize the maximum workload assigned to a roster. A comparison with the adapted algorithm of Bianco et al. (1992) shows that both present good results. A simulated annealing approach is developed for solving CCR in Ernst et al. (1998), which develops cyclic rosters from train trips based on the given number of crews at each depot, since the weekly rail schedules repeat. It is applied to freight train crew rostering in Australia. The problem involves wages and out-of town expenses as well as the penalty cost of over-coverage or under-coverage of a trip. The ALPI system for railway CCR is presented in Caprara et al. (1997), Caprara et al. (1998b), Caprara et al. (1999), and Caprara et al. (2001), which focus on a heuristic algorithm to find rosters with the optimal number of crews. A Lagrangian lower bound is described based on a defined graph, and is used to improve the effectiveness of the algorithm. Also, the results of the real-world test sets of up to 1000 duties show that the approach provides small gaps within a short computing time. Furthermore, Caprara et al. (1998a) published an approach that combined constraint logic programming and operations research techniques to solve the railway CCR problem. In Lee & Chen (2003), the train driver rostering problem aims at maximizing the cycle length and minimizing the weekly working time. It is solved as a constrained traveling salesman problem. The results obtained are compared with the ones implemented with a genetic algorithm, which generates better solutions. Drivers' preferences are considered in Constantino et al. (2006) by solving CCR. It solves the planning CCR by using a heuristic algorithm, which estimates the minimum number of train drivers. The distribution of workload is based on drivers' preferences; therefore the first phase of the heuristic is to establish a utility function, which measures their personal preferences. The CCR is formulated as a bottleneck assignment problem, which generates personal rosters based on a constructed cyclic master roster.

Short Summary

As shown above, the integrated CCR problem in public bus transit is paid relatively little attention, and most publications concentrate on sub-problems or different sequential approaches. Moreover, the solution approaches applied for solving the rail CCR problem are mostly heuristics. Therefore, there is a need to investigate the integrated CCR problem in public bus transit.

3.2. Non-Cyclic Crew Rostering (NCCR)

As described in Section 2.2.2, a non-cyclic crew rostering problem aims at generating a roster for each driver. This approach is widely used in the airline sector. We classify the papers about non-cyclic crew rostering according to which (sub-)problems they consider. Moreover, a review for airline crew rostering is shown separately, since non-cyclic crew rostering problems are mostly studied in the airline sector.

Days off scheduling

Days off scheduling for the crews of a Finnish bus transportation company is solved in Kyngäs & Nurmi (2011) by using a variation of the cooperative local search method (see Burke & Silva (2005)). The objective is to find a solution that minimizes the sum of weighted soft constraint violations without violating any hard constraints. A set of artificial test instances are used in this paper. The number of employees is up to 56, and the number of total weeks is limited to 36. Based on the days off scheduling in Kyngäs & Nurmi (2011), sequential days off and shift scheduling are solved in Nurmi et al. (2011) by using metaheuristic methods (simulated annealing, tabu search and ejection-chains) for a Finnish bus transportation company to minimize the weighted sum of the soft constraint violations.

Shift assignment

Carraresi & Gallo (1984) model the shift assignment as a multi-level bottleneck assignment problem by considering minimization of maximum workload, i.e. evenly distributing the workload among the crews. A heuristic algorithm has been used to produce asymptotically optimal solutions. Randomly generated and real life problems for five working days (in other words, one working week) were used for testing.

Duty assignment

Another model was proposed by Catanas & Paixão (1995) for solving the duty sequencing problem, which minimizes the maximum roster duration while the total roster cost is minimized. It is solved by column generation, where the master problem is a set covering problem, while the sub-problem is modeled as a shortest path problem with additional constraints. The approach is tested on randomly generated data sets.

Shift-duty assignment

Bianco et al. (1992) proposed a new iterative heuristic algorithm for solving the shift-duty assignment problem. It aims at finding the minimum-cost combination of rosters while minimizing the maximum roster workload. "Roster of type" is defined as a subset of the days of the time period, such as the ordered set 4,5,6,7,1, which represents a roster covering the days from Thursday to Monday. In each iteration the weekly rosters of type (five days) are generated by solving the multilevel bottleneck assignment problem on the subset of unassigned duties, which aims at minimizing the maximum workload. The algorithm terminates if no duties are available or it is not possible to generate rosters of any type. The solution is close to optimality, but larger computation times are needed compared with the algorithm proposed by Carraresi & Gallo (1984).

Sequential approach

One of the few publications about the railway NCCR is developed by De Pont (2006) for Netherlands Railways, in which the similar decomposition approach of Hartog et al. (2009) is proposed; however, the rosters are created for groups simultaneously instead of separately, which is shown to increase the fulfillment of crews' preferences. Firstly, rota scheduling is solved by enumeration of all legal sub-rosters, which are defined as pattern rosters (or in our words, rotas) with small roster periods, and link them to the complete rosters. The periods for sub-rosters are limited to eight days due to the large number of decision variables. Secondly, duty sequencing is formulated as an assignment problem with additional constraints, which aims at minimizing the sum of unfulfilled preferences, while finding a set of rosters, for which the maximum sum of unfulfilled preferences is minimized. The same roster groups for crews based in Utrecht as in Hartog et al. (2009) are tested with some modifications of roster groups and adjusted preference scenarios. It is shown that rosters with a length of 13 weeks can be generated for 96 drivers in an acceptable computational time because of the sequencing approach.

Integrated approach

Evolutionary heuristics for solving bi-objective NCCR have been proposed in Moz et al. (2009). This work minimizes the maximum overtime for drivers while minimizing the number of drivers during the rostering period. The test instances were designed to cope with the special case of a bus transport company in Portugal (the length of the rostering period is 4 weeks; the number of drivers is 45). Another paper on multi-objective modeling for solving NCCR (in Respício et al. (2007)) uses a specifically designed memetic algorithm considered within a preemptive goal programming framework, which combines the best features of both heuristics shown in Moz et al. (2009). Computational results show that the new method outperforms the results of those heuristics. Mesquita et al. (2011) use the goal programming approach to solve the binary bi-objective NCCR model, which aims at minimizing the number of drivers and the maximum overtime per driver. The optimal/near-optimal monthly solutions are obtained for instances with up to 1400 duties and 70 drivers.

A hybrid column generation approach is developed for urban transit NCCR in Yunes et al. (2005), in which the master problem is formulated as a set partitioning/covering problem, while the sub-problem is formulated as a constraint satisfaction problem to search for new feasible variables. The problem aims at minimizing the number of crews for the given period. This approach is tested on real-world instances with up to 40 crews; however, the planning horizon is limited to one week. An MIP model for solving NCCR is provided in Mesquita et al. (2011), which aims at minimizing the number of drivers while minimizing the maximum overtime for all drivers. The bi-objective problem is solved by a goal programming approach to obtain near-optimal rosters. The instances are limited to about 1300 duties and about 70 drivers. Prototype software for the multi-objective railway NCCR is developed in Hanne et al. (2009). The problem is solved using an evolutionary algorithm, which aims at minimizing the cost of assigned train drivers as well as undesired working hours, while congruity with holiday preferences is maximized. Optionally the hard constraints can be formulated as soft ones, and the violations can be summed up by penalty values in the objective function. The properties of solved instances are unknown. Visualization and navigation tools are provided to support the decision.

In the following, we summarize the publications about airline crew rostering, where an integrated approach is mostly applied.

Airline crew rostering

Airline crew rostering has attracted the most attention in the transportation sector because of its economic scale and impact. In terms of mathematical models, the following two relevant models are applied.

Firstly, the crew rostering problem can be formulated as a *set partitioning/covering problem* where each duty is defined as a row and each valid roster is represented as a column. It has been applied widely in an airline context, such as in Ryan (1992), Day & Ryan (1997), Gamache & Soumis (1998), Gamache et al. (1999), Freling et al. (2004), Medard & Sawhney (2007), Maenhout & Vanhoucke (2010). Most of them are solved using the column generation approach.

Ryan (1992) aims to assign rosters to crews with fair distribution of days off and pairings. In this paper, all feasible pairings are enumerated and the LP relaxation problem is solved with an efficient branching strategy. Up to 470 crews for three separate 28-day periods are analyzed to get feasible solutions. Sequential days off and shift-duty assignment problems are solved in Day & Ryan (1997) to minimize the desired days off structure and minimize the deviation from average duty hours, respectively. Both problems are solved by enumerating all five-day sub-rosters for 80 crew members and 610 duties over 14 days, and applying set partitioning technology. A re-rostering is used to repair the solution. Instead of using the sequential approach shown in Day & Ryan (1997), Gamache & Soumis (1998) consider the desired days off structure in the optimization process, and this way is proved to outperform the preassignment of days off. The column generation approach is used to solve this problem, where the master problem is the set partitioning problem, while the sub-problem generates disjoint pairings in each iteration. The problem aims to minimize the costs of selected rosters and idle times (or the number of employees). The test problems described in this paper include assigning 70 to 100 pairings to 10 to 20 pilots over two weeks.

A further development of Gamache & Soumis (1998) is presented in Gamache et al. (1999), which minimizes the idle times of employees. In order to solve large instances, the model has been simplified: fairness and preferences are not considered. The column generation approach is also used, where the sub-problem is a constrained shortest path problem. Instead of a constrained shortest path problem, the sub-problem is formulated as a constraint satisfaction problem in Sellmann et al. (2000), but with limited discussion of the techniques and results. The same approach is described in Fahle et al. (2002). The authors use the problem instances from a major European airline for the experiments, and they show that this approach reduces significantly the number of choice points during the generation of a new shortest path. The instances are limited to 67 crews and 280 activities, in order to run experiments within a reasonable time. Another heuristic approach using the technology of multi-objective simulated annealing is applied in Lučić & Teodorović (1999) to assign equal workloads to crews. It is based on an interactive approach, in which the decision maker can change the aspiration levels for different criteria, until he/she gets the most satisfactory solution. The approach is tested on an example in which 53 flight captains are assigned to 422 pairings during the next 30 days. Kohl & Karisch (2004) provide a comprehensive description of the real-world airline crew rostering problem. Also, simplified and extended mathematical models are developed to deal with different objectives and constraints. The methodology of a commercial crew rostering system (Carmen Crew Rostering), and some applications of this system in airlines and railways, are presented. A decision support system is discussed in Freling et al. (2004) for airline and railway crew planning problems. A generalized set partitioning model is formulated for crew scheduling and rostering problems and a state-of-the-art branch-and-price solver is developed for both problems. It aims at firstly minimizing the number of uncovered tasks, while secondly minimizing the total cost of the selected duties or rosters. An application for a case study in a European regional airline company is shown.

Medard & Sawhney (2007) provide solution techniques based on simple tree search and more sophisticated column generation and shortest path algorithms for the recovery process of crew scheduling and rostering problems. Both are formulated as set partitioning problems, which aims to minimize crew costs as well as the costs of selected rosters in the solution. The experiments are tested for large instances (up to 885 crews). A scatter search procedure is proposed in Maenhout & Vanhoucke (2010) for an airline crew rostering problem. Several objectives are considered in the model, such as minimizing the costs of using extra or freelance crew members, ensuring fairness to all regular crew members, and considering the crews' preferences. The results produced by the scatter search procedure are compared with those produced by a variable neighborhood search and optimal solutions based on the principles in Gamache et al. (1999), and are shown to outperform the vailable neighborhood search approach; they are near-optimal within a short running time.

However, such a set partitioning model is not popular in crew rostering in public bus transit, except for two applications for solving sub-problems: the duty sequencing in Catanas & Paixão (1995) and the days off scheduling in Pedrosa & Constantino (2001). Moreover, column generation is applied for solving a simplified NCCR problem in public transit in Yunes et al. (2005). According to Caprara et al. (2006), the network flow formulation is more suitable for railway crew rostering than the set partitioning formulation, since a relatively large number of duties should be scheduled in a roster, as well as complicated constraints being imposed on it. Therefore, for a similar reason, we use the network flow formulation in this thesis.

Secondly, the crew rostering problem can be cast as a *network based mathematical model*. A multicommodity network flow problem is modeled in Cappanera & Gallo (2004) for solving NCCR; in each network layer, activity arcs/nodes and connecting arcs are used to represent the activities and the compatible activities for an employee. A multicommodity network flow model with additional constraints is developed in Cappanera & Gallo (2004) for the air crew rostering problem, which aims at maximizing the number of covered activities. A path found on the network corresponds to the monthly schedule for an employee. Some families of valid inequalities are used to tighten the LP formulation of the model. Computational experiments are performed using the CPLEX solver for instances with up to 277 pairings and 50 employees. Instead, Respício et al. (2007), which we described before, adopt a multicommodity network flow to solve the bus driver NCCR problem, in which each network layer represents a day. Nodes represent the duties and days off while the connecting arcs represent linked pairs of nodes of consecutive layers.

Additionally, a new bi-criterion mathematical formulation for airline crew rostering is introduced by El Moudani et al. (2001), which aims at minimizing operational costs while maximizing crew satisfaction. A heuristic is generated for the initial population based on the acceptable satisfaction levels for the crews. Then, the genetic algorithm is developed to reduce operational costs. The approach is tested for a medium-sized instance, which includes 275 pairings and 75 crews. A multi-weight based heuristic is developed in Guo et al. (2006) to solve air crew rostering within partially integrated crew scheduling and rostering problems. It aims at creating balanced rosters among crews. Several metaheuristics are implemented in Lučić & Teodorović (2007) to solve the air crew rostering problem, i.e. simulated annealing, genetic algorithms, and tabu search. The initial solution is generated by a simple greedy heuristic, pilot-by-pilot. It aims at minimizing the deviations between the real flight time and ideal flight time for all crew members, minimizing the deviation between the real and ideal number of foreign trips per diem during the month for all crew members, and minimizing the deviation between the real and ideal number of weekend days on duty for all crew members. A simple weighted sum of these objectives is used in this paper. The different algorithms are tested on a real world example, which considers 422 pairings, 53 crews during a 30-day period, and some randomly generated instances. The results show that simulated annealing provides the best solutions.

Short Summary

Most of the NCCR problems in the airline sector are formulated either as a set partitioning problem or as a network flow problem. Since the set partitioning formulation is not suitable for the crew rostering problem in public transit, we use in this thesis the network flow problem to solve the NCCR problem. Moreover, the NCCR problems in public bus transit, especially the integrated approach, have been paid a little more attention in recent years, and are solved mostly with heuristics. However, large instances with complex rules and regulations cannot be tackled in an integrated manner. In addition to reduction of operational cost, the quality rules, especially the drivers' preferences, are not widely considered in the integrated approach in public bus transit, since they increase the complexity of this problem. The most considered preference in the literature is the balanced workload among all drivers. In addition to that, there are more aspects of preferences, which are described in Section 2.2.1. Therefore, a faster approach to generating good solutions is necessary for practical purposes.

3.3. Multi-Objective CCR and NCCR

If the crew rostering problem, either CCR or NCCR, considers different soft constraints, then it is often formulated as a multi-objective problem. Therefore, it is worthwhile to outline the solution approaches for solving this type of problem.

The goal programming approach is applied in Prakash et al. (1984) and Mesquita et al. (2011), and is considered to be an exact method to solve multi-objective problems. Moreover, a heuristic evolutionary algorithm is widely applied to solve the multi-objective optimization problem (such as in Moz et al. (2009), Respício et al. (2007), Hanne et al. (2009), and Lee & Chen (2003)). Another heuristic approach, the multi-objective simulated annealing approach, is applied in Lučić & Teodorović (1999).

However, most of the publications try to deal with one objective instead of multiple ones. The following methods are applied. Firstly, the drivers' preferences are pre-assigned, and then these preliminary skeleton rosters are completed to generate the complete rosters (see Ryan (1992), Day & Ryan (1997), Xie et al. (2012a), El Moudani et al. (2001), and Bianco et al. (1992)). Secondly, multi-objective crew rostering is considered as one objective problem using the sum of weighted objectives, which is widely used in literature due to its simple implementation (see Gamache & Soumis (1998), Catanas & Paixão (1995), De Pont (2006), Sodhi & Norris (2004), Emden-Weinert et al. (2000), Ernst et al. (1998), Kyngäs & Nurmi (2011), Burke & Silva (2005), Nurmi et al. (2011), Lučić & Teodorović (2007), and Maenhout & Vanhoucke (2010)).

Therefore, in this thesis we solve the multi-objective CCR and NCCR problems as one objective problem using the sum of weighted objectives; additionally, a multi-objective metaheuristic approach is applied.

3.4. Decision Support Systems

The concept of a decision support system (DSS) was introduced in the early 1970s. Different definitions of DSS have been given by many researchers. However, there is no single definition that is agreed by everyone. In this work we adopt the definition that was proposed in Gorry & Morton (1971):

> A DSS is an interactive computer-based system that helps decision makers to utilize data and models to solve unstructured problems.

Crew rostering is a complex problem, therefore there have been more DSSs appearing in literature or in practice in the last decade to help human planners to get good solutions without much human effort.

For the public transport area, the DISSY system in Emden-Weinert et al. (2000) is a decision support and simulation system for the bus and tram cyclic driver rostering problem. Solution approaches for sub-problems of the driver rostering problem are proposed. Additionally, different scheduling scenarios are evaluated in simulation to better adapt human resource management to new framework conditions. Moreover, different decision support systems have been developed in practice, such as MOVEO Profahr[1] and IUV.crew[2] in Germany. MOVEO Profahr provides solutions for cyclic and non-cyclic driver rostering problems separately using a sequential approach. Drivers' preferences and a balanced workload for all drivers are considered during the optimization. IVU.crew provides a version IVU.crew.roster.apd to optimize the crew rostering problem under consideration of drivers' preferences as well as a balanced workload, while another version, IVU.crew.Mobile, is used to allow drivers to enter their preferences and further information online, as well as access their plans using mobile devices.

In the airline and railway sectors, the Carmen Crew Rostering system is developed and applied to different practical crew rostering problems in eight airlines in Europe and North America, and in the Swedish State Railways and Deutsche Bahn. More details can be found in Kohl & Karisch (2004). According to Bengtsson et al. (2007), this system is used by all major European airlines, and also used by several operators in North America and Asia. Another DSS in the airline and railway sectors, Harmony CDR, is developed in Freling et al. (2004) for crew scheduling and rostering. A state-of-the-art Branch-and-Price algorithm is developed to solve both problems sequentially and within one step. Other applications for airline crew scheduling and rostering include the AD OPT Altitude system in Desrosiers et al. (2000), which includes a three-module optimization package for aircraft routing, crew pairing and crew rostering problems. A DSS for airline crew recovery is developed in Guo (2005). Hartog et al. (2009) concentrate on solving the decomposed cyclic train driver rostering problem in an automatic way.

Most of the DSSs in literature for crew rostering problems are traditional DSSs, apart from an application in the Carmen Preferential Bidding system (see Kohl & Karisch (2004)), which supports a web-based bidding interface for crews. The crews receive immediate feedback while they bid. Moreover, some web applications for bus driver rostering are provided in practice, especially to support the functions for drivers, such as IVU.crew.Mobile.

By the mid-1990s, the first of a series of papers were published in Bhargava et al. (1995a) and Bhargava et al. (1995b) on DecisionNet, electronic marketplace of web-based DSSs, since they saw the new opportunities created by World Wide Web and Internet technologies for building and deploying decision support systems. More about the historical perspectives and how the web technologies influence the development of a DSS can be found in Bhargava et al. (2007). Moreover, many prototype applications of web-based DSSs in different areas were reported starting at the beginning of the 20th century, such as hospital management (Kohli et al. (2001)), personalized e-services (Yu (2004)), service contract management (Sundarraj (2004)), risk analysis for e-commerce development (Ngai & Wat (2005)), integrated pest management (Jones et al. (2010)), and assessing regional water quality conditions and management actions (Booth et al. (2011)). More examples of development of software for web-based DSSs can be found in Power & Kaparthi (2002) and Bhargava et al. (2007).

Due to wide applications of web-based DSSs in other sectors and the rapid development of web technologies, we develop in this thesis a novel prototype of a web-based DSS for

[1]MOVEO Profahr: `http://www.moveo-software.com/cms/produkte/profahr/index.html`
[2]IVU.crew: `http://www.ivu.de/produkte-loesungen/ivusuite/disposition/ivucrew.html`

different users in bus companies, for the purpose of reducing the human effort in the planning and (simplified) operative process of the crew rostering problem.

4. Required Work and Scope of the Thesis

In the previous chapter, we discussed how CCR and NCCR problems are solved in transportation sectors according to the literature. Both are widely studied in the literature, but they are solved separately, regardless of their similarities. To our knowledge, this is the first study showing different approaches for both kinds of bus driver rostering problems. The goal of this thesis is to investigate, design and develop solution approaches to solve both CCR and NCCR problems (see Chapters 5 and 7). We have outlined which mathematical optimization models and solution approaches are used in literature. In order to cope with complex rules and regulations in the crew rostering problem, many human planners decompose the CCR or NCCR problem into sub-problems. Until recently, it was not possible to solve large instances in an integrated manner to cope with those rules and preferences of both the management and the drivers.

In addition to cost reduction, which is the preference of management, the preferences of drivers are considered as an important aspect. Therefore, the crew rostering problem is formulated as a multi-objective problem to deal with different interests. If the weight of one objective dominates that of another, this may be handled by decomposition techniques that focus on this objective in one of the first phases of the decomposition (see Section 3.3). Therefore, an additional promising research direction is to develop multi-objective metaheuristics that support the planner in determining the weight of each objective (see Section 7.5).

The rules and regulations might differ from one bus company to another. Moreover, there are different suitable solution approaches for different sizes of problems. As shown in the literature, there is an apparent lack of such a state-of-the-art DSS that can flexibly support various constraints and provide suitable solver(s) to different problems. Additionally, such a DSS provides support for planners to select the preferred weights to solve the multi-objective crew rostering problem. Moreover, a web-based DSS simplifies the usage of a DSS without any installation of software and enables remote data access, which is independent of specific operating system and hardware platforms (mobile phone, PC, or laptop).

Altogether, the main goals of our research are twofold:

- To develop models and techniques for the integrated approach to both CCR and NCCR problems in public bus transit that will make it possible to tackle large real-world instances.
- To develop a web-based decision support system to support different requirements and reduce human effort.

As explained before, the set partitioning formulation is not suitable for the crew rostering problem, therefore we present in this thesis a novel multicommodity network model which is similar to the model developed for the airline crew rostering problem by Cappanera & Gallo (2004) for both cyclic and non-cyclic rostering problems (see Chapter 5). We do not adopt another multicommodity network model shown in Respício et al. (2007) because its structure is not suitable for considering the individual preferences of each driver. We extend the network flow model of Cappanera & Gallo (2004) in the following way.

- A set of additional soft constraints is integrated, which is necessary for bus crew rostering (see quality rules in Section 2.2.1).
- The costs of the activities and the combinations of activities depend on the personal preferences of the employees.
- Some constraints, such as forbidden sequences, can be extended to more than two consecutive days in bus traffic.
- The previous planning period is considered as well.

Moreover, the most widely used approaches for solving crew rostering problems are heuristics, including construction heuristics, metaheuristics, and column generation. Therefore, in this thesis we apply different solution approaches to solve CCR and NCCR problems, i.e. column generation and metaheuristics including simulated annealing, ant colony optimization, and tabu search (see Chapter 7). The differences to the existing implementations are discussed in Chapter 7 as well. And we compare the results obtained by using the integrated approach with the ones produced by the sequential approach.

Part II.

Solution Approaches

5. Mathematical Programming and Optimal Crew Rostering

We first describe the network used for solving the crew rostering problem in Section 5.1. We have the same network design for the rota scheduling problem (a sub-problem of the crew rostering problem) as for the integrated problem, for both CCR and NCCR problems. Based on the network, an overview of the mathematical formulations for solving the decomposed and integrated NCCR problems will be given in Section 5.2. A small modification of the models is then presented in Section 5.3 for solving the CCR problems. A description of real-world instances, along with the results, will be presented in Chapter 6.

5.1. The Underlying Network

As mentioned before, the NCCR problem in this work is formulated as a multicommodity flow network, where each network layer represents the valid activities on each day for a driver, and possible connections between them. Recall that an activity can be a shift, a standby, a day off, or a fixed activity, such as a training period or annual leave. The activity arcs are only connected if they are compatible, i.e. the sequence of both activities does not violate any work regulation, such as the minimum rest period between two consecutive shifts. A path on the network corresponds to a schedule for an employee for the planning horizon (for example: two months). On each network layer, the cost of each activity is defined to reflect the daily desire of the driver, while the cost of each connection arc is used to reflect the combination of desires of activities for the driver. An example of the combination of desires for a driver is that similar shifts are connected. The arcs representing the less-desired activities and less-desired combinations of activities receive higher costs. An illustration of the network layer for driver $d1$ in the example in Figure 2.4 is shown in Figure 5.1, in which the different types of activity arcs are represented as nodes for illustration purposes. The nodes with letters E, M, and L represent sorted shift types: early, midday, and late shifts respectively; while the ones with numbers 1 and 2 represent the single-offs and double-offs respectively. The marked nodes are the activities that driver $d1$ prefers. Additionally, a start and an end node are defined on each layer.

Only the feasible activities are generated as activity arcs for each driver. If a fixed activity exists on one day, then there is only one activity on that day, and one connection arc between two fixed activities is generated. One exception is a fixed single day off on the actual planning horizon, for example, the fixed day off on the 11th day in Figure 5.1. The single- and double-off activities on that day are generated for the open case, where a day off on day 10 or 12 may be selected. The following techniques are used to reduce the complexity of the network shown in Figure 5.1.

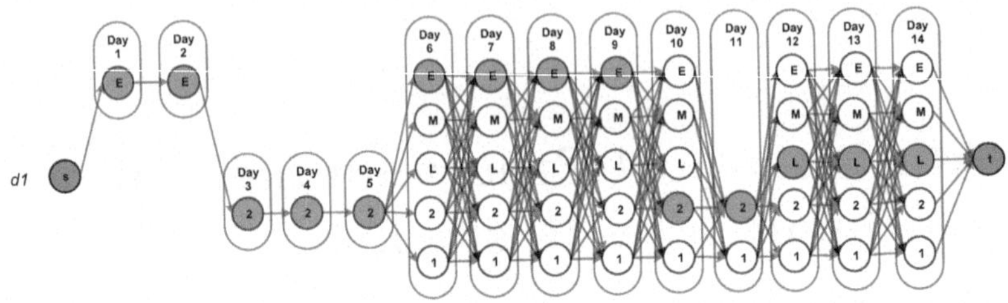

Figure 5.1. Illustration of the network layer for driver $d1$ in the NCCR problem in Figure 2.4.

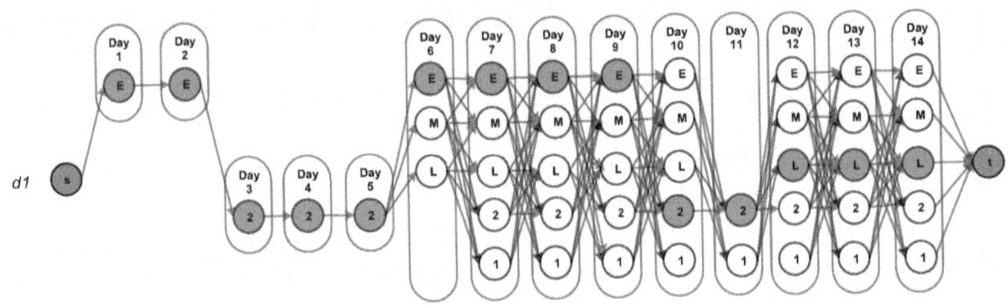

Figure 5.2. Illustration of the reduced network layer in Figure 5.1.

- We assume the maximum block of days off is three days. Therefore, on the 6th day only work-related activities are possible and single- and double-off activities are deleted (see Figure 5.2). Moreover, only the compatible and desirable connections for each pair of consecutive days are generated as connection arcs. Any connection arcs between forbidden sequences that include two activities, and any that violate a single-off or double-off, are eliminated. The forbidden sequences that include two activities in this example include (L, E) and (E, L).

- Activity arcs without incoming or outgoing arcs should be eliminated. The single-off on day 10 and 12 for driver $d1$ can be eliminated. Figure 5.3 shows the reduced network for drivers $d1$ and $d2$.

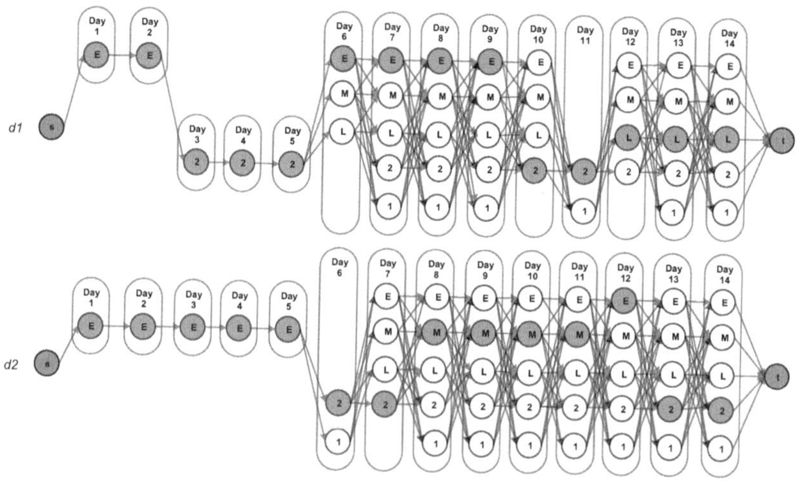

Figure 5.3. Illustration of the reduced network layers of the example in Figure 2.4.

The same network design, and the reducing techniques for NCCR, can be used for solving the CCR problem, but with the following modifications. Figure 5.4 shows the reduced network for the example shown in Figure 2.3.

- We consider each driver group as one driver.
- For each driver there might be a different planning period, which is calculated as the number of drivers in the driver group multiplied by the number of days within a week (i.e. seven).
- The capacity of each work-related activity or day off activity is no longer restricted by calendar dates, but by days of the week (see vertical rules in Section 2.2.1).
- Due to the properties of CCR, the compatibility of the assigned activity on the last day with the one on the first day should be checked. Additionally, the length of work days, days off blocks, and the maximal distance between two double-off arcs should be checked. In order to retain the acyclic network, a sequence of artificial days is appended to the planning period, with a length equal to the largest block length we consider (such as the maximal distance between two double-off arcs). The available activity arcs for these artificial days are the same as those available at the beginning of the planning period.

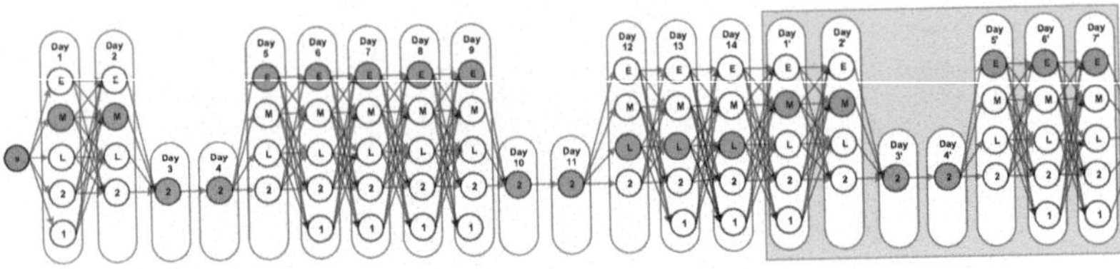

Figure 5.4. Illustration of the network layer of the CCR problem in Figure 2.3.

We have two variations of design of the network for the integrated problem. The first variation is to generate each duty, instead of each shift, as an activity arc. The problem with this is that the size of the network explodes, and most of the constraints we considered ignore the duty information, except for the objective of minimizing maximum working time. The second variation is to maintain the network used for solving the sub-problems. However, some sequences that include two activities, and are forbidden due to violating the required overnight rest time, still remain in the network. For example, the forbidden sequence (L, E) remains in Figures 5.3 and 5.4 for the integrated approach. Recall that the reason of that is described with Example 3 in Section 2.2.3. Moreover, some constraints about the feasibility of assigning duties are added to the network model. Details can be found in Sections 5.2.3 and 5.3.3.

5.2. The Mathematical Model of NCCR

The models for sequential rota scheduling and duty sequencing, as well as the integrated models of NCCR, are shown. This includes the basic and specialized index-sets, all necessary parameters and variables, the constraints and the objective function.

5.2.1. Rota Scheduling for NCCR

Index-sets

$\mathcal{M}$	Set of all employees.
$\mathcal{T}_m$	Partially ordered set of all discrete time-elements t (here: days) of the planning horizon, which means $\mathcal{T}_m = \{1, \ldots, T_m\}\ \forall m \in \mathcal{M}$.
$\mathcal{D}$	Set of all activities d.
$\mathcal{D}_w \subseteq \mathcal{D}$	Set of all work-related activities.
$\mathcal{D}_b \subseteq \mathcal{D}_w$	Set of all standby activities.
$\mathcal{D}_s \subseteq \mathcal{D}_w$	Set of all shift activities.
$\mathcal{D}_f \subseteq \mathcal{D}$	Set of all day off activities.
$\mathcal{D}_{df} \subseteq \mathcal{D}_f$	Set of all double-off activities.
$\mathcal{D}_{sf} \subseteq \mathcal{D}_f$	Set of all single-off activities.
$\mathcal{D}_{mf} \subseteq \mathcal{D}_f$	Set of all moved day off activities.
$\mathcal{D}_{mfw} \subseteq \mathcal{D}_f$	Set of all moved day off activities at a weekend.

$\mathcal{D}_{du} \subseteq \mathcal{D}$	Set of all dummy activities.
$\mathcal{E} = \mathcal{A} \cup \mathcal{C}$	Set of all edges e. This set includes the set of all activity arcs $\mathcal{A}$ implied by the given activities with the set of all compatibility arcs $\mathcal{C}$.
$\mathcal{A} \subset \mathcal{E}$	Set of all activity arcs.
$\mathcal{A}^s \subset \mathcal{E}$	Set of all activity arcs e including the extended source e^s_m and sink-edges e^e_m per employee $m \in \mathcal{M}$. That is, $\mathcal{A}^s = \bigcup_{m \in \mathcal{M}} \{e^s_m, e^e_m\} \cup \mathcal{A}$.
$\mathcal{A}_{m,t,d} \subseteq \mathcal{A}$	Subset of $\mathcal{A}$ that only contains the activities available to a given employee $m \in \mathcal{M}$ on day $t \in \mathcal{T}_m$ referring to an activity $d \in \mathcal{D}$.
$\mathcal{C} \subset \mathcal{E}$	Set of all compatibility arcs e, which connect compatible activity-arcs.
$\mathcal{F}_e \subset \mathcal{C}$	Set of all compatibility-arcs outgoing from activity-arc e, which link to all compatible activity arcs of the following day for a specific employee. The so-called "Forward-Star" (see also Cappanera & Gallo (2004)), with $e \in \mathcal{A}^s$.
$\mathcal{B}_e \subset \mathcal{C}$	Set of all compatibility arcs incoming to activity arc e, which link to all compatible activity arcs of the preceding day for a specific employee. The so-called "Backward-Star" (see also Cappanera & Gallo (2004)) with $e \in \mathcal{A}^s$.
$\mathcal{S}$	Contains all sets s of sequencing activity arcs, which are forbidden to be simultaneously active in a feasible solution. This means, for example, $(e_i, \ldots, e_j) \in \mathcal{S}$ with $e_i, \ldots, e_j \in \mathcal{A}$. These sets of edges are implied by the given forbidden sequences. Due to the reduction in the network each $\lvert s \rvert > 2$.

Parameters

T_m	Count of days on the planning horizon for employee m.
D	Maximal distance between two double-off arcs.
L^R_m	Maximal length of consecutive day off activities for employee m.
L^W_m	Maximal length of consecutive work-related activities for employee m.
C^d	Penalty cost for not satisfying the maximal distance, defined by D, between two double-off activities.
C^f	Penalty cost for falling short of the minimal amount of day off activities per employee.
C^g	Penalty cost for exceeding the maximal amount of single-off activities per employee.
C^p	Penalty cost for falling below the minimal count of standbys for an employee.
C^u	Penalty cost for an unallocated shift/duty.
C^{m1}	Penalty cost for activating an activity which indicates a moved day off activity.

C^{m2}	Penalty cost for activating an activity which indicates a moved day off activity at a weekend.
C^{o}	Penalty cost for the maximum overtime for all drivers.
C^{a}_{e}	Cost which appears when using the activity e.
C^{du}	Penalty cost for an unassigned day per employee.
I_d	Count of units of an activity $d \in \mathcal{D}_w \cup \mathcal{D}_f$ which are planned to be allocated.
W_d	Work time consumed when using an activity belonging to the work-related activity $d \in \mathcal{D}_w$.
T_d	The day of the work-related activity $d \in \mathcal{D}_w$.
F_m	Minimal count of days off for employee m.
E_m	Maximal count of single-off activities for employee m.
V_m	Minimal count of standbys for employee m.
R_m	Desired amount of working hours for employee m. When this value is exceeded for the correlating employee the resulting surplus will be considered overtime.

Variables

x^{a}_{e}	Binary variable that depicts the flow over the activity arc $e \in \mathcal{A}^s$.
x^{c}_{e}	Binary variable that depicts the flow over the compatibility arc $e \in \mathcal{C}$.
e^{s}_{m}	Binary variable for defining the source edge of employee $m \in \mathcal{M}$.
e^{e}_{m}	Binary variable for defining the sink edge of employee $m \in \mathcal{M}$.
σ_m	Sum of the days off for the employee m described through an integer variable with the bounds $l = 0$ and $u = T^m$.
v_m	Binary variable that indicates if the sum of days off is satisfactory for the corresponding employee m.
τ_m	Sum of single-off activities for the employee m depicted by an integer variable with the bounds $l = 0$ and $u = T^m$.
w_m	Binary variable that indicates if the sum of single-off activities is overflowed for the employee m.
ψ_m	Sum of the standbys for the employee m. This integer variable is bounded between $l = 0$ and $u = T^m$.
p_m	Binary variable that indicates if the sum of used standbys is falling short for employee m.
λ_d	Sum of unallocated units of activity d depicted by an integer variable within the bounds $l = 0$ and $u = I_d$.
δ_m	Binary variable that indicates if a violation of the maximal distance between two double-off activities is present for the employee m.
ϕ	Maximal overtime over all employees as a positive continuous variable.
z_m	Integer variable that indicates the sum of open days for the employee m, since it is possible that there are some days without assigned activities for the employee m.

Hard constraints

As described above, the rota scheduling is formulated as a multicommodity network flow problem, which contains the following *network constraints*. The set of constraints (5.1) makes sure that the value of an activity arc matches the sum of all compatibility arcs of the backward-star as well as the sum of all compatibility arcs of the forward-star (*flow conservation*), while the set of constraints (5.2) ensures that exactly one activity is selected for each driver per day (*demand satisfaction*). The units of each activity are restricted in the *flow capacity* constraint (5.7). In each network layer, a resource constrained shortest path has to be determined. The *resources* include the maximal block length of work-related days (see constraint set (5.3)) as well as days off for each driver (see constraint set (5.4)). Additionally, the double-off and forbidden sequences are defined in the constraints (5.5) and (5.6), respectively.

$$x^a_e = \sum_{e' \in \mathcal{F}_e} x^c_{e'} \qquad \forall e \in \mathcal{A}^s \qquad (5.1)$$
$$x^a_e = \sum_{e' \in \mathcal{B}_e} x^c_{e'} \qquad \forall e \in \mathcal{A}^s$$

$$e^s_m = 1 \qquad \forall m \in \mathcal{M} \qquad (5.2)$$
$$e^e_m = 1 \qquad \forall m \in \mathcal{M}$$

$$\sum_{t'=t}^{t+L^W_m} \sum_{e \in \mathcal{A}_{m,t',d}} x^a_e \geq 1 \qquad \forall m \in \mathcal{M}, t \in \{1, ..., T_m - L^W_m\}, d \in \mathcal{D}_f \qquad (5.3)$$

$$\sum_{t'=t}^{t+L^R_m} \sum_{e \in \mathcal{A}_{m,t',d}} x^a_e \geq 1 \qquad \forall m \in \mathcal{M}, t \in \{1, ..., T_m - L^R_m\}, d \in \mathcal{D}_w \qquad (5.4)$$

$$\sum_{e \in \mathcal{A}_{m,t,d}} x^a_e \geq \sum_{e \in \mathcal{A}_{m,t+1,d}} x^a_e \qquad \forall m \in \mathcal{M}, t \in \{1, ..., T_m - 1\}, d \in \mathcal{D}_{df} \qquad (5.5)$$

$$\sum_{e \in s} x^a_e \leq |s| - 1 \qquad \forall s \in \mathcal{S} \qquad (5.6)$$

$$\sum_{m \in \mathcal{M}} \sum_{e \in \mathcal{A}_{m,t,d}} x^a_e \leq I_d \qquad \forall d \in \mathcal{D}_w \cup \mathcal{D}_f, t = T_d \qquad (5.7)$$

Soft constraints

Besides the hard constraints listed above, some constraints are soft and can be weighted by applying specific penalty costs to them. The number of unassigned shifts is counted as λ_d in the constraint set (5.8). The fulfillment of the minimal sum of days off per driver is achieved by the constraint set (5.9). The first group of constraints sums the count of days off per driver, while the second group determines whether the minimal sum of days off is met. The constraint set (5.10) limits the number of unpopular single-off activities. Furthermore, a maximal distance between two double-off activities should be satisfied (see constraint set (5.11)). Additionally, if a given number of standbys falls short for a driver, the corresponding penalty costs will be added to the objective function (see constraint set (5.12)). In order to avoid the case where there is no activity possible for a driver on a day, a dummy activity is selected. In constraint set (5.13), the sum of all open days for driver m is stored in the integer variable z_m. Moreover, in order to prevent large differences in overtimes among drivers, the constraint set (5.14) defines the maximal overtime for all drivers. Note that the working time of each shift type is defined as the average working time of the duties for the particular shift type.

$$I_d - \sum_{m\in\mathcal{M}} \sum_{e\in\mathcal{A}_{m,t,d}} x_e^a = \lambda_d \qquad \forall d \in \mathcal{D}_s, t = T_d \tag{5.8}$$

$$\sum_{e\in\mathcal{A}_{m,t,d}} x_e^a = \sigma_m \qquad \forall m \in \mathcal{M}, t \in \mathcal{T}_m, d \in \mathcal{D}_f \tag{5.9}$$

$$F_m - v_m \cdot T^m \leq \sigma_m \qquad \forall m \in \mathcal{M}$$

$$\sum_{e\in\mathcal{A}_{m,t,d}} x_e^a = \tau_m \qquad \forall m \in \mathcal{M}, t \in \mathcal{T}_m, d \in \mathcal{D}_{sf} \tag{5.10}$$

$$E_m + w_m \cdot T^m \geq \tau_m \qquad \forall m \in \mathcal{M}$$

$$\sum_{t'=t}^{t+D} \sum_{e\in\mathcal{A}_{m,t',d}} x_e^a \geq 1 - \delta_m \qquad \forall m \in \mathcal{M}, d \in \mathcal{D}_{df}, t \in \{1, \ldots, T_m - D\} \tag{5.11}$$

$$\sum_{e\in\mathcal{A}_{m,t,d}} x_e^a = \psi_m \qquad \forall m \in \mathcal{M}, t \in \mathcal{T}_m, d \in \mathcal{D}_b \tag{5.12}$$

$$\psi_m \geq V_m - V_m \cdot p_m \qquad \forall m \in \mathcal{M}$$

$$\sum_{t\in\mathcal{T}_m} \sum_{d\in\mathcal{D}_{du}} \sum_{e\in\mathcal{A}_{m,t,d}} x_e^a = z_m \qquad \forall m \in \mathcal{M} \tag{5.13}$$

$$\sum_{t\in\mathcal{T}_m} \sum_{d\in\mathcal{D}_w} \sum_{e\in\mathcal{A}_{m,t,d}} W_d \cdot x_e^a - R_m \leq \phi \qquad \forall m \in \mathcal{M} \tag{5.14}$$

Objective function

There are three types of objectives that typically have to be considered in crew rostering problems.

1. *Objectives related to real costs*
   The number of unassigned activities, such as shift activities (5.22), standby activities (5.21), and the number of open days (5.23), should be minimized in the objective function, since additional costs have to be paid, e.g. for hiring new (part-time) drivers or asking drivers to work overtime. Additionally, the overtime should be paid. In some cases overtime should be avoided, for example, when some drivers work overtime while others work substantially less than the regular working time (also a fairness aspect). Therefore, the maximum overtime among all drivers should be minimized in the objective function (5.24).

2. *Objectives related to the fairness among drivers*
   One aspect of even distribution of workload (overtime) is considered in the last category (5.24). Another one, i.e. the given number of days off for each driver, should be satisfied as far as possible (5.18). Moreover, the other aspects of fairness, such as the distribution of unpopular activities, are embedded in drivers' preferences (5.15) (i.e. the desirability of an activity on one particular day).

3. *Objectives related to preferences*
   One cost category reflects the desirability of an activity on one particular day. This category includes the costs of selected activities (5.15) and the costs for moved days off (5.16) (at weekends (5.17)). Another cost reflects the desirability of the frequency of a desired/undesired activity, which contains the costs of underrun days off (5.18) and the costs of overflowed single-off activities (5.19). Additionally, the violation of the maximal distance between two double-off activities should be minimized (5.20).

$$\min z^R_{NCCR}$$

$$= \sum_{e \in \mathcal{A}^s} C^a_e \cdot x^a_e \qquad \text{(Costs of selected activities)} \tag{5.15}$$

$$+ \sum_{m \in \mathcal{M}} \sum_{d \in \mathcal{D}_{mf}} \sum_{e \in \mathcal{A}_{m,T_d,d}} C^{m1} \cdot x^a_e \qquad \text{(Costs of moved days off)} \tag{5.16}$$

$$+ \sum_{m \in \mathcal{M}} \sum_{d \in \mathcal{D}_{mfw}} \sum_{e \in \mathcal{A}_{m,T_d,d}} C^{m2} \cdot x^a_e \qquad \text{(Costs of moved days off at weekends)} \tag{5.17}$$

$$+ \sum_{m \in \mathcal{M}} C^f \cdot v_m \qquad \text{(Costs of underrun days off)} \tag{5.18}$$

$$+ \sum_{m \in \mathcal{M}} C^g \cdot w_m \qquad \text{(Costs of overflowed single-offs)} \tag{5.19}$$

$$+ \sum_{m \in \mathcal{M}} C^d \cdot \delta_m \qquad \text{(Violated max. dist. btwn double-offs)} \tag{5.20}$$

$$+ \sum_{m \in \mathcal{M}} C^p \cdot p_m \qquad \text{(Costs of underrun standbys)} \tag{5.21}$$

$$+ \sum_{d \in \mathcal{D}_s} C^u \cdot \lambda_d \qquad \text{(Costs of unassigned shifts)} \tag{5.22}$$

$$+ \sum_{m \in \mathcal{M}} C^{du} \cdot z_m \qquad \text{(Costs of open days)} \tag{5.23}$$

$$+ C^o \cdot \phi \qquad \text{(Overtime)} \tag{5.24}$$

5.2.2. Duty Sequencing for NCCR

Let the set of duties be $\mathcal{J}$ and $\mathcal{J}_e$ be the set of duties belonging to the shift activity arc e, where $e \in \mathcal{A}_m^{a,w}$, which is defined as the set of selected shift activities after solving the rota scheduling for the driver $m \in \mathcal{M}$. A set $\mathcal{A}_m^w$ is defined as all assigned work-related activities, which contains the subset $\mathcal{A}_m^{a,w}$. Let T_e be the day of the activity arc $e \in \mathcal{A}_m^{a,w}$, and $\mathcal{A}_j$ be a set of assigned shift activity arcs, which contains the duty j. We define $\mathcal{S}^o$ as the set of sequencing duties, which are forbidden to be simultaneously active in a feasible solution due to violating the overnight rest period. Let $y_{e,j}$ be a binary variable, which is equal to 1, if the duty j is assigned to the selected shift activity arc $e \in \mathcal{A}_m^{a,w}$. Additionally, for each assigned shift activity a binary variable for the open day is defined as z_e, and each of them should be punished in the objective function with the cost factor C^{du}, which is the same for the open days in the rota scheduling. Moreover, a parameter W_j is defined as the working time of the duty $j \in \mathcal{J}$, while a parameter W is defined as the standard working time of each standby activity $d \in \mathcal{D}_b$.

Hard restrictions

Each duty might be available to several shift activity arcs, therefore the constraints (5.25) make sure that each duty is selected at most once. The constraints (5.26) forbid an impossible combination of duties.

$$\sum_{e \in \mathcal{A}_j} y_{e,j} \leq 1 \qquad \forall j \in \mathcal{J} \tag{5.25}$$

$$y_{e,j} + y_{e',j'} \leq 1 \qquad \forall e, e' \in \mathcal{A}_m^{a,w}, m \in \mathcal{M}, T_e = T_{e'} - 1, (j, j') \in \mathcal{S}^o \tag{5.26}$$

Soft restrictions

The constraints (5.27) ensure the relationship between duty and the selected shift activity arc, i.e. one duty or dummy is needed for each selected shift activity arc. The dummies are needed due to the sequencing approach. The constraints (5.14a) redefine the calculation of maximal overtime for all drivers.

$$x_e^a = \sum_{j \in \mathcal{J}_e} y_{e,j} + z_e \qquad \forall e \in \mathcal{A}_m^{a,w}, m \in \mathcal{M} \tag{5.27}$$

$$\sum_{e \in \mathcal{A}_m^w \setminus \mathcal{A}_m^{a,w}} W \cdot x_e^a + \sum_{e \in \mathcal{A}_m^{a,w}} \sum_{j \in \mathcal{J}_e} W_j \cdot y_{e,j} - R_m \leq \phi' \qquad \forall m \in \mathcal{M} \tag{5.14a}$$

Objectives

The duty sequencing problem aims to assign duties to the selected shifts fairly without violating any constraints. The fairness refers to minimizing the maximum overtime. Additionally, some more open days, or more precisely, some unassigned duties, might be caused.

$$\min z_{NCCR}^D = C^o \cdot \phi' \qquad \text{(Overtime)} \tag{5.24a}$$

$$+ \sum_{m \in \mathcal{M}} \sum_{e \in \mathcal{A}_m^{a,w}} C^{du} \cdot z_e \qquad \text{(Open days/unassigned duties)} \tag{5.28}$$

5.2.3. Integrated Problem for NCCR

Recall that the set of duties is defined as $\mathcal{J}$. Let $\mathcal{J}'_e$ be a set of duties belonging to the activity arc e, where $e \in \mathcal{A}^a_m, m \in \mathcal{M}$. We define $\mathcal{A}^a$ be the set of all shift activity arcs, and $\mathcal{A}^a_m \subset \mathcal{A}^a$ be the set of all shift activity arcs for driver $m \in \mathcal{M}$. The set $\mathcal{A}'_j$ is a set of possible shift activity arcs, to which the duty j can be assigned. Let $y'_{e,j}$ be a binary variable that is equal to 1 if the duty j is assigned to the activity arc $e \in \mathcal{A}^a_m$ of the driver m, and 0 otherwise.

Hard restrictions

The set of hard constraints (5.1) to (5.7) remains the same as in Section 5.2.1. Additionally, each duty might belong to several shift activity arcs, therefore the constraints (5.25*a*) make sure that each duty is selected at most once. Moreover, the constraints (5.26*a*) forbid an impossible combination of duties. Constraints (5.27*a*) ensure each assigned shift activity arc gets a duty.

$$(5.1), (5.2), (5.3), (5.4), (5.5), (5.6), (5.7)$$

$$\sum_{e \in \mathcal{A}'_j} y'_{e,j} \leq 1 \qquad \forall j \in \mathcal{J} \tag{5.25a}$$

$$y'_{e,j} + y'_{e',j'} \leq 1 \qquad \forall e \in \mathcal{A}'_j, e' \in \mathcal{A}'_{j'}, (j,j') \in \mathcal{S}^o \tag{5.26a}$$

$$x^a_e = \sum_{j \in \mathcal{J}'_e} y'_{e,j} \qquad \forall e \in \mathcal{A}^a_m, m \in \mathcal{M} \tag{5.27a}$$

Soft restrictions

The set of soft constraints (5.8) to (5.13) in Section 5.2.1 remains the same. Additionally, the constraints (5.14*b*) replace (5.14) and redefine the calculation of maximal overtime ϕ'' for all drivers.

$$(5.8), (5.9), (5.10), (5.11), (5.12), (5.13)$$

$$\sum_{d \in \mathcal{D}_w \backslash \mathcal{D}_s} \sum_{e \in \mathcal{A}_{m,T_d,d}} W_d \cdot x^a_e + \sum_{e \in \mathcal{A}^a_m} \sum_{j \in \mathcal{J}'_e} W_j \cdot y'_{e,j} - R_m \leq \phi'' \quad \forall m \in \mathcal{M} \tag{5.14b}$$

Objectives

The objectives (5.15) to (5.23) remain. The new calculated maximum overtime is minimized in the objective function.

$$\min z^I_{NCCR} = (5.15) + ... + (5.23)$$
$$+ C^o \cdot \phi'' \qquad \text{(Overtime)} \tag{5.24b}$$

5.3. The Mathematical Model of CCR

The network model of CCR is similar to the one of NCCR. The differences between them are shown in Section 5.1. In this section, the modifications to the mathematical models in Section 5.2 for the CCR problem are shown, both for the sequential and integrated approaches.

5.3.1. Rota Scheduling for CCR

Hard restrictions

As mentioned before, the capacities of work-related activities and day off activities are no longer restricted by calendar dates, but by days of the week (5.7a). Therefore, T_d' is defined as the day of the week for the work-related activity or day off activity $d \in \mathcal{D}_w \cup \mathcal{D}_f$. Note that $\mathcal{T}_m$ is defined as the days for driver m in the network, including the artificial days for the CCR problem. A set $\mathcal{T}_{m,t}$ is used to define the days (but not including artificial days) in the network for the day t of the week for the driver $m \in \mathcal{M}$. For example, the day t of the week is equal to 1, so a set $\mathcal{T}_{m,t}$ might be $\{1, 8, 15, ...\}$. The number of artificial days for each driver m is stored in b_m^{art}. Let $\mathcal{D}_t$ be the set of all available activities on day $t \in \mathcal{T}_m$. Constraints (5.29) make sure the selected activity on each artificial day $T_m - b_m^{art} + i$ is equal to the selected one on the day i, where $i \in \{1, 2, ..., b_m^{art}\}$. The rest remains the same as in Section 5.2.1.

$$(5.1), (5.2), (5.3), (5.4), (5.5), (5.6)$$

$$\sum_{m\in\mathcal{M}} \sum_{t'\in\mathcal{T}_{m,t}} \sum_{e\in\mathcal{A}_{m,t',d}} x_e^a \leq I_d \qquad \forall d \in \mathcal{D}_w \cup \mathcal{D}_f, t = T_d' \tag{5.7a}$$

$$x_e^a = x_{e'}^a \qquad \forall m \in \mathcal{M}, i \in \{1, 2, ..., b_m^{art}\} \quad d \in \mathcal{D}_i, e \in \mathcal{A}_{m,T_m - b_m^{art}+i,d}, e' \in \mathcal{A}_{m,i,d} \tag{5.29}$$

Soft restrictions

$\mathcal{T}_m^{art} \subset \mathcal{T}_m$ is defined as the set of artificial days in the network for driver m. Additionally, the artificial days should be ignored by the constraints of calculations of unassigned shifts (5.8a), underrun days off (5.9a), overflowed single-offs (5.10a), underun of standbys (5.12a), unassigned days (5.13a), and the maximum amount of overtime (5.14c). However, a maximal distance between two double-off activities should also be checked on the artificial days (see constraint set (5.11)).

$$(5.11)$$

$$I_d - \sum_{m\in\mathcal{M}} \sum_{t'\in\mathcal{T}_{m,t}} \sum_{e\in\mathcal{A}_{m,t',d}} x_e^a = \lambda_d' \qquad \forall d \in \mathcal{D}_s, t = T_d' \tag{5.8a}$$

$$\sum_{e\in\mathcal{A}_{m,t,d}} x_e^a = \sigma_m' \qquad \forall m \in \mathcal{M}, d \in \mathcal{D}_f, t \in \mathcal{T}_m \setminus \mathcal{T}_m^{art} \tag{5.9a}$$

$$F_m - v_m{}' \cdot T^m \leq \sigma_m{}' \qquad \forall m \in \mathcal{M}$$

$$\sum_{e \in \mathcal{A}_{m,t,d}} x_e^a = \tau_m{}' \qquad \forall m \in \mathcal{M}, d \in \mathcal{D}_{sf}, t \in \mathcal{T}_m \setminus \mathcal{T}_m^{art} \tag{5.10a}$$

$$E_m + w_m{}' \cdot T^m \geq \tau_m{}' \qquad \forall m \in \mathcal{M}$$

$$\sum_{e \in \mathcal{A}_{m,t,d}} x_e^a = \psi_m{}' \qquad \forall m \in \mathcal{M}, d \in \mathcal{D}_b, t \in \mathcal{T}_m \setminus \mathcal{T}_m^{art} \tag{5.12a}$$

$$\psi_m{}' \geq V_m - p_m{}' \cdot V_m \qquad \forall m \in \mathcal{M}$$

$$\sum_{t \in \mathcal{T}_m \setminus \mathcal{T}_m^{art}} \sum_{d \in \mathcal{D}_{du}} \sum_{e \in \mathcal{A}_{m,t,d}} x_e^a = z_m{}' \qquad \forall m \in \mathcal{M} \tag{5.13a}$$

$$\sum_{t \in \mathcal{T}_m \setminus \mathcal{T}_m^{art}} \sum_{d \in \mathcal{D}_w} \sum_{e \in \mathcal{A}_{m,t,d}} W_d \cdot x_e^a - R_m \leq \phi''' \qquad \forall m \in \mathcal{M} \tag{5.14c}$$

Objectives

The objective is modified according to the altered soft constraints.

$$\min z_{CCR}^R = (5.15) + (5.16) + (5.17) + (5.20)$$

$$+ \sum_{m \in \mathcal{M}} C^f \cdot v_m{}' \qquad \text{(Costs of underrun days off)} \tag{5.18a}$$

$$+ \sum_{m \in \mathcal{M}} C^g \cdot w_m{}' \qquad \text{(Costs of overflowed single-offs)} \tag{5.19a}$$

$$+ \sum_{m \in \mathcal{M}} C^p \cdot p_m{}' \qquad \text{(Costs of underrun standbys)} \tag{5.21a}$$

$$+ \sum_{d \in \mathcal{D}_s} C^u \cdot \lambda'_d \qquad \text{(Costs of unassigned shifts)} \tag{5.22a}$$

$$+ \sum_{m \in \mathcal{M}} C^{du} \cdot z_m{}' \qquad \text{(Costs of open days)} \tag{5.23a}$$

$$+ C^o \cdot \phi''' \qquad \text{(Overtime)} \tag{5.24c}$$

5.3.2. Duty Sequencing for CCR

We assume that the sets $\mathcal{A}_j$, $\mathcal{A}_m^{a,w}$, and $\mathcal{A}_m^{w}$ do not contain the arcs on artificial days. Therefore, the constraints (5.25), (5.27), (5.14a), as well as the objective, remain the same as in Section 5.2.2. Let $\mathcal{A}_m^{a,art}$ be the assigned shift activity arcs in the artificial days for driver m.

Hard restrictions

The combination of duties should also be checked in the artificial days, therefore, the constraints (5.26) should be changed to (5.26b). Moreover, a set of constraints in (5.30) makes sure that the same duties are assigned in the artificial days and the original days.

$$(5.25)$$

$$y_{e,j} + y_{e',j'} \leq 1 \qquad \forall e, e' \in \mathcal{A}_m^{a,w} \cup \mathcal{A}_m^{a,art}, T_e = T_{e'} - 1, \; (j, j') \in \mathcal{S}^o, m \in \mathcal{M} \tag{5.26b}$$

$$y_{e,j} = y_{e',j} \qquad \forall m \in \mathcal{M}, T_e \in \{1, 2, ..., b_m^{art}\}, e \in \mathcal{A}_m^{a,w}, e' \in \mathcal{A}_m^{a,art} \; T_{e'} = T_m - b_m^{art} + T_e, j \in \mathcal{J}_e \tag{5.30}$$

Soft restrictions

Since the sets $\mathcal{A}_m^{a,w}$ and $\mathcal{A}_m^{w}$ do not contain the arcs on artificial days, the constraints (5.27), about the relationship between duty and the selected shift activity arc, and the constraints (5.14a) of defining maximum overtime for all drivers, remain.

$$(5.27), (5.14a)$$

Objectives

The objective remains as same as the one in duty sequencing for NCCR.

$$\min z_{CCR}^D = \min z_{NCCR}^D$$

5.3.3. Integrated Problem for CCR

The model for CCR in integrated planning is considered as an extended model of the rota scheduling in Section 5.3.1. The hard and soft constraints about duties are extended.

Hard restrictions

The constraints (5.1) to (5.29) in Section 5.3.1 remain the same. We assume that $\mathcal{A}'_j$ does not contain the shift activities on the artificial days. Therefore, the constraints (5.25a), (5.26a) and (5.27a) from Section 5.2.3 remain. (5.30a) replaces (5.30) to make sure the assigned duties on the artificial days are equal to those on the original days.

$$(5.1), ..., (5.6), (5.7a), (5.29)(5.25a), (5.26a), (5.27a)$$

$$y'_{e,j} = y'_{e',j} \quad \forall m \in \mathcal{M}, T_e \in \{1, 2, ..., b^{art}_m\}, e, e' \in \mathcal{A}^a_m, T_{e'} = T_m - b^{art}_m + T_e, j \in \mathcal{J}'_e \quad (5.30a)$$

Soft restrictions

The soft constraints in Section 5.3.1 from (5.8a) to (5.13a) remain for the formulation of this problem. Additionally, the calculation of maximum overtime ϕ'''' should avoid the duties on artificial days in constraint set (5.14d). The relationship between a duty and its possible shift activity arcs is the same as in Section 5.2.3.

$$(5.8a), (5.9a), (5.10a), (5.11), (5.12a), (5.13a)$$

$$\sum_{t \in \mathcal{T}_m \setminus \mathcal{T}^{art}_m} \sum_{d \in \mathcal{D}_w \setminus \mathcal{D}_s} \sum_{e \in \mathcal{A}_{m,t,d}} W_d \cdot x^a_e + \sum_{e \in \mathcal{A}^a_m} \sum_{j \in \mathcal{J}'_e} W_j \cdot y'_{e,j} - R_m \leq \phi'''' \quad \forall m \in \mathcal{M} \quad (5.14d)$$

Objectives

All objectives in Section 5.3.1 are included, except for a small modification to maximum overtime ϕ''''.

$$\begin{aligned} \min z^I_{CCR} = & (5.15) + (5.16) + (5.17) + (5.18a) \\ & + (5.19a) + (5.20) + (5.21a) + (5.22a) + (5.23a) \\ & + C^o \cdot \phi'''' \qquad \text{(Overtime)} \qquad (5.24d) \end{aligned}$$

6. Computational Experiments for the MIP Models

In this section we begin by introducing a set of real-world instances from different German bus companies in Section 6.1; this is followed by a description of the solutions achieved with different solvers, namely the Gurobi Optimizer (see Gurobi Optimization (2014)) and the IBM ILOG CPLEX Optimizer 12.0 (see IBM Corporation (2014)) for the sequential and integrated approaches in Sections 6.2 and 6.3. Additionally, a comparison of the sequential and integrated approaches is shown there.

6.1. Properties of the Real-World Data Instances

We test our solution approaches on 16 real-world instances for which the number of duties varies between 1,013 and 19,486. The number of drivers in the instances varies between 48 and 629. The names of the instances include the number of drivers (NCCR) / groups of drivers (CCR), the number of planning days, and the number of included shift types.

Instance	Duties	Standbys	Days off	ϕAlt.	Act.arcs(fixed)	Com.arcs
48-75-6	1,313	454	1,472	2.2	10,516 (12.7%)	34,584
52-73-6	1,288	664	1,487	2.2	11,367 (12.2%)	37,907
52-75-6	1,321	488	1,509	2.2	11,072 (15.5%)	36,113
9-238-11*	1,013	303	483	4.7	6,672 (12.4%)	30,457
393-45-37	5,420	2,619	8,030	1.5	45,035 (23.8%)	145,491
392-45-37	5,815	2,342	8,364	1.3	43,367 (26.2%)	134,974
397-40-37	4,917	2,717	7,438	1.4	38,277 (26.3%)	115,236
96-70-8	3,200	876	1,936	5	38,413 (6.3%)	287,490
87-70-8	3,273	796	1,708	4.5	38,944 (4.1%)	301,374
89-70-8	3,260	671	1,758	4.8	40,392 (4.8%)	326,505
214-45-34	3,966	1,472	3,240	6.6	55,366 (8.7%)	472,958
211-45-34	4,003	1,447	3,029	7	55,376 (8.9%)	490,521
221-45-30	4,214	1,646	3,222	6.7	64,576 (7.6%)	624,520
629-46-26	11,073	4,292	9,246	5	150,616 (11.8%)	1,212,486
606-70-26	18,739	4,977	13,612	5.3	255,657 (7.5%)	2,158,525
607-70-26	19,486	4,549	13,364	5.1	258,075 (7.3%)	2,205,303

Table 6.1. Characteristics of the test set instances. The star (*) indicates the instance for the CCR problem.

In Table 6.1, the important properties of the instances are shown, including the number of activities, i.e. duties, standbys, and days off, the average alternatives (ϕAlt.), the number of activity arcs (Act.arcs), the percentage of fixed activity arcs in parentheses, and the number of compatibility arcs (Com.arcs). These are some of the factors causing difficulties in solving the instances. As we consider more activities (duties, standbys, days off) and drivers, more activity and compatibility arcs are generated in our network. If more alternatives for desired activities of drivers are provided, that also causes more activity and compatibility arcs. However, if we consider more fixed activity arcs, then this problem is easier to solve (such as the instances 96-70-8 vs. 89-70-8). The instances are sorted according to the gap to optimum after 24 hours for solving the integrated problem.

Besides those factors shown in Table 6.1, another important factor is how many quality rules are considered in those instances. Most of the instances in Table 6.1 consider all quality rules in Section 2.2.1, but the instances 392-45-37, 393-45-37 and 397-40-37 only consider the objectives (5.15), (5.22), (5.23), and (5.24) and their corresponding soft constraints. This is one of the reasons why these instances can be solved more easily compared with, for example, 221-45-30.

The instance 9-238-11 is used to solve the CCR problem. It includes nine groups of drivers (total 256 drivers) with different sizes, in which the maximum number of drivers in a group is 32, therefore there are at most 224 planning days for a group. 14 artificial days are needed to expand the planning period, because there is a 14-day distance between two double-off activities. Therefore, we consider nine drivers in a planning period of at most 238 days. The instance size for the CCR problem is, in practice, usually small compared with the instance size for the NCCR problem. The instance 9-238-11 is a large instance, which is available from German bus companies. The rest are provided to solve the NCCR problem. These instances are available at the web page `http://dsor.upb.de/crewrostering`.

The model we present is a multi-objective optimization model. The weight of each objective given by bus companies is shown in Table 6.2. The quality and the running time of the solution depend on the weights of the objectives. For example, we change the given C^u to be $2e7$ in instance 96-70-8, and the other weights remain. The optimal solution and the running time of the altered weights differ from the optimal solution determined with weights from the bus company (see Table 6.3). The number of unassigned shifts is reduced to 187 from 200, and the running time is reduced by about 86%.

All experiments in this chapter were conducted on an Intel Core i7-940 2.93 GHz processor with 32 GB of RAM running Windows 7 Professional (64 bit).

6.2. Results of Solving the Sequential Planning

An overview of the size of sub-problems, i.e. rota scheduling (RS) and duty sequencing (DS), is given in Table 6.4. The largest RS problems with 606, 607 and 629 drivers result in an optimization problem which ranges in the class of the extra-large set of the MIPLIB 2010 (see Zuse Institute Berlin (2014)) regarding the counts of variables, constraints and non-zeros.

As shown in literature (such as Sodhi & Norris (2004)), the duty sequencing problem is usually easier to solve compared with the rota scheduling problem, due to the assigned

Instance	C_e^a	C^u	C^{du}	C^f	C^{m2}	C^{m1}	C^d	C^p	C^g	C^o
48-75-6	1	1e6	1e7	5e6	1e5	9e5	1.5e6	1e4	5e5	1e4
52-73-6	1	1e6	1e7	5e6	1e5	9e5	1.5e6	1e4	5e5	1e4
52-75-6	1	1e6	1e7	5e6	1e5	9e5	1.5e6	1e4	5e5	1e4
9-238-11	1	1e6	1e7	5e6	1e5	2.1e6	2.5e6	1e4	5e5	1e3
393-45-37	1	1e6	1e7	0	0	0	0	0	0	1e1
392-45-37	1	1e6	1e7	0	0	0	0	0	0	1e1
397-40-37	1	1e6	1e7	0	0	0	0	0	0	1e1
96-70-8	1	1e6	1e7	5e6	1e5	2.1e6	2.5e6	1e4	5e5	1e3
87-70-8	1	1e6	1e7	5e6	1e5	2.1e6	2.5e6	1e4	5e5	1e3
89-70-8	1	1e6	1e7	5e6	1e5	2.1e6	2.5e6	1e4	5e5	1e3
214-45-34	1	1e8	5e7	1.5e7	5e5	5e6	3e7	1e5	5e5	5e2
211-45-34	1	5e7	5e7	2e7	1e5	1e7	1e7	1e5	5e5	1e3
221-45-30	1	5e7	5e7	2e7	1e5	1e7	1e7	1e5	5e5	1e3
629-46-26	1	1e6	1e7	5e6	1e5	9e5	1.5e6	1e5	5e5	1e3
606-70-26	1	1e6	1e7	5e6	1e5	9e5	1.5e6	1e5	5e5	1e3
607-70-26	1	1e6	1e7	5e6	1e5	9e5	1.5e6	1e5	5e5	1e3

Table 6.2. The weights of all objectives in all instances.

Information	96-70-8 (given w.)	96-70-8 (changed w.)
# Unassigned shifts	200	187
# Underrun standbys	1	1
# Used moved days off	1	13
# Used moved days off on weekends	8	13
# Underrun days off	0	0
# Single-off overflow	0	0
# Double-off distance violations	0	2
Maximal overtime (in hours)	0.41	1.6
Selected activity costs	2,963,383	2,741,173
Running time (in seconds)	27,284	4,069

Table 6.3. The comparison of solutions after solving rota scheduling for the instance 96-70-8 by using different weights of the objectives.

shifts and other activities. Moreover, fewer restrictions are considered in this problem (see the model description in Sections 5.2.2 and 5.3.2). The duty sequencing problem for all instances can be solved optimally within one hour, either using CPLEX or Gurobi as a solver. Note that the solution quality of this sequential approach depends highly on the solution to the rota scheduling problem. Therefore, we list only the solutions to the rota scheduling problem in Figure 6.1, in which the solutions obtained by two solvers are illustrated.

Instance	Stage	Int	Bin	Cols	Rows	NZs
48-75-6	RS	459	37,800	38,260	29,940	161,024
	DS	0	37,468	37,469	4,392	50,548
52-73-6	RS	461	41,714	42,176	32,084	174,557
	DS	0	41,613	41,614	3,969	53,764
52-75-6	RS	469	39,562	40,032	31,261	166,968
	DS	0	39,426	39,427	4,460	52,289
9-238-11	RS	93	54,210	54,304	21,479	174,660
	DS	0	100,821	100,822	61,295	254,775
393-45-37	RS	1,998	137,567	139,566	122,084	592,645
	DS	0	206,233	206,234	70,410	410,168
392-45-37	RS	1,958	128,225	130,184	116,666	558,222
	DS	0	222,085	222,086	78,042	447,784
397-40-37	RS	1,826	113,395	115,222	103,317	490,472
	DS	0	204,248	204,249	92,132	462,509
96-70-8	RS	658	264,238	264,897	154,439	1,078,099
	DS	0	235,227	235,228	46,204	374,940
87-70-8	RS	627	276,383	277,011	162,425	1,131,938
	DS	0	252,058	252,059	39,280	386,600
89-70-8	RS	631	303,541	304,173	175,855	1,231,574
	DS	0	261,922	261,923	46,124	409,105
214-45-34	RS	1,338	435,951	437,290	185,623	1,547,708
	DS	0	312,771	312,772	42,630	438,848
211-45-34	RS	1,287	457,029	458,317	183,363	1,576,977
	DS	0	315,070	315,071	63,111	479,735
221-45-30	RS	1,404	587,103	588,508	225,444	1,998,863
	DS	0	378,505	378,506	40,121	505,613
629-46-26	RS	2,507	1,095,668	1,098,176	675,251	4,446,551
	DS	0	2,197,945	2,197,946	366,693	3,456,166
606-70-26	RS	2,890	1,952,636	1,955,527	1,196,006	8,060,000
	DS	0	3,822,694	3,822,695	640,384	5,967,647
607-70-26	RS	2,916	2,000,713	2,003,630	1,239,754	8,304,197
	DS	0	3,903,682	3,903,683	285,569	5,069,953

Table 6.4. Characteristics of the test-set optimization models of the rota scheduling (RS) and duty sequencing (DS) problems.

According to Figure 6.1, the Gurobi solver is suitable for the smaller instances (see Figures 6.1a and 6.1b), especially instances 96-70-8 and 87-70-8, since the computational time is much shorter than for the solutions obtained by the CPLEX solver. However, the CPLEX solver is the better choice for the rest (running times are limited to 24 hours), except the instance 221-45-30. In order to solve the instances with Gurobi more quickly, we perform parameter tuning. Only a small set of instances (48-75-6, 392-45-37, and 96-70-8)

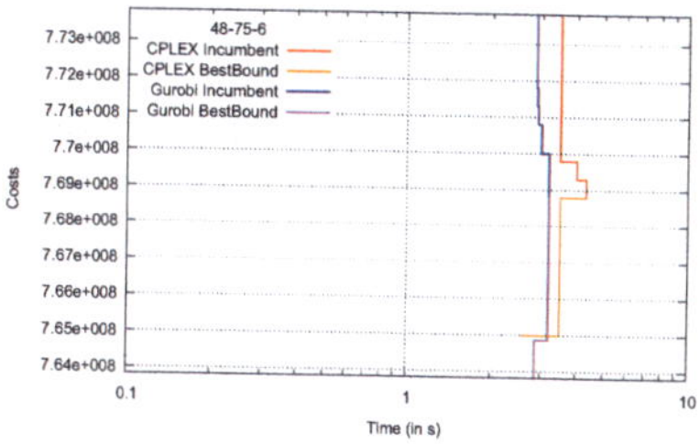

(a) Performance statistics for the instance 48-75-6. The statistics are similar for the instances 52-73-6, 52-75-6, 9-238-11, 393-45-37, 392-45-37, and 397-40-37. They are solvable within a minute.

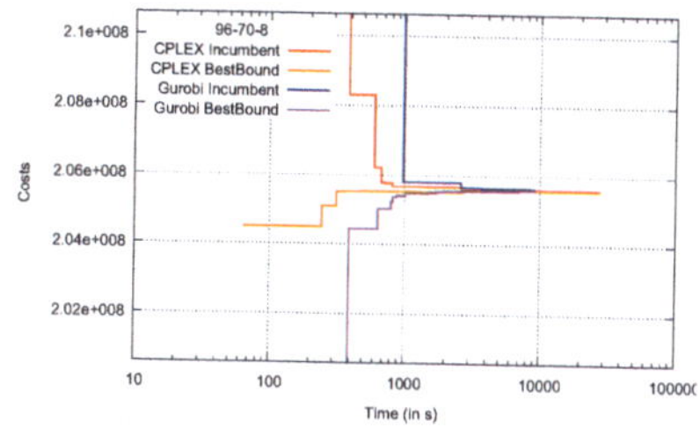

(b) Performance statistics for the instance 96-70-8. The statistics are similar for the instance 87-70-8.

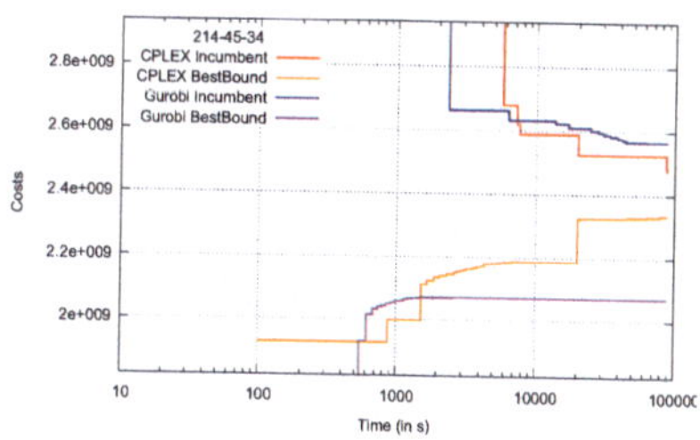

(c) Performance statistics for the instance 214-45-34. The statistics are similar for the instances 211-45-34, 89-70-8, 629-46-26, 606-70-26, and 607-70-26, but with different gaps after 24 hours.

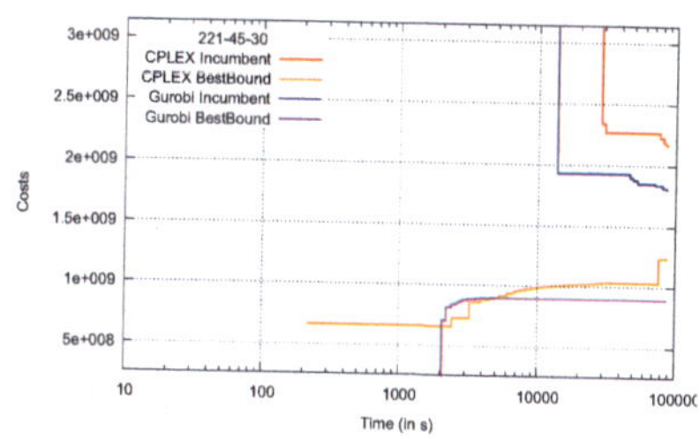

(d) Performance statistics for the instance 221-45-30.

Figure 6.1. Performance statistics of using the CPLEX and Gurobi solvers after 24 hours of computation for the rota scheduling.

is chosen, due to the long running time of tuning. The default method in Gurobi for the MIP problem in this thesis is 1, i.e. the dual method is chosen automatically for the MIP root node. We tried the barrier method, but it did not work appropriately for all instances. Note that the barrier method (method 2 in Gurobi) is a recommendation arising from the tuning. It is shown that the CPLEX solver is the better choice for most of the instances, especially the large ones. Therefore, we choose CPLEX as the standard solver for solving the integrated planning in the next subsection.

6.3. Results of Solving the Integrated Planning

The characteristics of the models of integrated planning are shown in Table 6.5. It is obvious that the integrated problem is more complex compared with sub-problems, especially the Rows and NZs. The integrated models of the largest instances, 629-46-26, 606-70-26, and 607-70-26, are too large to be generated using our limited computational memory.

Instance	Int	Bin	Cols	Rows	NZs
48-75-6	459	67,382	67,842	122,224	418,477
52-73-6	461	75,252	75,714	136,282	466,202
52-75-6	469	70,612	71,082	128,887	438,855
9-238-11	102	151,350	151,444	2,336,654	5,080,561
393-45-37	1,998	328,298	330,297	795,443	2,427,350
392-45-37	1,958	331,597	333,556	1,092,803	3,042,083
397-40-37	1,826	297,923	299,750	1,032,050	2,835,595
96-70-8	658	500,361	501,020	2,750,243	6,898,857
87-70-8	627	532,129	532,757	3,037,455	7,565,810
89-70-8	631	571,633	572,265	3,364,690	8,324,919
214-45-34	1,338	807,350	808,689	4,530,971	11,202,248
211-45-34	1,287	828,050	829,338	5,149,397	12,469,394
221-45-30	1,404	983,899	985,304	6,075,659	14,742,199
629-46-26	-	-	-	-	-
606-70-26	-	-	-	-	-
607-70-26	-	-	-	-	-

Table 6.5. Characteristics of the test-set optimization models of integrated planning; the dash "-" indicates unknown characteristics due to running out of memory.

The performance statistics for rota scheduling and integrated planning are shown in Table 6.6. In general, the integrated planning of all instances needs more running time. The running times of the duty sequencing sub-problem can be ignored. Details about the solutions solved by the sequential approach are shown together with the solutions solved by the integrated approach in Table 6.7. The integrated approach is shown to outperform the sequential one in terms of quality for all criteria, especially for the reduction of the numbers of unassigned duties and open days; for example, the percentage of unassigned duties of the instance 87-70-8 is reduced from 4% to 0.2%.

It is common that not all duties can be assigned in the optimization for real-world instances (also in the optimal solution solved by the integrated approach). One reason for this is the shortage of drivers. Some more (part-time) drivers are required/hired to cover the unassigned duties. In this thesis, the number of unassigned duties is intended to be minimized (because of the high punishment cost of each unassigned duty). The decision on the number of additional drivers is not part of this thesis. Another reason for the unassigned duties is the large number of forbidden sequences, which might result in fewer compatible duties. Furthermore, a bad duty plan might be generated in the crew scheduling problem without considering the driver information. This also results in unassigned duties. The comparison shows that the sequential approach causes more unassigned duties and open days, and the integrated approach brings generally better solutions, but with longer running times.

Instance	RS gap	RS time (sec.)	Int. gap	Int. time (sec.)
48-75-6	0%	6	0%	27
52-73-6	0%	6	0%	50
52-75-6	0%	5	0%	59
9-238-11	0%	7	0%	5,483
393-45-37	0%	17	1.68%	86,400
392-45-37	0%	17	9%	24,600*
397-40-37	0%	15	4.86%	86,400
96-70-8	0%	27,284	0%	48,100
87-70-8	0%	51,907	12.5%	86,400
89-70-8	39.8%	86,400	86.5%	86,400
221-45-30	42.9%	86,400	82.3%	86,400
214-45-34	5.8%	86,400	93%	86,400
211-45-34	13.7%	86,400	99%	86,400
629-46-26	10.9%	86,400	*	*
606-70-26	74.1%	86,400	*	*
607-70-26	97.7%	86,400	*	*

Table 6.6. Performance statistics of using CPLEX solver after 24 hours of computation for rota scheduling (RS) and integrated planning (Int.). A star (*) indicates the available memory was exceeded.

Moreover, the costs of assigning less desirable duties reflect the effectiveness of the solution. The costs are categorized and represented in Figure 6.2. A cost of 0 means that the most-preferred activities are selected while a larger cost means that less-attractive activities are assigned. As expected, most-preferred activities have been assigned in all solutions, in both the sequential and integrated approaches. The integrated approach provides a few more assigned activities as desired, since more duties, including the most desired ones, are not assigned in the sequential approach. For all instances, there are fewer unfulfilled preferences are present for each driver. Such unfulfilled preferences could be an expected day off, etc. However, the driver could swap the undesired activity with another driver, and a small number of swaps would not reflect the quality of the solution and would not incur much operational expense. Alternatively, these drivers could be compensated by means of extra vacation, etc. If we ignore the penalty of preferences in the objective function, then more drivers get, for example in instances 48-75-6, 52-73-6, and 52-75-6, fewer-desired jobs (more than 10 % of activities are assigned as undesired).

Instance	Unassigned duties(%)			# unassigned days			# underrun standbys		# moved days off		# moved days off (weekends)		# underrun days off		# overflowed single-offs		# double-off dis. vio.		Maximal overtime (in hr.)	
	RS	DS	int.	RS	DS	int.	seq.	int.	seq.	int.	seq.	int.	seq.	int.	seq.	int.	seq.	int.	seq.	int.
48-75-6	0.3	1.1	0.3	0	14	0	0	1	0	0	0	0	48	48	0	0	0	0	80.7	80.2
52-73-6	0	0.5	0	0	7	0	1	2	0	0	0	0	52	52	1	1	0	0	57.9	60.3
52-75-6	0	0.5	0	0	16	0	1	2	0	0	0	0	52	52	0	0	0	0	60.8	53.8
9-238-11	1.5	4.8	1.5	8	49	8	0	0	0	0	0	0	0	0	0	0	0	0	0	0
393-45-37	6.0	2.6	4.4	0	141	0	0	0	0	0	0	0	0	0	0	0	0	0	81.3	81.3
392-45-37	14	2.9	11.1	0	165	0	0	0	0	0	0	0	0	0	0	0	0	0	82.9	82.9
397-40-37	6.4	2.6	3.8	0	132	0	0	0	0	0	0	0	0	0	0	0	0	0	73.9	73.9
96-70-8	6.3	5.4	6.3	0	174	0	1	0	1	1	8	8	0	0	0	0	0	0	0	0
87-70-8	0.2	3.8	0.2	0	127	0	12	12	0	0	3	3	0	0	0	0	0	0	1.1	0

Table 6.7. Detailed breakdown of the characteristics of the solutions of the integrated (int.) vs. the sequential (seq.) approaches (CPLEX). RS means rota scheduling and DS is duty sequencing.

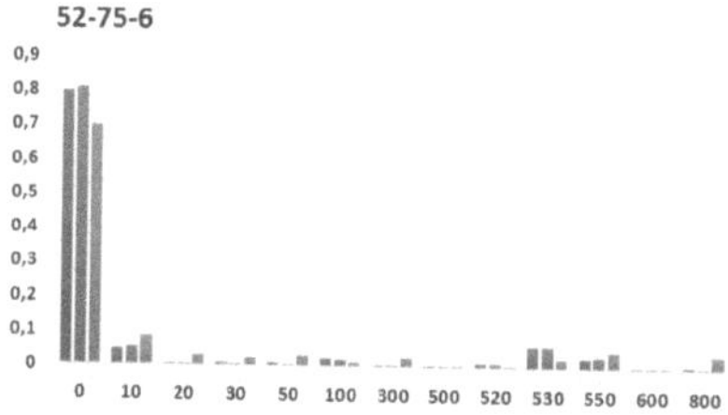

(a) The distribution of penalty costs against preferences for the instance 52-75-6. The distribution is similar for 48-75-6 and 52-74-6.

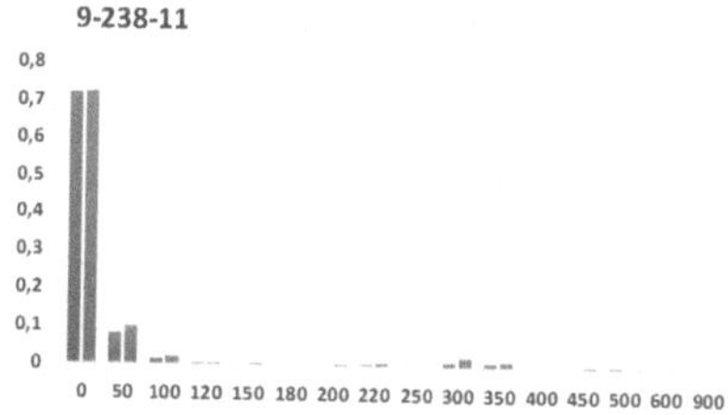

(b) The distribution of penalty costs against preferences for the instance 9-238-11.

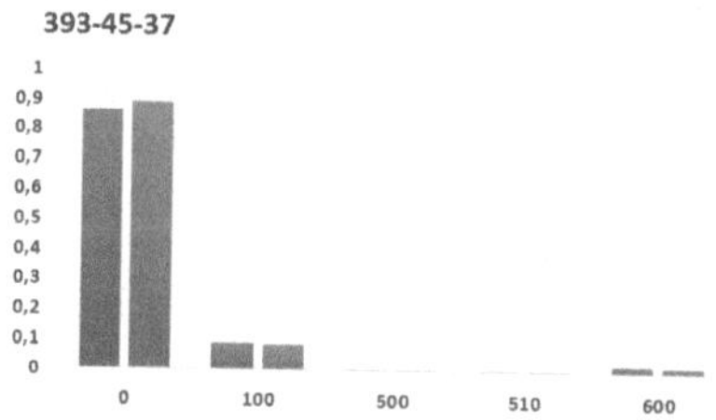

(c) The distribution of penalty costs against preferences for the instance 393-45-37. The distribution is similar for 392-45-37 and 397-40-37.

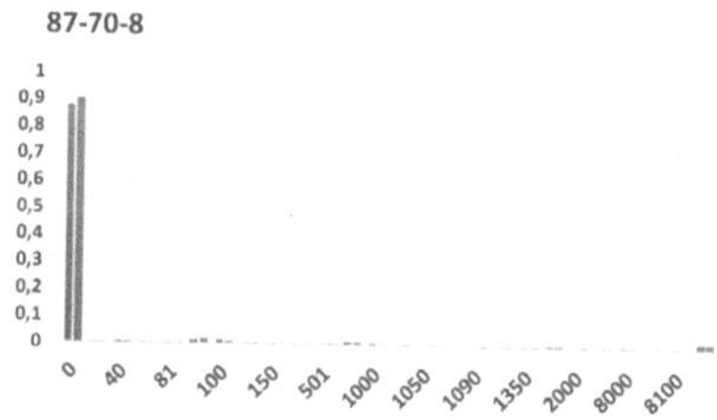

(d) The distribution of penalty costs against preferences for the instance 87-70-8. The distribution is similar for 96-70-8.

Figure 6.2. The distribution of penalty costs in x-axis against the driver preferences in y-axis (from left to right: sequential, integrated, integrated without considering preferences (optional)).

6.4. Summary

In Chapter 5, we developed a multicommodity network flow formulation of the cyclic and non-cyclic crew rostering problems, an appropriate implementation, and solver bindings for CPLEX and Gurobi. In the literature, the crew rostering problem is mostly solved using a sequential approach to deal with the sizes of real-world instances, such as rota scheduling first and duty sequencing second. For the sequential and integrated approaches, some of the given real-world instances were solved successfully in acceptable solution times considering the size of the correlated optimization model. The integrated approach was proved to produce better solutions compared with the sequential one. On average 3.5% more duties were assigned, and all open/unassigned days resulting from the sequential approach can be avoided, for example, 165 unassigned days were avoided by the integrated approach for the instance 392-45-37. Moreover, as shown in Figure 6.2, more desired duties were assigned. Our work about the concept behind Chapter 5 and the results in this chapter was published in Xie & Suhl (2014).

Due to the given real-world instances in German bus companies, we consider only the law and labor union rules that apply to those companies. However, our model can be modified/extended to adopt other rules, such as the percentage of weekends off.

However, considering that some instances can not be solved optimally within 24 hours with commercial solvers (especially with the integrated approach), a faster approach for generating feasible solutions is necessary for practical purposes. One possibility is a column generation implementation, which is described in Sections 7.4.1 and 7.4.2.

Another approach is a metaheuristic-based method such as simulated annealing and tabu search. Furthermore, an ant colony optimization-based approach might be a good choice since it works directly on the graph by nature. Therefore, it will always result in a feasible solution regarding the flow conservation constraints. Details about the implementations of these metaheuristics and the results can be found in the next chapter.

Moreover, there are several objectives in our network model. The weight of each objective is provided by bus companies, based on experience. As shown in Table 6.3, a different weight combination might bring a different solution and a different running time. Thus, it would be very attractive to research the multi-objective crew rostering problem, which will support the human planner to define the preferred weight of each objective (see Section 7.5).

7. Heuristics for Solving the Crew Rostering Problem

As shown in Chapter 6, some instances can not be solved optimally within 24 hours with solvers or are unsolvable due to a shortage of memory (especially with the integrated approach). Therefore, in this chapter we try to develop some heuristics to identify good solutions to the crew rostering problem. We begin this chapter with some information in Section 7.1 shared by the heuristics, i.e. update of meta-information, local search operators, and generation of an initial solution. In Section 7.2, different metaheuristics are developed to solve the rota scheduling problem of the NCCR problem. The best metaheuristic is chosen to solve the integrated problem of the NCCR and CCR problems in Section 7.3. Column generation approaches for the rota scheduling problem, and for the integrated problem of both NCCR and CCR problems, are then described in Sections 7.4.1 and 7.4.2. Next, a multi-objective metaheuristic is described in Section 7.5. Finally, the experimental results are shown in Section 7.6. The notation used in this chapter, including the sets, parameters, and variables, is the same as in Chapter 5.

7.1. Characteristics of Heuristics

The descriptions of the basic procedures for all heuristics, i.e. metaheuristics including ant colony algorithms, simulated annealing, and tabu search, and column generation, are shown in Section 2.3. We begin this section with descriptions of some characteristics that are shared by some of the heuristics. Firstly, we will show the method for updating meta-information (Section 7.1.1), which includes actual information about the hard and soft constraints; for example, a counter for the number of unassigned duties. Secondly, different local search operators will be described (Section 7.1.2); these will be applied in simulated annealing and tabu search algorithms. Finally, the procedure for generating an initial solution, to be used by all heuristics, will be shown in Section 7.1.3.

7.1.1. Update of Meta-Information

The update of meta-information occurs not only for the generation of a feasible initial solution but also for the δ-evaluation using local search operators. Meta-information includes the actual information about the hard constraints, such as block length, forbidden sequences, and capacity of activities, as well as the counters of all soft constraints (λ_d for each activity d, σ_m, τ_m, ψ_m, z_m for each driver m). Additionally, the costs of the personal preferences of the selected activities and actual overtimes are stored. Since each soft constraint can be managed with a counter or a storage value, they will not be explained in more detail. The capacity of each activity is updated for all drivers on each calendar

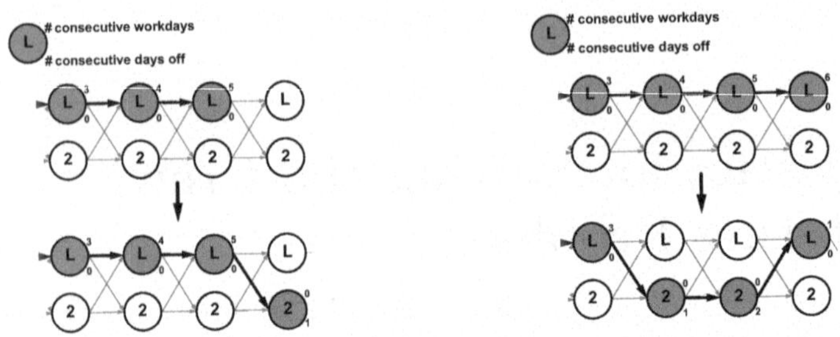

(a) Update of block length during the generation of a solution.

(b) Update of block length during a switch in a local search operator or backtracking.

Figure 7.1. Tracking of block length.

date (for NCCR)/ day of the week (for CCR). However, the updates of block lengths and forbidden sequences are somewhat complex, therefore they are described with examples as follows.

Block lengths Figure 7.1 shows two examples of tracking block lengths of work-related and days-off activities. For each node (activity) the accumulated lengths of consecutive work-related and days-off activities are stored during the generation process (see Figure 7.1a), while they are updated for each switch during backtracking or local search in Figure 7.1b.

Forbidden sequences We build all forbidden sequences as branches of trees, in order to avoid unnecessary searches for all forbidden sequences during the generation of a solution or when switching activities. In the example shown in Figure 7.2, three forbidden sequences are considered, which are illustrated as branches of trees, i.e. (L, E), (L, M, E), and (E, L). A check on the validity of adding an activity can be done by checking its corresponding node in the tree up to the root nodes and down to all leaves, if necessary. The reference between each activity and itself in each forbidden tree is attached during the generation of a solution. Each reference is illustrated by a dotted line. In this example, if the early shift (E) is added to the actual solution, then this shift is attached to the leaf of the tree (by a dotted line). That means this early shift is forbidden to be added to the actual solution, since the late and midday shifts on the previous two days are selected sequentially (the forbidden sequence (L, M, E)). In this case, the check for all forbidden sequences can be avoided. For the same reason, the structure of the tree can speed up the validation of switching activities. When backtracking occurs, the state of the previous activity can be restored by saving the related nodes of the trees to the activities.

7.1.2. Local Search Operators

This subsection introduces the different operators used by our local search-based methods, i.e. the simulated annealing and tabu search algorithms in Sections 7.2.2 and 7.2.3. In Lučić

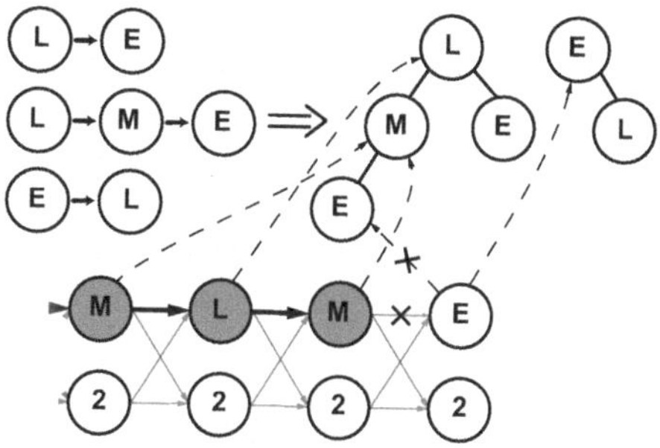

Figure 7.2. Tracking of forbidden sequences during generation of a solution.

& Teodorović (2007), a simple operator is applied to exchange duties between two crews. However, we develop different operators based on the properties of our crew rostering problem, such as the Crawl operator, which is defined to cope with the definition of double-offs. It is worth noting that each operator should satisfy all hard constraints to generate a feasible solution.

Simple-Switch The *Simple-Switch* operator is the most primitive operator in terms of the changes made to the current solution. With this operator, usually only one activity for a specific driver on a specific day is substituted by a new activity. The new activity has to satisfy all hard constraints; this is checked before the switch is performed. However, one special case has to be coped with here. Since a double-off activity has to be linked to at least one other double-off activity, exchanging one of them would obviously lead to invalid solutions. If this case occurs, the two double-off activities are exchanged with the other two activities. This case is illustrated in Figure 7.3, where double-offs on days 10 and 11 are exchanged with an early shift and a single-off, respectively.

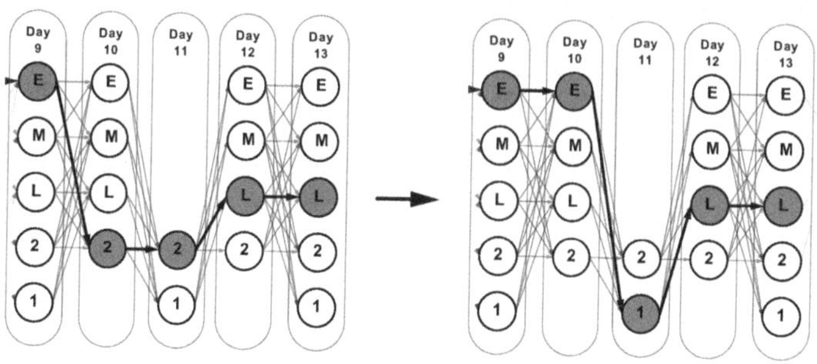

Figure 7.3. An example of the Simple-Switch operator performing a two-day exchange.

Multi-Switch The *Multi-Switch* operator performs a limited number of Simple-Switches in a row, while the affected days are consecutive. An example of exchanges with a depth of three is shown in Figure 7.4. It begins on day 9, and a Simple-Switch has occurred. On days 10 and 11 the same Simple-Switch involving two double-offs; this is shown as in Figure 7.3. After that, a Simple-Switch is applied on day 12. All possible exchanges are tested, and the best is chosen. This operator is implemented to allow bigger leaps when modifying a solution.

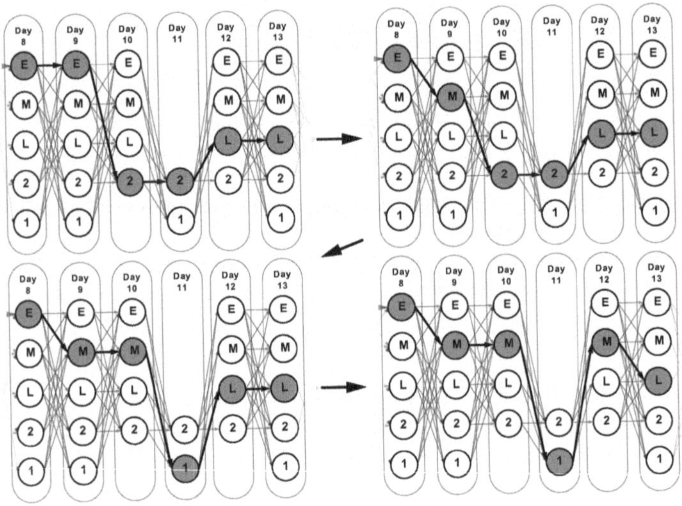

Figure 7.4. An example of the Multi-Switch operator.

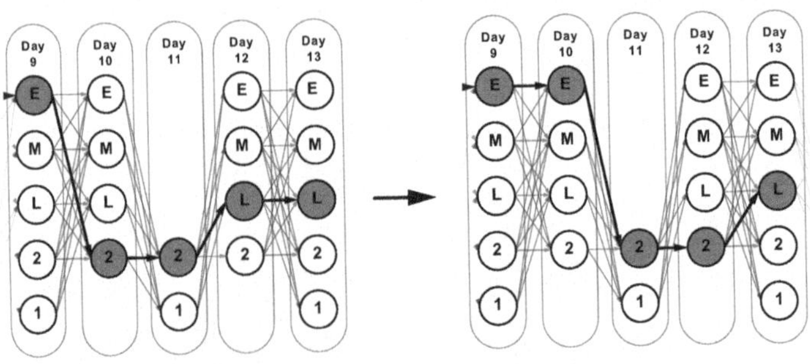

Figure 7.5. An example of the Crawl operator.

Crawl The *Crawl* operator is used to shift a sequence of double-offs to the earlier or later days. This is required because removing a sequence of double-offs often leads to a violation of the given distance between two subsequent double-offs. Therefore, it causes penalty costs in the evaluation value. For that reason, the exchange should be removed in the local search. To overcome this, the complete sequence of double-offs is moved by using the Crawl operator. Figure 7.5 illustrates an example where two double-offs on days 10 and 11 are shifted to days 11 and 12. Technically, the Crawl operator can be considered as two Simple-Switches. A Simple-Switch is applied on day 10 to change double-off to other activity, while another Simple-Switch is applied to change the activity on day 12 to a double-off.

Shift-Switch The last operator that is implemented is the Shift-Switch. This operator is used to move a selected shift from one driver to another. It works as follows, with an example shown in Figure 7.6. First, an early shift (E) for a driver $d1$ on day 9 is substituted with a randomly selected valid activity (in this case: a midday shift M). Secondly, the selected shift on day 9 (M) for the second driver ($d2$) is changed to another activity. The aims of this operator include, for example, reducing the request for early shifts on day 9 without changing the actual assigned amount for the midday shift, since the early shifts on day 9 are over-requested.

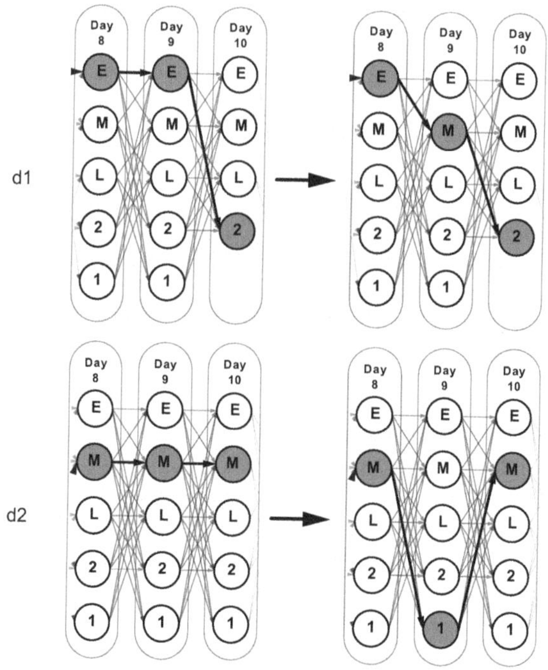

Figure 7.6. An example of the Shift-Switch operator.

7.1.3. Initial Solution

An initial solution $\mathcal{X}$ can be achieved by the construction heuristic *DriverByDriver* with *BacktrackRepair* (see Algorithms 7.1 and 7.2). Let $\mathcal{X}$ be a set of vectors (activities, duties). The horizontal and vertical rules are considered in the construction heuristic, i.e. the generated solution for each driver is feasible. Let a parameter A_e be the outgoing activity arc of the compatibility arc $e \in \mathcal{C}$. In $\mathcal{F}'_n$ the compatibility arcs e are collected such that adding their corresponding activity arcs $e' = A_e$ to the current solution does not violate any maximum block lengths or generate forbidden sequences. Moreover, the capacity of each activity should be controlled during the generation process. Recall that $\mathcal{J}_{e'}$ is the set of duties belonging to the shift activity arc e'. If no valid choice exists, then backtracking (Algorithm 7.2) is activated until a valid choice is available or the source-node is reached (lines 16-20).

Algorithm 7.1: DriverByDriver

1 **output:** $\mathcal{X}$
2 $\mathcal{X} \leftarrow \emptyset$
3 **foreach** $m \in \mathcal{M}$ **do**
4     $n \leftarrow e^s_m$
5   **while** $n \neq nil$ **do**
6         $\mathcal{F}'_n \leftarrow$ Subset of randomly sorted feasible outbound compatibility arcs $e \in \mathcal{F}_n$
7   **if** $\mathcal{F}'_n = \emptyset$ **then**
8             $n \leftarrow$ BACKTRACKREPAIR($\mathcal{X}$)
9         $e \leftarrow Pop(\mathcal{F}'_n)$
10   **while** $e \neq nil$ **do**
11             $e' \leftarrow A_e$
12   **if** $\mathcal{J}_{e'} \neq \emptyset$ **then**
13   **if** $\exists$ *a feasible duty* $j \in \mathcal{J}_{e'}$ **then**
14                     $\mathcal{X} \leftarrow \mathcal{X} \cup \{(e', j)\}$, UPDATEMETAINFO, $n \leftarrow e'$
15   **break**
16   **else**
17                     $e \leftarrow Pop(\mathcal{F}'_n)$
18   **if** $e == nil$ **then**
19                         $n \leftarrow$ BACKTRACKREPAIR($\mathcal{X}$)
20   **break**
21   **else**
22                 $\mathcal{X} \leftarrow \mathcal{X} \cup \{(e', nil)\}$, UPDATEMETAINFO, $n \leftarrow e'$
23   **break**

Algorithm 7.1 is suitable for both CCR and NCCR problems, as well as for the associated rota scheduling and integrated problems. For the integrated problem, the check on the selection of a feasible duty is shown in lines 12 to 20. For the rota scheduling problem, only activities are selected (see lines 21-23). For the CCR problem, the activities selected on artificial days should be the same as ones on the original days. Moreover, the check for the limited capacity of each activity is restricted by its day of the week.

In the backtracking procedure, $\mathcal{K}$ is defined as a set of activity arcs, similar to a tabu list, which are stored to ensure that the same path will not be selected again. It is done by removing the last added activity k from the solution, while the link to k is marked as forbidden. Then the outgoing valid options for the new last node are evaluated. Since the last used link is forbidden there is no possibility of using the same path again. If there are still no other options left, the last activity is removed and the forbidden link is updated to the new one, since the first forbidden link could possibly belong to an alternative path. This is repeated until no valid options are available or a sink node of the previous driver is the current last node. The algorithm gives activity arc k as output, which indicates the closest possible activity to backtrack. From that activity the search for the rest of the initial solution begins.

In the function UpdateMetaInfo in Algorithms 7.1 and 7.2, the actual block length of working days and days off, and the capacity of an activity etc., are updated. An example illustrated in Figure 7.1a shows that, after the checking of feasibility, the block lengths of working days and days off are updated. The capacity of each activity is updated for all drivers on each calendar date (for NCCR)/ day of the week (for CCR).

Algorithm 7.2: BacktrackRepair

input:$\mathcal{X}$
output:k
$k \leftarrow Pop(\mathcal{X})[0]$
UPDATEMETAINFO
$\mathcal{K} \leftarrow \mathcal{K} \cup k$
while $\mathcal{F}'_k = \emptyset$ **do**
    if $k \neq nil$ **then**
        $\mathcal{K} \leftarrow \mathcal{K} \setminus \{k\}$
    $k \leftarrow Pop(\mathcal{X})[0]$
    UPDATEMETAINFO
    $\mathcal{K} \leftarrow \mathcal{K} \cup k$

7.2. Metaheuristics for Solving the Rota Scheduling Problem

In this subsection, we describe three implemented metaheuristics for solving the rota scheduling problem of the NCCR problem. A comparison of the solutions achieved by these three metaheuristics follows.

7.2.1. Ant Colony Algorithm

Algorithm 7.3 shows the new structure of ACO applied to the crew rostering problem in the literature. The main differences from the basic ACO algorithm shown in Algorithm 2.3 are the updating of heuristic information for every h-th iteration (see lines 11 to 12) and the construction of ant solutions in parallel (see lines 6 to 7).

Algorithm 7.3: ACO algorithm for the crew rostering problem

```
1  input: Colony, α, β, ρ, F^base, I^stag, h, N^min, N^max
2  output: Colony[a_best].X
3  Initialization
4  i ← 0
5  while termination condition not met do
6      forall the a ∈ Colony in parallel do
7          Colony[a].X ← AntWalk(a)
8      a_best ← arg min_{a∈Colony} f(Colony[a].X)
9      ApplyLocalSearch
10     UpdatePheromones
11     if i mod h = 0 then
12         UpdateHeuristicInformation
13     i ← i + 1
```

Algorithm 7.4: AntWalk

```
input: ant a
output: X
Q ← Randomly ordered queue of sub-graph start-nodes e^s_m for all employees m ∈ M
X ← ∅
forall the n ∈ Q do
    while n ≠ nil do
        F'_n ← Subset of feasible outbound edges of F_n
        if F'_n = ∅ then
            n ← BacktrackRepair(X)
        Probabilistically choose e ∈ F'_n depending on p_e
        e' ← A_e
        X ← X ∪ {e'}, UpdateMetaInfo
        n ← e'
```

Initialization At the beginning of the ACO algorithm, parameters (such as h, t_0) are set and all pheromone variables are set to a value τ_0.

AntWalk In lines 6 and 7 of Algorithm 7.3, an AntWalk algorithm is applied to generate a solution for each ant a (see Algorithm 7.4). This is similar to Algorithm 7.1 (DriverBy-Driver). $\mathcal{X}$ is the set of all activity arcs in a feasible solution for all drivers. Each artificial ant walks through the randomly ordered network layers and stops when it reaches the sink-node of the last network layer. Instead of randomly choosing a feasible outgoing edge $e \in \mathcal{F}'_n \subset \mathcal{F}_n$ as in Algorithm 7.1, an edge is chosen based on the weighted probability p_e (in line 8). We assume an ant chooses a node n on day i. From day i to day $i+1$, the subsequent construction step is done with probability

$$p_e = \begin{cases} \frac{\tau_e^\alpha \cdot \eta_e^\beta}{\sum\limits_{e' \in \mathcal{F}'_n} \tau_{e'}^\alpha \cdot \eta_{e'}^\beta} & e \in \mathcal{F}'_n \\ 0 & otherwise \end{cases} \tag{7.1}$$

where τ_e is defined as *pheromone value* of $e \in \mathcal{F}'_n$, while η_e is the *heuristic information* of e. This is called a *state transition rule*. The exponents α and β are positive parameters, which indicate the relationship between the pheromone value and heuristic information. If $\alpha = 0$, then an arc $e \in \mathcal{F}'_n$ is chosen dependent only on the heuristic information. If $\beta = 0$, then the choice depends only on the pheromone value of that arc e. For the purpose of comparison, the initial solution obtained by the ant-walk algorithm is also applied in the simulated annealing and tabu search algorithms for solving the rota scheduling problem (see Sections 7.2.2 and 7.2.3).

In this step, *parallelization* is implemented to gain a speed-up. Instead of the parallel independent execution of multiple colonies introduced by Randall & Lewis (2002) and Stützle (1998), we adopt another approach described in Randall & Lewis (2002), where the construction and the evaluation of ants within a colony are implemented in parallel. The first reason is the limitation of memory, while the second one ist that the influence of randomness is quite low. Thus, multiple executions will not have a significant effect on the quality of the solution. This is one of the extensions we implemented compared with the basic ACO algorithm to get a better solution quickly. Another one is the update of heuristic information, which we will describe later.

ApplyLocalSearch In lines 8 and 9 of Algorithm 7.3, the value obtained by the function $f(\mathcal{X})$ is defined as the evaluation value of a solution $\mathcal{X}$. And the best-so-far solution Colony$[a_{best}].\mathcal{X}$ is improved by an iterative improvement directly from the start of the simulated annealing, which will be described in Section 7.2.2, i.e. the initial temperature t_0 is set to be zero.

UpdatePheromones The pheromone τ_e on each edge e is updated in line 8 of the ACO algorithm as follows:

$$\tau_e = (1-\rho) \cdot \tau_e + \rho \cdot \Delta\tau_e \tag{7.2}$$

where

$$\Delta\tau_e = \begin{cases} \dfrac{F^{base} \cdot f(\mathcal{X}^1)}{f(\text{Colony}[a_{best}].\mathcal{X})} & e \in \text{Colony}[a_{best}].\mathcal{X} \\ 0 & \text{otherwise} \end{cases} \tag{7.3}$$

That is, we treat the update of the pheromones on the edges that are included in the best solution differently from those that are included in other solutions. The parameter $\rho \in (0, 1)$ is defined as a pheromone decay parameter, and F^{base} is defined as a coefficient for pheromone update.

UpdateHeuristicInformation The *heuristic information* is often problem-dependent and static throughout the algorithm. However, although the model shown in Section 5.2 has many different penalty costs in soft constraints, the use of the latest information from the best obtained solution seems to be useful. Let $\mathcal{C}$ be a set of cost categories; while the generation of feasible solutions for nearly all cases succeeds due to the enforcement of feasibility, the quality of the generated solutions is usually poor and improves very slowly. Therefore, the heuristic values η_e are updated by every h iteration for each edge e of the best-so-far solution Colony$[a_{best}].\mathcal{X}$ (see Constraint (7.6)). The parameter h is defined to control how often the update of heuristic information occurs.

The value δ_e in Constraint (7.6) can be a positive or negative update for an edge e depending on whether the edge is causing high costs or not. The influencing data on the value δ_e of an edge e consists of the related weight w_i of each cost category $i \in \mathcal{C}$ in Constraint (7.4), and the impact of the edge e for the cost category i, $\xi_{e,i}$. We define $\xi_{e,i}$ as a dynamic value, which depicts the positive or negative influence of the cost-category i on the edge e. For example, a violation of the minimal number of days off might exist in the incumbent solution. During the update of heuristic-values a slight increase of η_e is performed for each edge e, which leads to more days off for drivers with insufficient days off. The calculation of the value δ_c is shown in Constraint (7.5).

To avoid extreme heuristic values, which might drain the influence of the pheromone-values, a normalization is required after each update to transform all heuristic values into a predetermined range $[0, 1]$ (see Equation (7.7)). Let N_{min} and N_{max} be parameters that define the minimum and maximum of the normalized heuristic values. η^{min} and η^{max} are defined as the updated minimum and maximum of heuristic values of all edges.

$$w_i := \frac{C_i}{\sum\limits_{j \in \mathcal{C}} C_j} \quad \text{with } \mathcal{C} \text{ as the set of cost-indices and the costs } C \tag{7.4}$$

$$\delta_e := \sum_{i \in \mathcal{C}} \xi_{e,i} \cdot w_i \tag{7.5}$$

$$\eta_e := \eta_e + \delta_e \tag{7.6}$$

$$\eta_e := N^{min} + (N^{max} - N^{min}) \cdot \frac{\eta_e - \eta^{min}}{\eta^{max} - \eta^{min}} \quad \forall \eta_e > 0 \tag{7.7}$$

Termination The whole procedure is iterated until one of the specified termination criteria is met. In particular, the termination criteria are a given CPU-time limit, a certain number of solution constructions or when an evaluation value stagnates over limited iterations (stored in parameter I^{stag}).

ACS and MMAS In this thesis two ant colony optimization variants are implemented. The first one is derived from the Ant Colony System (ACS) introduced by Dorigo & Gambardella (1997), but we do not implement the local pheronome updating, since the length of the network layers is static for all ants. Thus, no differential length effect can be exploited. Algorithm 7.5 shows the procedure of the ACS algorithm. The second variant is based on the *Max-Min* Ant System (MMAS) introduced by Stützle & Hoos (2000), where the limit to the range of pheromone values is set to $[\tau_{min}, \tau_{max}]$ to prevent the search from stagnating.

Algorithm 7.5: The ACS algorithm

initialization
while *termination condition not met* **do**
  foreach *ant* **do**
    applies an extended state transition rule (see constraint (7.8)) to incrementally build a solution
  A pheromone updating rule is applied

Algorithm 7.6: The MMAS algorithm

initialization
$\tau_0 \leftarrow \tau_{max}$
while *termination condition not met* **do**
  foreach *ant* **do**
    applies a state transition rule (see constraint (7.1)) to incrementally build a solution
  A pheromone updating rule is applied (limit to $[\tau_{min}, \tau_{max}]$)

According to Algorithms 7.5 and 7.6, the difference between ACS and MMAS lies in the transition rule and the update of pheromones. For MMAS a classic stochastic variant is chosen as shown above in (7.1). However, the transition rule of ACS extends the transition rule in (7.1) in the following way:

$$e = \begin{cases} \arg\max\limits_{e \in \mathcal{F}_n} \left\{ \tau_e^{\alpha} \cdot \eta_e^{\beta} \right\} & \text{if } q \leq q_0 \\ X & \textit{otherwise} \end{cases} \tag{7.8}$$

where q is a random number uniformly distributed in $[0...1]$, and q_0 is a parameter between 0 and 1. If $q \leq q_0$ then the best edge is chosen, otherwise a probabilistic decision according to (7.1) is made. $X : \Omega \to \mathcal{F}_n$ is defined as a random variable with $\mathcal{P}(\{x = e\}) = p_e$. The heuristic-values η_e are initiated as described previously in this section, considering dynamic weights w_i.

For the pheromone values, the MMAS algorithm uses an explicit lower bound $\tau_{min} > 0$ and an upper bound $\tau_{max} > 0$ to limit the pheromone values. If a new best-so-far solution is found, then the bounds are dynamically updated (for more detail see Stützle & Hoos (2000)):

$$\tau_{max} = 1/((1-\rho) \cdot F(\text{Colony}[a_{best}].\mathcal{X})) \tag{7.9}$$

$$\tau_{min} = (\tau_{max} \cdot (1 - \sqrt[n]{p_{best}}))/((avg-1) \cdot \sqrt[n]{p_{best}}) \tag{7.10}$$

where p_{best} is defined as the probability of finding the best solution. The parameter avg is defined as the mean of all possible solutions at each choice point of an ant, i.e. the average number of outgoing arcs for each compatibility arc.

7.2.2. Simulated Annealing

The algorithm used here is depicted in Algorithm 7.7 (extended from Algorithm 2.4 in Section 2.3), and the basic procedure is similar to a typical Simulated Annealing implementation (see Burke & Kendall (2005)).

First, an initial solution is generated using Algorithm 7.4 (ant-walk). Then an operator is selected by a weighted random choice from the available set of local search operators described in Section 7.1.2 (called *RandomlySelectOperator()*). The weights are given by the parameter values $W^{simple}, W^{multi}, W^{crawl}, W^{shift}$. After that an activity is chosen randomly based on the initial solution $\mathcal{X}$ and the selected operator *op*. For the Crawl operator a double-off will be chosen and for the ShiftSwitch operator a shift activity is necessary, while for the other operators no particular activity type for the selected edge has to be considered. After applying the selected operator, a new fitness $F(\mathcal{X}')$ will be evaluated for the modified solution $\mathcal{X}'$. If it is better than the global best one $F(\mathcal{X}^{best})$, the new solution replaces the old one. Otherwise, it is still possible to select a poorer solution that depends on a random variable y between 0 and 1, the current temperature t, and the deterioration of the evaluation values $F(\mathcal{X}') - F(\mathcal{X}^{best})$. If the following formulation is true, then the solution $\mathcal{X}'$ is selected.

$$y < e^{-\frac{f(\mathcal{X}') - F(\mathcal{X}^{best})}{t}} \tag{7.11}$$

Let I^{max} be the parameter defining the number of iterations on a temperature level: the temperature will be cooled down if this number of iterations is achieved. The geometric cooling schedule ($t \leftarrow \alpha \cdot t$) is used to reduce the temperature t gradually, where α is defined between $[0.8, 0.99]$.

This procedure is repeated while the temperature is reduced. The termination condition is met when the temperature is equal to 0 or when the time limit is reached.

As mentioned above, this procedure is used as the local search sub-routine in the ACO approach (see Algorithm 7.3). In this case the initial solution is provided rather than generating a new one. Since the temperature t is already selected as 0, only improved solutions will be accepted, such that the SA procedure in this case is considered as a greedy iterative improvement.

7.2.3. Tabu Search

A simple tabu search is developed in this work (see Algorithm 7.8 extended from Algorithm 2.5).

Algorithm 7.7: SA algorithm for crew rostering problem

```
input: t_0, I^max, α
output: X^best
initialization
t ← t_0
i ← 0
X ← AntWalk
X^best ← X
while termination condition not met do
    if i ≤ I^max then
        op ← RandomlySelectOperator()
        e ← RandomlyChooseActivity(X, op)
        if op = SimpleSwitch then
            X' ← SimpleSwitch(X, e)
        else
            if op = MultiSwitch then
                X' ← MultiSwitch(X, e)
            else
                if op = Crawl then
                    X' ← Crawl(X, e)
                else
                    if op = ShiftSwitch then
                        X' ← ShiftSwitch(X, e)
        y ← random(0, 1)
        if F(X') ≤ F(X^best) then
            X ← X', X^best ← X'
        else
            if t > 0 ∧ y < e^(−(f(X') − F(X^best))/t) then
                X ← X'
        i ← i + 1
    else
        i ← 0
        t ← α · t
```

Some of the operators described in Section 7.1.2 are applied here as well. Similar to SA, the initial solution is also generated by Algorithm 7.4. The implementation of the tabu search algorithm is similar to the one described in Burke & Kendall (2005). In each iteration, every possible switch based on the Crawl, SimpleSwitch and MultiSwitch operators is used to generate new solution $\mathcal{X}'$, which is stored in a set $\mathcal{X}^{storage}$. At the beginning of Algorithm 7.8, every double-off is shifted to the left and the right, where $\mathcal{X}^{s=2}$ is defined as the set of active double-off activities. Then all available SimpleSwitch

Algorithm 7.8: TS algorithm for crew rostering problem

input: d^{rec}
output: $\mathcal{X}$
initialization
$i \leftarrow 0$
$\mathcal{X} \leftarrow$ AntWalk
$\mathcal{X}^{storage} \leftarrow \{\mathcal{X}\}$
while *termination condition not met* **do**
  forall the $e \in \mathcal{X}^{S=2}$ **do**
    $\mathcal{X}' \leftarrow$ Crawl$(\mathcal{X}, e)$
    $\mathcal{X}^{storage} \leftarrow \mathcal{X}^{storage} \cup \mathcal{X}'$
  forall the $e \in \mathcal{X}$ **do**
    $\mathcal{X}' \leftarrow$ SimpleSwitch$(\mathcal{X}, e)$
    $\mathcal{X}^{storage} \leftarrow \mathcal{X}^{storage} \cup \mathcal{X}'$
    $\mathcal{X}' \leftarrow$ MultiSwitch$(\mathcal{X}, e)$
    $\mathcal{X}^{storage} \leftarrow \mathcal{X}^{storage} \cup \mathcal{X}'$
  $\mathcal{X}^{best} \leftarrow \underset{\mathcal{X}' \in \{\mathcal{X}' \in \mathcal{X}^{storage} \mid i - rec(\mathcal{X}') > d^{rec}\}}{\arg\min} f(\mathcal{X}')$
  $\mathcal{X} \leftarrow \mathcal{X}^{best}$
  $\mathcal{X}^{storage} \leftarrow \{\mathcal{X}\}$
  $i \leftarrow i + 1$

and MultiSwitch exchanges are evaluated. At the end of each iteration the best available exchange is executed. Exchanges unavailable to this selection are the ones which are tabu. An exchange is tabu if it affects an employee on a specific day which has been exchanged during the last d^{rec} iterations, and the parameter $rec(\mathcal{X}')$ records the number of the iteration in which $\mathcal{X}'$ was generated. This is repeated until no further exchanges are available due to the *recency* (see Section 2.3.5), or either the time limit or maximum number of iterations is reached.

7.2.4. Computational Results

In this section, the results of different applied metaheuristics for the rota scheduling problem are compared. All experiments in this section, including parameter tunings for all three metaheuristics and the results solved by solvers, were performed on six technically identical machines with 8 GB of main memory and Intel Core2Quad CPUs at 2.83 GHz running Microsoft Windows 7. The tunings of parameters are used to analyze a suitable configuration for our implemented metaheuristics for the driver rostering problem. According to Ansótegui et al. (2009) a large set of instances is required for an automatic algorithm configuration to avoid an over-tuning effect. Due to our limited number of real-world instances, such an automatic algorithm configuration is not adopted in this thesis. Although evaluating each parameter set on all available instances takes a lot of time, 10,368 combinations with two repetitions were tested on all instances. The selected parameters are shown in Table 7.1.

Metaheuristic	Parameter	Description	Value
ACO/ACS/MMAS			
	$\lvert Colony \rvert$	number of ants within a colony	10
	α	influence of pheromone value	1
	β	influence of heuristic information	1
	ρ	pheromone decay parameter	0.7
	F^{base}	coefficient for pheromone update	10
	I^{stag}	number of iterations due to stagnation	100
	h	interval of updating heuristic information	1
	N^{min}	minimum of normalized heuristic value	0.1
	N^{max}	maximum of normalized heuristic value	1
	q_0	the probability of exploitation	0.01
	P_{best}	parameter to influence τ_{min}	0.05
	τ_{min}	lower bound of pheromone value	0.1
	τ_{max}	upper bound of pheromone value	1
SA			
	t_0	initial temperature	1e7
	I^{max}	maximum iterations	1e5
	α	temperature reduction	0.9
TS			
	d^{rec}	number of iterations of recency	50

Table 7.1. The values of parameters applied in the metaheuristics.

Due to the size of the large instances, especially the bus companies with more than 600 drivers, the number of ants is limited to 10 to avoid memory overflows for these instances and keep the solutions comparable to those of smaller instances. Based on our experiment, this restriction does not limit the overall performance of the ACO algorithm, since there is less difference between the evaluation values obtained by 10 ants and those obtained by 15, 30, and 50 ants.

In this thesis, we develop three additional functionalities compared with classic ACO, i.e. parallelization, updating heuristic information, and embedded local search. We test the benefits of those developments, including ACS, ACS with parallelization (in short: ACSPara), MMAS, and MMAS with parallelization (in short: MMAPara).

During the evaluation two physical cores are available; the parallelized variant gains an average speed-up of about 1.78 for the ACS compared with the original variant and about 1.8 for the MMAS (see Table 7.2). Besides that, the structure of the problem influences the time needed for an artificial ant to generate a feasible solution. Furthermore, some time might be lost because of the updates of the heuristic values and pheromones. Anyway, a speed-up is achieved across all instances. Figure 7.7 shows a speed-up for the ACS and MMAS for the instance 629-46-26. Similar results can be obtained for any other instances (see Figure A.1).

Moreover, changing heuristic information periodically implies a speed-up. Although the same initial solution and the same values of initial heuristic information are used, periodic update of the heuristic information brings an improvement to the solution at

Instance	ACS	ACSPara	Speed-up	MMAS	MMASPara	Speed-up
48-75-6	69.09	32.99	2.09	69.44	33.05	2.10
52-73-6	77.54	36.86	2.10	77.25	36.42	2.12
52-75-6	75.48	36.92	2.04	76.20	36.37	2.09
393-45-37	343.56	180.95	1.90	345.77	168.25	2.06
392-45-37	336.89	170.56	1.98	339.21	167.74	2.02
397-40-37	303.58	152.61	1.99	316.10	160.17	1.97
96-70-8	330.53	193.91	1.70	334.48	194.22	1.72
87-70-8	308.89	180.50	1.71	306.06	177.99	1.72
89-70-8	356.31	207.96	1.71	347.45	208.78	1.66
221-45-30	727.75	464.35	1.57	716.28	455.44	1.57
211-45-34	445.10	272.97	1.63	438.79	272.26	1.61
214-45-34	570.70	335.44	1.70	575.64	338.52	1.70
629-46-26	1362.00	794.77	1.71	1393.75	815.15	1.71
606-70-26	2816.89	1777.88	1.58	2844.88	1728.66	1.65
607-70-26	2805.16	1705.26	1.65	2762.45	1719.46	1.61
Average			1.78			1.80

Table 7.2. Results of the parallelization evaluation (CPU-runtime in seconds and the relative speed-up).

an early stage, for both ACS and MMAS. After that, the algorithm is able to exploit a superior neighborhood of solutions and terminates with a much better one. For example, we show distributions with the activated vs. deactivated update of heuristic information for the large instance 629-46-26 in Figure 7.8. Similar results can be obtained for all other instances (see Figures A.2, A.3, A.4, and A.5).

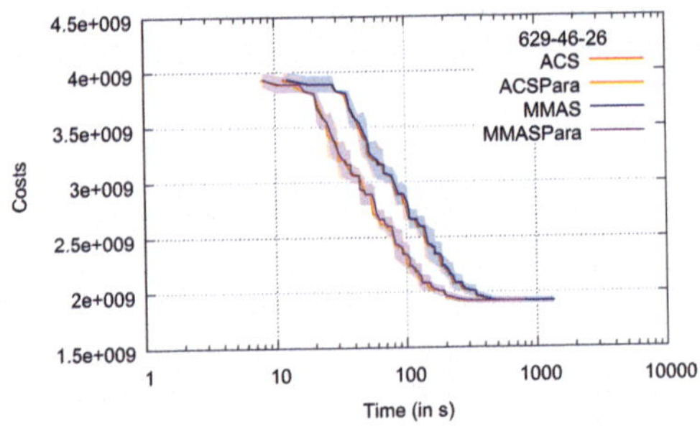

Figure 7.7. Behavior of the different ACO methods for instance 629-46-26 (logarithmic x-scale).

However, the local search method was deactivated during both evaluations above, since its great impact on the performance overshadows the two aspects above. Moreover, the local search algorithm consumes some time, but it is necessary in order to achieve good solutions for solving the driver rostering problem; for example, Figure 7.9 shows the example of all

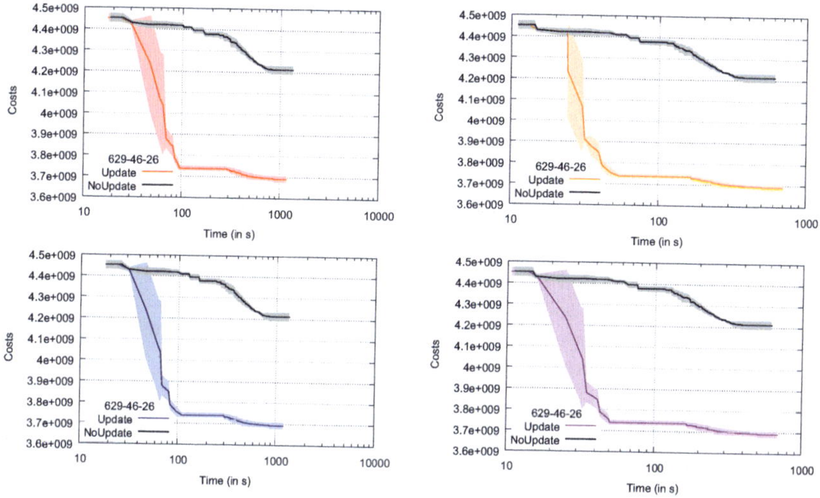

Figure 7.8. Behavior of different ACO methods (from top left to bottom right: ACS, ACSPara, MMAS, MMASPara) with the activated update of the heuristic information vs. the deactivated update for instance 629-46-26 (logarithmic x-scale).

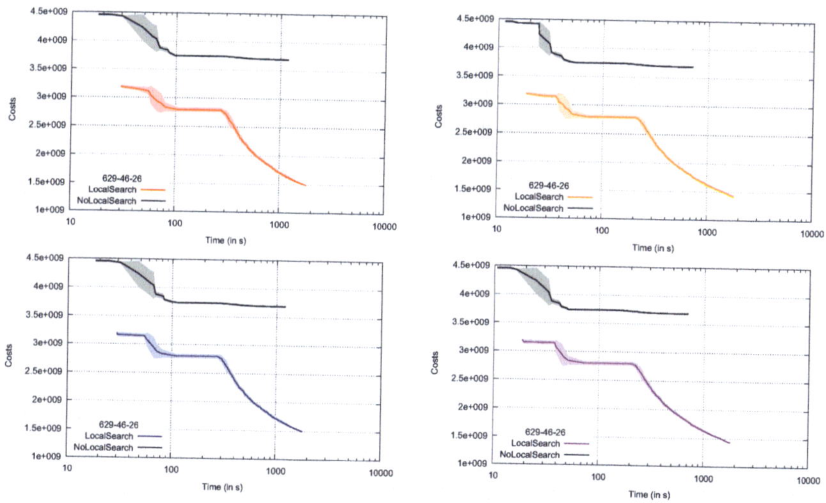

Figure 7.9. Behavior of different ACO methods (from top left to bottom right: ACS, ACSPara, MMAS, MMASPara) with the activated local search vs. the deactivated local search for instance 629-46-26 (logarithmic x-scale).

ACO methods with activated and deactivated local search for the instance 629-46-26. The local search improves the solutions from the beginning. In this test, the update of heuristic information is not included. Similar results can be obtained using all ACO methods for all instances in Figures A.6, A.7, A.8, and A.9.

In Figure 7.10, the results of ACO methods (including ACS, ACSPara, MMAS, and MMASPara with update of heuristic information, as well as applying the local search) are compared with those obtained by simulated annealing (SA), Tabu search (TS), the Gurobi solver, and the CPLEX solver. The time limit is set to 30 minutes. Furthermore, 10 repetitions were done for all metaheuristic methods to minimize the influence of randomness. This results in 900 performed tests. For some instances, the parallelization in ACO methods does not work significantly, such as 397-40-37 and 211-45-34. Moreover, all ACO methods tend to generate a very good solution at the early stage, while SA and TS have poorer starts, although their start solutions are generated by the same ACO method (ant-walk algorithm). TS generally produces weak solutions, so the best two of our implemented metaheuristics are the SA and ACO methods.

Instance	ACS	ACSPara	MMAS	MMASPara	SA	TS	Gurobi	CPLEX
48-75-6	1.02	1.02	1.02	1.02	1.25	1.26	1.00	1.00
52-73-6	1.00	1.00	1.00	1.00	1.00	1.01	1.00	1.00
52-75-6	1.00	1.00	1.00	1.00	1.00	1.01	1.00	1.00
393-45-37	1.30	1.29	1.30	1.29	1.19	2.81	1.00	1.00
392-45-37	1.08	1.08	1.08	1.08	1.05	1.57	1.00	1.00
397-40-37	1.19	1.19	1.19	1.19	1.13	2.57	1.00	1.00
96-70-8	1.27	1.24	1.27	1.24	1.16	1.66	1.00	1.00
87-70-8	3.25	3.08	3.26	3.08	1.81	15.49	1.00	1.00
89-70-8	1.31	1.26	1.31	1.27	1.00	4.34	2.57	1.00
221-45-30	1.17	1.16	1.17	1.16	1.00	1.31	n.a.	6.99
211-45-34	1.90	1.89	1.91	1.89	1.70	2.27	1.00	24.64
214-45-34	2.13	2.11	2.13	2.11	2.01	2.52	1.00	15.60
629-46-26	1.61	1.55	1.62	1.55	1.00	3.07	n.a.	7.13
606-70-26	1.59	1.56	1.58	1.55	1.00	2.50	n.a.	n.a.
607-70-26	1.65	1.62	1.64	1.61	1.00	2.40	n.a.	n.a.

Table 7.3. Evaluation overview — the obtained evaluation values relative to the particular best value of each instance at the end of the 30 minute time limit. "n.a." means that no solution is obtained.

Additionally, Table 7.3 provides details of the evaluation, where the relationship between each evaluation value and the best one is shown for each instance.

It is obvious that the ACO methods can compete with SA only on small instances with about 50 drivers. SA obtains generally better or equal solutions for all instances compared with all ACO methods, except for the instance 48-75-6. The agility of the SA method might explain why it is the best method for our problem. As shown in Table 7.4, the number of iterations per second is higher with SA than with any other approaches, since only some parts of solutions might be altered while using the δ-evaluation instead of creating a new one. This probably enables SA to dive into good solutions very fast, while the ACO

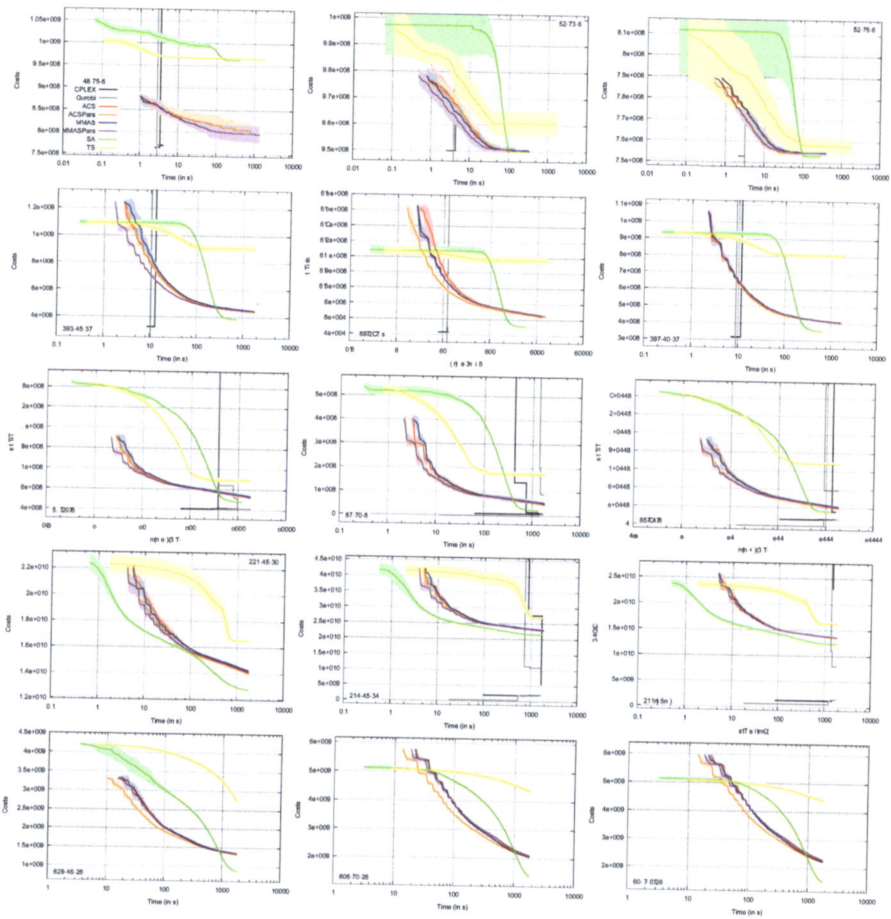

Figure 7.10. Behavior of the different methods for all instances (logarithmic x-scale).

approaches need more time on each iteration to generate new solutions for most of the instances.

Moreover, the solutions obtained by solvers perform well on smaller instances (such as instances 48-75-6 to 89-70-8), but are unable to generate one feasible solution within the time limit for a larger instance, such as 606-70-26 or 607-70-26. In such cases, the SA method brings good solutions within 30 minutes; for instance, the CPLEX solver obtains a solution seven times worse than the one obtained by the SA method for the instance 629-46-26. According to our experiments, longer running times (the time limit is not set) for all metaheuristics approaches do not bring significantly better solutions.

Instance	ACS	ACSPara	MMAS	MMASPara	SA	TS
48-75-6	0.37	0.41	0.38	0.41	11,438.29	17.32
52-73-6	1.16	1.68	1.17	1.67	18,650.84	18.63
52-75-6	1.19	1.72	1.20	1.66	18,802.83	18.01
393-45-37	0.31	0.42	0.30	0.42	7,389.54	5.03
392-45-37	0.33	0.46	0.32	0.47	9,358.61	3.63
397-40-37	0.35	0.50	0.35	0.50	8,630.59	5.12
96-70-8	0.35	0.44	0.35	0.44	4,328.90	1.26
87-70-8	0.35	0.44	0.35	0.44	4,371.06	1.33
89-70-8	0.33	0.41	0.33	0.41	4,397.49	1.21
221-45-30	0.18	0.22	0.19	0.22	3,102.91	0.59
211-45-34	0.21	0.26	0.21	0.26	3,255.13	0.61
214-45-34	0.20	0.25	0.21	0.26	2,912.51	0.51
629-46-26	0.07	0.09	0.07	0.09	1,647.82	0.15
606-70-26	0.05	0.05	0.05	0.05	1,461.38	0.11
607-70-26	0.05	0.05	0.05	0.05	1,585.37	0.12
Overall	0.44	0.55	0.43	0.54	6,493.02	10.52

Table 7.4. Overview of the average iterations per second for the different approaches.

The SA method is the best metaheuristic we implemented, therefore, it is worth taking a deeper look at the local search operators used in the SA method (see Section 7.1.2), which are different from the existing operators used in Lučić & Teodorović (2007). In order to see the influence of each operator on the quality of the solution, different combinations of their weights are tested (the order: $W^{simple} - W^{multi} - W^{crawl} - W^{shift}$). In Figure 7.11, one of the local search operators is activated. The Crawl operator brings the worst solutions (the normalized evaluation values) for all instances. We know this in advance, since this operator is only an assistant operator to support the others. The second worst operator is the Shift-Switch operator, but for some small instances, such as 52-73-6 and 52-75-6, this operator alone provides good solutions. The classical Simple- and Multi-Switch operators generally bring good solutions. Therefore, we would like to see the influence of deactivating one of the operators in Figure 7.12. Without Simple-Switch and Crawl operators the solutions for very large instances are worse, while the solutions for medium-sized and large instances are worse without the Shift-Switch operator. The activating of all operators brings the best or second-best solution (the difference to the best one is less than 1%) for all instances.

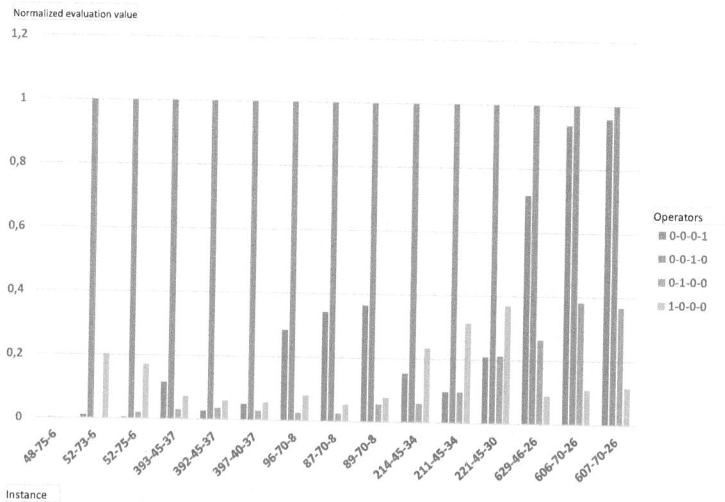

Figure 7.11. The results obtained for all instances using SA by activating one of the local search operators (the order: $W^{simple} - W^{multi} - W^{crawl} - W^{shift}$).

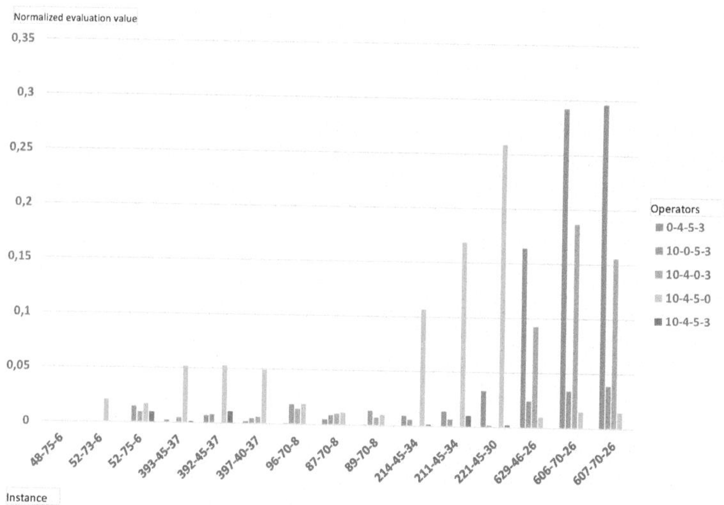

Figure 7.12. The results all instances using SA after deactivating one of the local search operators and activating all operators (the order: $W^{simple} - W^{multi} - W^{crawl} - W^{shift}$).

7.3. Simulated Annealing for the Integrated Problem

Based on the experimental results shown in Section 7.2.4, simulated annealing is the best choice among several metaheuristics for solving the rota scheduling problem. Therefore, we use simulated annealing to solve the integrated NCCR and CCR problems. The simulated annealing approach described in Section 7.2.2 remains; however, the constraints about duties (see constraints (5.25a), (5.27a), (5.26a), and (5.14b)) for the NCCR problem should be checked during the generation of the initial driver-by-driver solution as well as during the switching. A similar thing is done for the CCR problem by checking constraints about duties (see constraints (5.25a), (5.27a), (5.26a), (5.14d), and (5.30a)).

7.4. Column Generation for the Crew Rostering Problem

As shown in Section 7.2.4, most of the solutions obtained by using metaheuristics can not compete with the ones solved by commercial solvers. Therefore, an efficient method is required. According to the literature, the most-applied method in the airline sector is column generation. There is an implementation shown in Yunes et al. (2005) for solving the NCCR problem in public bus transport. However, our implementation is different from the existing one in the following ways:

- We formulate the crew rostering problem as a multicommodity flow network problem (see Section 5.1) instead of a classical set-partitioning problem.
- We solve both CCR and NCCR problems with the same column generation approach.
- We consider a more complex crew rostering problem (see rules in Section 2.2.1), including components such as multiple objectives, balanced workloads, feasibility checks from the previous period to the current one, fixed activities in the current planning period, personal requirements (not only the need for the required number of days off, but also considering the daily desired activities including a day off on each calendar day, etc.).
- We generate in each pricing problem a roster with the smallest negative reduced cost. The problem is formulated as an integer program instead of a constraint satisfaction problem.
- We test our approach for larger real-world instances for an entire planning horizon (more than one month) instead of one week.

7.4.1. Column Generation for NCCR

We firstly describe the column generation approach for the NCCR problem, including the master and pricing problems, and a similar approach for the sub-problem, i.e. the rota scheduling problem.

The Master Problem

The master problem aims at minimizing all soft constraints (quality rules, described in Section 2.2.1), while vertical rules (capacity constraints) should be held. We reuse the objective and some constraints described in Section 5.2.3.

Preferences The costs of selected undesired activities are considered in objectives (5.15), while the costs for moved days off (at weekends) are considered in objectives (5.16) and (5.17). Additionally, another cost reflects the desirability of the frequency of a desired/undesired activity, which contains the costs of underrun days off. The fulfillment of the minimal sum of days off per driver is achieved by the constraint set (5.9). The first group of constraints sums the count of days off per driver, while the second group determines whether the minimal number of days off is met. If it is not met for a driver, then the penalty cost in objective (5.18) is activated. The same is true for overrun single-off activities (see constraint set (5.10) and objective (5.19)). Moreover, constraint set (5.11) checks weather at least one violation of the maximal distance between two double-off activities occurs for each driver. In that case, objective (5.20) is activated.

Real costs They are considered as follows. The number of unassigned shifts is counted as λ_d in the constraint set (5.8) and minimized in objective (5.22). Additionally, if a given number of standbys falls short for a driver, the corresponding penalty costs will be added to the objective function (see constraint set (5.12) and objective (5.21)). In order to avoid the case where there is no activity possible for a driver on a day, a dummy activity is selected. In (5.13), the sum of all open days for a driver m is stored in the integer variable z_m. The number of these is minimized in objective (5.23). Moreover, in order to prevent large differences in overtimes among drivers, the constraint set (5.14*b*) defines the maximal overtime for all drivers, which is minimized in objective (5.24*b*).

Fairness An even distribution of workload (overtime) is considered in constraints (5.14*b*) and objective (5.24*b*). The other fairness factor, i.e. the given number of days off for each driver, should be satisfied as far as possible (see constraint set (5.9) and objective (5.18)).

Constraints As described above, NCCR is formulated as a multicommodity network flow problem, therefore the *network constraints* should be considered, i.e. flow conservation constraints (5.1), demand satisfaction constraints (5.2), and capacity constraints (5.7) and (5.25*a*) in the vertical rules. Moreover, the relationship between each shift activity arc and its corresponding duties is taken into account (see constraint set (5.27*a*)), i.e. each assigned shift gets a corresponding duty. We do not consider all variables in the master problem, but only some of them. Therefore, this problem is called the *restricted master problem*. All variables are relaxed, i.e. they are linear variables.

$$\min z^M_{NCCR}$$

$$= \sum_{e \in \mathcal{A}^s} C^a_e \cdot x^a_e \qquad \text{(Costs of selected activities)} \qquad (5.15)$$

$$+ \sum_{m \in \mathcal{M}} \sum_{d \in \mathcal{D}_{mf}} \sum_{e \in \mathcal{A}_{m,T_d,d}} C^{m1} \cdot x_e^a \qquad \text{(Costs of moved days off)} \qquad (5.16)$$

$$+ \sum_{m \in \mathcal{M}} \sum_{d \in \mathcal{D}_{mfw}} \sum_{e \in \mathcal{A}_{m,T_d,d}} C^{m2} \cdot x_e^a \qquad \text{(Costs of moved days off at weekends)} \qquad (5.17)$$

$$+ \sum_{m \in \mathcal{M}} C^f \cdot v_m \qquad \text{(Costs of underrun days off)} \qquad (5.18)$$

$$+ \sum_{m \in \mathcal{M}} C^g \cdot w_m \qquad \text{(Costs of overflowed single-offs)} \qquad (5.19)$$

$$+ \sum_{m \in \mathcal{M}} C^d \cdot \delta_m \qquad \text{(Violated distance between double-offs)} \qquad (5.20)$$

$$+ \sum_{m \in \mathcal{M}} C^p \cdot p_m \qquad \text{(Cost of underrun standbys)} \qquad (5.21)$$

$$+ \sum_{d \in \mathcal{D}_s} C^u \cdot \lambda_d \qquad \text{(Costs of unassigned shifts)} \qquad (5.22)$$

$$+ \sum_{m \in \mathcal{M}} C^{du} \cdot z_m \qquad \text{(Costs of open days)} \qquad (5.23)$$

$$+ C^o \cdot \phi'' \qquad \text{(Overtime)} \qquad (5.24b)$$

s.t.

$$x_e^a = \sum_{e' \in \mathcal{F}_e} x_{e'}^c \qquad \forall e \in \mathcal{A}^s \qquad (5.1)$$

$$x_e^a = \sum_{e' \in \mathcal{B}_e} x_{e'}^c \qquad \forall e \in \mathcal{A}^s$$

$$e_m^s = 1 \qquad \forall m \in \mathcal{M} \qquad (5.2)$$

$$e_m^e = 1 \qquad \forall m \in \mathcal{M}$$

$$I_d - \sum_{m \in \mathcal{M}} \sum_{e \in \mathcal{A}_{m,t,d}} x_e^a = \lambda_d \qquad \forall d \in \mathcal{D}_s, t = T_d \qquad (5.8)$$

$$\sum_{e \in \mathcal{A}_{m,t,d}} x_e^a = \sigma_m \qquad \forall m \in \mathcal{M}, t \in \mathcal{T}_m, d \in \mathcal{D}_f \qquad (5.9)$$

$$F_m - v_m \cdot T^m \leq \sigma_m \qquad \forall m \in \mathcal{M}$$

$$\sum_{e \in \mathcal{A}_{m,t,d}} x_e^a = \tau_m \qquad \forall m \in \mathcal{M}, t \in \mathcal{T}_m, d \in \mathcal{D}_{sf} \qquad (5.10)$$

$$E_m + w_m \cdot T^m \geq \tau_m \qquad \forall m \in \mathcal{M}$$

$$\sum_{t'=t}^{t+D} \sum_{e \in \mathcal{A}_{m,t',d}} x_e^a \geq 1 - \delta_m \qquad \forall m \in \mathcal{M}, d \in \mathcal{D}_{df}, t \in \{1, \ldots, T_m - D\} \qquad (5.11)$$

$$\sum_{e \in \mathcal{A}_{m,t,d}} x_e^a = \psi_m \qquad \forall m \in \mathcal{M}, t \in \mathcal{T}_m, d \in \mathcal{D}_b \qquad (5.12)$$

$$\psi_m \geq V_m - p_m \cdot V_m \qquad \forall m \in \mathcal{M}$$

$$\sum_{d \in \mathcal{D}_{du}} \sum_{e \in \mathcal{A}_{m,t,d}} x_e^a = z_m \qquad \forall m \in \mathcal{M} \tag{5.13}$$

$$\sum_{m \in \mathcal{M}} \sum_{e \in \mathcal{A}_{m,t,d}} x_e^a \leq I_d \qquad \forall d \in \mathcal{D}_w \cup \mathcal{D}_f, t = T_d \tag{5.7}$$

$$\sum_{e \in \mathcal{A}'_j} y'_{e,j} \leq 1 \qquad \forall j \in \mathcal{J} \tag{5.25a}$$

$$x_e^a = \sum_{j \in \mathcal{J}'_e} y'_{e,j} \qquad \forall e \in \mathcal{A}_m^a, m \in \mathcal{M} \tag{5.27a}$$

$$\sum_{d \in \mathcal{D}_w \setminus \mathcal{D}_s} \sum_{e \in \mathcal{A}_{m,T_d,d}} W_d \cdot x_e^a + \sum_{e \in \mathcal{A}_m^a} \sum_{j \in \mathcal{J}'_e} W_j \cdot y'_{e,j} - R_m \leq \phi'' \qquad \forall m \in \mathcal{M} \tag{5.14b}$$

The Pricing Problem

The pricing problem aims to generate a feasible roster by considering horizontal rules (in Section 2.2.1) with minimal reduced costs for each driver in objective (7.12). Let $\mathcal{A}_m^s$ be the subset of $\mathcal{A}^s$ that contains all activity arcs including the extended source e_m^s and sink-edges e_m^e of the employee $m \in \mathcal{M}$. We define C_e^r as the reduced cost of selecting the activity arc $e \in \mathcal{A}_m^s$ for the employee $m \in \mathcal{M}$. And C_j^r is the reduced cost of selecting the duty $j \in \mathcal{J}_e$ of the activity arc $e \in \mathcal{A}_m^s$ for the employee $m \in \mathcal{M}$. These are updated after the master problem has been solved. Let $\mathcal{S}_m$ be the subset of $\mathcal{S}$, which contains a set s of forbidden sequencing activity arcs for the driver m. Additionally, let $\mathcal{S}_m^o$ be a superset of all sets s of sequencing duties (with a length of 2) for the driver m, which are forbidden to be simultaneously active in a feasible solution due to violating the overnight rest period. The following pricing model is run in parallel for each driver $m \in \mathcal{M}$. It is based on the hard constraints of the integrated model for NCCR in Section 5.2.3, but without the capacity constraints. Moreover, constraints (5.27am) ensure each assigned shift activity arc gets an assigned duty, while constraints (5.26a) forbid an impossible combination of duties.

We consider in each pricing problem only one network layer for a driver. Therefore, the network constraints for a single network layer are considered during the generation of a feasible schedule for a driver. The flow conservation constraints (5.1m) and the demand satisfaction constraints (5.2m) are defined for each driver. Additionally, a resource constrained shortest path (see Section 2.3.2 for an introduction) has to be determined in each network layer. The resources include the maximal block length of work-related days (see constraint set (5.3)) and the maximal block length of days off for the driver m (see constraint set (5.4)). Additionally, the double-off and forbidden sequences are defined in the constraints (5.5) and (5.6), respectively. All variables in the pricing problem are binary variables.

$$\min z_{NCCR}^P = \sum_{d \in \mathcal{D}_s} \sum_{e \in \mathcal{A}_{m,T_d,d}} (C_e^r \cdot x_e^a + \sum_{j \in \mathcal{J}'_e} C_j^r \cdot y'_{e,j}) + \sum_{d \in \mathcal{D} \setminus \mathcal{D}_s} \sum_{e \in \mathcal{A}_{m,T_d,d}} C_e^r \cdot x_e^a \tag{7.12}$$

s.t.

$$x_e^a = \sum_{e' \in \mathcal{F}_e} x_{e'}^c \qquad \forall e \in \mathcal{A}_m^s \tag{5.1m}$$

$$x_e^a = \sum_{e' \in \mathcal{B}_e} x_{e'}^c \qquad \forall e \in \mathcal{A}_m^s$$

$$e_m^s = 1 \tag{5.2m}$$

$$e_m^e = 1$$

$$\sum_{t'=t}^{t+L_m^W} \sum_{e \in \mathcal{A}_{m,t',d}} x_e^a \geq 1 \qquad t \in \{1, ..., T_m - L_m^W\}, d \in \mathcal{D}_f \tag{5.3m}$$

$$\sum_{t'=t}^{t+L_m^R} \sum_{e \in \mathcal{A}_{m,t',d}} x_e^a \geq 1 \qquad t \in \{1, ..., T_m - L_m^R\}, d \in \mathcal{D}_w \tag{5.4m}$$

$$\sum_{e \in \mathcal{A}_{m,t,d}} x_e^a \geq \sum_{e \in \mathcal{A}_{m,t+1,d}} x_e^a \qquad t \in \{1, ..., T_m - 1\}, d \in \mathcal{D}_{df} \tag{5.5m}$$

$$\sum_{e \in s} x_e^a \leq |s| - 1 \qquad \forall s \in \mathcal{S}_m \tag{5.6m}$$

$$y'_{e,j} + y'_{e',j'} \leq 1 \qquad \forall e \in \mathcal{A}'_j, e' \in \mathcal{A}'_{j'}, (j, j') \in \mathcal{S}_m^o \tag{5.26am}$$

$$x_e^a = \sum_{j \in \mathcal{J}'_e} y'_{e,j} \qquad \forall e \in \mathcal{A}_m^a \tag{5.27am}$$

Sub-Problem: Rota Scheduling (RS)

As shown in Section 5.2.1, the rota scheduling problem is hard to solve, therefore, a similar column generation approach is also applied to solve this problem. The mathematical model of its sequencing process, i.e. the duty sequencing problem, can be found in Section 5.2.2.

The Master Problem

All constraints in the master problem of integrated planning for NCCR in Section 7.4.1 are also considered in the model of this problem, except for the constraints about duties, (5.25a) and (5.27a). Moreover, the constraint set defining the maximum overtime for all drivers (5.14b) is modified by (5.14) and its corresponding objective (5.24).

$$\min z_{NCCR}^{M,RS} = (5.15) + (5.16) + (5.17) + (5.18) + (5.19) + (5.20) + (5.21) + (5.22) + (5.23) + C^o \cdot \phi \tag{5.24}$$

s.t.

$$(5.1), (5.2), (5.8), (5.9), (5.10), (5.11), (5.12), (5.13), (5.7)$$

$$\sum_{t\in\mathcal{T}_m}\sum_{d\in\mathcal{D}_w}\sum_{e\in\mathcal{A}_{m,t,d}} W_d \cdot x_e^a - R_m \leq \phi \qquad \forall m \in \mathcal{M} \qquad (5.14)$$

The Pricing Problem

This problem aims at finding a feasible combination of activities for the driver m with the lowest reduced cost (see objective (7.12a)). All constraints in the pricing problem of the crew rostering problem in Section 7.4.1 are also considered in the model of this problem, except for the constraints about duties (5.26a) and (5.27am).

$$\min z_{NCCR}^{P,RS} = \sum_{e\in\mathcal{A}_m^s} C_e^r \cdot x_e^a \qquad \text{(Reduced costs)} \qquad (7.12a)$$

s.t.

$$(5.1\text{m}), (5.2\text{m}), (5.3\text{m}), (5.4\text{m}), (5.5\text{m}), (5.6\text{m})$$

7.4.2. Column Generation for CCR

As mentioned in Section 5.1, one difference between this problem and the NCCR problem is that the capacity of each work-related activity is no longer restricted by calendar dates, but by days of the week. Additionally, the constraints about artificial days should be considered. Note that we use the similar initial driver-by-driver solution as shown in Section 7.1.3 for the NCCR problem.

The Master Problem

We reuse the objective and some constraints described in Section 5.3.3. Artificial days should be ignored by the constraints of calculations of unassigned shifts (5.8a), insufficient days off (5.9a), overrun single-offs (5.10a), insufficient standbys (5.12a), unassigned days (5.13a), and maximum overtime (5.14d). However, artificial days are considered in the constraints of flow conservation (5.1), demand satisfaction (5.2), and checking maximal distance between two double-off activities (5.11). Constraints (5.8a) and (5.7a) make sure that the work-related activities are restricted by days of the week. Constraints (5.29) and (5.30a) make sure the selected activity and duty on each artificial day $T_m - b_m^{art} + i$ are equal to the selected ones on the day i, where $i \in \{1, 2, ..., b_m^{art}\}$. Additionally, the relationship between a shift activity arc and its possible duties is guaranteed in (5.27a), and the duty capacity constraints in (5.25a) should be considered as well.

$$\min z_{CCR}^{M} = \qquad (5.15) + (5.16) + (5.17) + (5.20)$$

$$+ \sum_{m\in\mathcal{M}} C^f \cdot v_m{}' \qquad \text{(Costs of underrun days off)} \qquad (5.18a)$$

$$+ \sum_{m \in \mathcal{M}} C^g \cdot w_m{}' \qquad \text{(Costs of overflowed single-offs)} \qquad (5.19a)$$
$$+ \sum_{m \in \mathcal{M}} C^p \cdot p_m{}' \qquad \text{(Costs of underrun standbys)} \qquad (5.21a)$$
$$+ \sum_{d \in \mathcal{D}_s} C^u \cdot \lambda_d{}' \qquad \text{(Costs of unassigned shifts)} \qquad (5.22a)$$
$$+ \sum_{m \in \mathcal{M}} C^{du} \cdot z_m{}' \qquad \text{(Costs of open days)} \qquad (5.23a)$$
$$+ C^o \cdot \phi'''' \qquad \text{(Overtime)} \qquad (5.14d)$$

s.t.

$$(5.1), (5.2), (5.11), (5.25a), (5.27a)$$

$$I_d - \sum_{m \in \mathcal{M}} \sum_{t' \in \mathcal{T}_{m,t}} \sum_{e \in \mathcal{A}_{m,t',d}} x_e^a = \lambda_d{}' \qquad \forall d \in \mathcal{D}_s, t = T_d{}' \qquad (5.8a)$$
$$\sum_{e \in \mathcal{A}_{m,t,d}} x_e^a = \sigma_m{}' \qquad \forall m \in \mathcal{M}, d \in \mathcal{D}_f, t \in \mathcal{T}_m \setminus \mathcal{T}_m^{art} \qquad (5.9a)$$
$$F_m - v_m{}' \cdot T^m \leq \sigma_m{}' \qquad \forall m \in \mathcal{M}$$
$$\sum_{e \in \mathcal{A}_{m,t,d}} x_e^a = \tau_m{}' \qquad \forall m \in \mathcal{M}, d \in \mathcal{D}_{sf}, t \in \mathcal{T}_m \setminus \mathcal{T}_m^{art} \qquad (5.10a)$$
$$E_m + w_m{}' \cdot T^m \geq \tau_m{}' \qquad \forall m \in \mathcal{M}$$
$$\sum_{e \in \mathcal{A}_{m,t,d}} x_e^a = \psi_m{}' \qquad \forall m \in \mathcal{M}, d \in \mathcal{D}_b, t \in \mathcal{T}_m \setminus \mathcal{T}_m^{art} \qquad (5.12a)$$
$$\psi_m{}' \geq V_m - p_m{}' \cdot V_m \qquad \forall m \in \mathcal{M}$$
$$\sum_{t \in \mathcal{T}_m \setminus \mathcal{T}_m^{art}} \sum_{d \in \mathcal{D}_{du}} \sum_{e \in \mathcal{A}_{m,t,d}} x_e^a = z_m{}' \qquad \forall m \in \mathcal{M} \qquad (5.13a)$$
$$\sum_{m \in \mathcal{M}} \sum_{t' \in \mathcal{T}_{m,t}} \sum_{e \in \mathcal{A}_{m,t',d}} x_e^a \leq I_d \qquad \forall d \in \mathcal{D}_w, t = T_d{}' \qquad (5.7a)$$
$$\sum_{t \in \mathcal{T}_m \setminus \mathcal{T}_m^{art}} \sum_{d \in \mathcal{D}_w \setminus \mathcal{D}_s} \sum_{e \in \mathcal{A}_{m,t,d}} W_d \cdot x_e^a + \sum_{e \in \mathcal{A}_m^a} \sum_{j \in \mathcal{J}_e'} W_j \cdot y_{e,j}' - R_m \leq \phi'''' \quad \forall m \in \mathcal{M} \quad (5.14d)$$
$$x_e^a = x_{e'}^a \quad \forall m \in \mathcal{M}, i \in \{1, 2, ..., b_m^{art}\}, d \in \mathcal{D}_i, e \in \mathcal{A}_{m, T_m - b_m^{art} + i, d}, e' \in \mathcal{A}_{m,i,d} \quad (5.29)$$
$$y_{e,j}' = y_{e',j}' \quad \forall m \in \mathcal{M}, T_e \in \{1, 2, ..., b_m^{art}\}, e, e' \in \mathcal{A}_m^a, T_{e'} = T_m - b_m^{art} + T_e, j \in \mathcal{J}_e' \quad (5.30a)$$

The Pricing Problem

We extend the pricing problem for the NCCR problem (constraints (5.1m) to (5.27am)) with constraints (5.29m) and (5.30am) to make sure the selected activity and duty on each artificial day are equal to the selected ones on the original day for the driver m. Additionally, it is known that the duties are dependent on the day of the week, therefore we have to make sure that each duty can only be assigned to a driver once.

$$\min z^{P}_{CCR} = \sum_{t\in\mathcal{T}_m\setminus\mathcal{T}^{art}_m} \sum_{d\in\mathcal{D}_{s,t}} \sum_{e\in\mathcal{A}_{m,t,d}} (C^{r}_{e}\cdot x^{a}_{e} + \sum_{j\in\mathcal{J}_e} C^{r}_{j}\cdot y_{e,j}) \quad \text{(Reduced costs)} \qquad (7.12b)$$
$$+ \sum_{t\in\mathcal{T}_m\setminus\mathcal{T}^{art}_m} \sum_{d\in\mathcal{D}_{w,t}\setminus\mathcal{D}_{s,t}} \sum_{e\in\mathcal{A}_{m,t,d}} C^{r}_{e}\cdot x^{a}_{e}$$

s.t.

$$(5.1\text{m}), (5.2\text{m}), (5.3\text{m}), (5.4\text{m}), (5.5\text{m}), (5.6\text{m}), (5.26am), (5.27am)$$

$$x^{a}_{e} = x^{a}_{e'} \qquad i\in\{1,2,...,b^{art}_{m}\}, d\in\mathcal{D}_i, e\in\mathcal{A}_{m,T_m-b^{art}_m+i,d}, e'\in\mathcal{A}_{m,i,d} \qquad (5.29\text{m})$$
$$y'_{e,j} = y'_{e',j} \qquad T_e\in\{1,2,...,b^{art}_{m}\}, e,e'\in\mathcal{A}^{a}_{m}, T_{e'} = T_m - b^{art}_{m} + T_e, j\in\mathcal{J}'_e \qquad (5.30am)$$

Sub-Problem: Rota Scheduling (RS)

Similar to Section 7.4.1, all constraints in the master and pricing problem of CCR in Sections 7.4.2 and 7.4.2 are considered in the models of this section, except for the constraints about duties in the master problem (5.25a), (5.27a), (5.26a), and (5.30a), and the constraints in the pricing problem (5.25a), (5.27am), (5.26a), and (5.30am).

The Master Problem

The constraint set about maximum overtime is replaced with (5.24c).

$$\min z^{M,RS}_{CCR}$$
$$= (5.15) + (5.16) + (5.17) + (5.18a) + (5.19a)$$
$$+ (5.20) + (5.21a) + (5.22a) + (5.23a)$$
$$+ C^{o}\cdot\phi''' \qquad (5.24c)$$

s.t.

$$(5.1), (5.2), (5.8a), (5.9a), (5.10a), (5.11), (5.12a), (5.13a), (5.7a), (5.29)$$

$$\sum_{t\in\mathcal{T}_m\setminus\mathcal{T}^{art}_m} \sum_{d\in\mathcal{D}_w} \sum_{e\in\mathcal{A}_{m,t,d}} W_d\cdot x^{a}_{e} - R_m \le \phi''' \qquad \forall m\in\mathcal{M} \qquad (5.14c)$$

The Pricing Problem

The objective is changed as in (7.12c), which considers only the reduced costs of activity arcs.

$$\min z^{P,RS}_{CCR} = \sum_{t\in\mathcal{T}_m\setminus\mathcal{T}^{art}_m} \sum_{d\in\mathcal{D}_{w,t}} \sum_{e\in\mathcal{A}_{m,t,d}} C^{r}_{e}\cdot x^{a}_{e} \quad \text{(Reduced costs)} \qquad (7.12c)$$

s.t.

$$(5.1\text{m}), (5.2\text{m}), (5.3\text{m}), (5.4\text{m}), (5.5\text{m}), (5.6\text{m}), (5.29\text{m})$$

7.5. Multi-Objective Simulated Annealing for the Crew Rostering Problem

As mentioned before, the crew rostering problem in this thesis considers the interests of the management and the drivers. In this subsection, we explicitly consider each objective as an objective function (see Objectives 7.13 to 7.22) instead of considering all objectives within an objective function (see Section 5.2.1); i.e. instead of seeking an optimal solution as in the single objective function, we look for a set of solutions, which spread the solution space as far as possible. Therefore, the human planner can see the different solutions for further decisions about the weight for each objective.

$$f_1 = \sum_{e \in \mathcal{A}^s} C_e^a \cdot x_e^a \quad \rightarrow \min(\text{Costs of selected activities}) \tag{7.13}$$

$$f_2 = \sum_{m \in \mathcal{M}} \sum_{d \in \mathcal{D}_{mf}} \sum_{e \in \mathcal{A}_{m,T_d,d}} x_e^a \quad \rightarrow \min(\#\text{ moved days off}) \tag{7.14}$$

$$f_3 = \sum_{m \in \mathcal{M}} \sum_{d \in \mathcal{D}_{mfw}} \sum_{e \in \mathcal{A}_{m,T_d,d}} x_e^a \quad \rightarrow \min(\#\text{ moved days off at weekends}) \tag{7.15}$$

$$f_4 = \sum_{m \in \mathcal{M}} v_m \quad \rightarrow \min(\#\text{ underrun days off}) \tag{7.16}$$

$$f_5 = \sum_{m \in \mathcal{M}} w_m \quad \rightarrow \min(\#\text{ overflowed single-offs}) \tag{7.17}$$

$$f_6 = \sum_{m \in \mathcal{M}} \delta_m \quad \rightarrow \min(\#\text{ violated dist. btwn double-offs}) \tag{7.18}$$

$$f_7 = \sum_{m \in \mathcal{M}} p_m \quad \rightarrow \min(\#\text{ underrun standbys}) \tag{7.19}$$

$$f_8 = \sum_{d \in \mathcal{D}_s} \lambda_d \quad \rightarrow \min(\#\text{ unassigned shifts}) \tag{7.20}$$

$$f_9 = \sum_{m \in \mathcal{M}} z_m \quad \rightarrow \min(\#\text{ open days}) \tag{7.21}$$

$$f_{10} = \phi'' \quad \rightarrow \min(\text{Overtime}) \tag{7.22}$$

In the literature, Lučić & Teodorović (1999) describe a multi-objective simulated annealing (MOSA) approach for solving the aircrew NCCR problem, and an interactive method is provided. We use a similar scalar ordering (fitness) function $F : \mathbb{R}^n \rightarrow \mathbb{R}$ to determine the preference structure within a normal SA as described in Algorithm 7.7:

$$F(f) = \sum_{i=1}^{n} w_i \cdot f_i \tag{7.23}$$

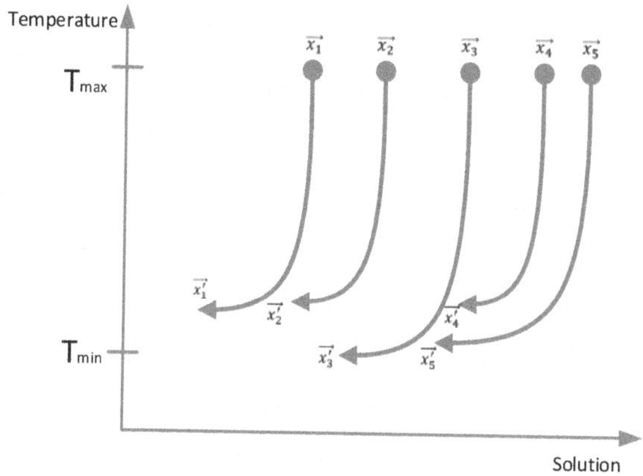

Figure 7.13. The basic idea of multi-objective simulated annealing.

where all weights w_i are non-negative and randomly generated numbers of 2^j with $j = 1, ..., n$, since our primary goal is to provide a set of spreading non-dominated solutions. This is different to Lučić & Teodorović (1999), where the weights are provided by the planner subjectively. Other ordering approaches can be found in Serafini (1994). Since we have extreme $f_i, i \in \{1, ..., n\}$, which might drain the influence of the scalar function F, we use N_i for each $f_i, i \in \{1, ..., n\}$ as shown in (7.24) for the normalization:

$$f_i \leftarrow f_i/N_i \quad \forall i \in \{1, ..., n\} \tag{7.24}$$

As illustrated in Figure 7.13 and described in Algorithm 7.9, a new solution $\vec{x'_j}$ is achieved by SA for an initial solution $\vec{x_j}$ in each iteration j. Then the new solution is compared with the existing pool of solutions by using the following dominance test.

We assume we have n objectives, and $\vec{x} \in \mathbb{R}^n$ and $\vec{y} \in \mathbb{R}^n$ are the old and new solutions, respectively. One of the following three alternatives for the comparison must be satisfied.

- $\vec{x} \prec \vec{y}$ ($\vec{x}$ is preferred to / dominates $\vec{y}$) $\leftrightarrow x_i \leq y_i, \forall i \in \{1, ..., n\}$ and $x_i < y_i, \exists i \in \{1, ..., n\}$
- $\vec{x} \succ \vec{y}$ ($\vec{y}$ is preferred to / dominates $\vec{x}$) $\leftrightarrow y_i \leq x_i, \forall i \in \{1, ..., n\}$ and $y_i < x_i, \exists i \in \{1, ..., n\}$
- $\vec{x} \sim \vec{y}$ ($\vec{x}$ and $\vec{y}$ are indifferent) $\leftrightarrow y_i = x_i, \forall i \in \{1, ..., n\}$

Let $\mathcal{N}$ be the set of non-dominated solutions. After that, the dominance test is carried out between $\vec{y}$ and each solution $\vec{x} \in \mathcal{N}$, and the new set of non-dominated solutions $\mathcal{N}'$ can be obtained. This is different from the one in Lučić & Teodorović (1999), which uses scalar ordering to determine the preference structure, such as $\vec{x} \prec \vec{y} \leftrightarrow F(f(\vec{x})) < F(f(\vec{y}))$. The algorithm stops if the limit of $\mathcal{N}$ is achieved, or the time limit or maximum number of iterations is reached. According to our experimental observation, the values of $N_i, i \in \{1, ..., n\}$ are set as follows:

$$N_1 \leftarrow |\mathcal{A}|, N_{10} \leftarrow |\mathcal{D}|, N_2, ..., N_9 \leftarrow 1$$

Algorithm 7.9: MOSA algorithm for crew rostering problem

initialization
$\mathcal{N} \leftarrow \emptyset$
while *termination condition not met* **do**
    $\mathcal{N}' \leftarrow \emptyset$
    calculate a new fitness value $F(f_1, ..., f_n)$
    $\vec{y} \leftarrow \mathrm{SA}(t_0, F(f_1, ..., f_n))$
    if $\mathcal{N}$ *is empty* **then**
        $\mathcal{N} \leftarrow \mathcal{N} \cup \{\vec{x}\}$
    foreach $\vec{x} \in \mathcal{N}$ **do**
        if $\vec{y} \prec \vec{x}$ *or* $\vec{x} \sim \vec{y}$ **then**
            $\mathcal{N}' \leftarrow \mathcal{N}' \cup \{\vec{y}\}$
        else
            if $\vec{x} \prec \vec{y}$ **then**
                $\mathcal{N}' \leftarrow \mathcal{N}' \cup \{\vec{x}\}$
    $\mathcal{N} \leftarrow \mathcal{N}'$

7.6. Advanced Computational Results

We compare the solutions of the implemented heuristics with the ones solved by the CPLEX solver. The comparisons were conducted on an Intel Core i7-740 2.93 GHz processor with 32 GB of RAM running Windows 7 Professional (64 bit).

Results of Column Generation

The criteria for the termination of column generation are shown below.

- There is no new pricing solution with a negative reduced cost.
- The maximal running time is reached (in our case: 24 hours).

In our pricing problem, we generate feasible pricing solutions for drivers in parallel. According to our experiments, the Gurobi solver appears to deal with parallelism better. Therefore, we test the CPLEX and Gurobi solvers separately for solving with column generation. After that, all inactive variables in column generation remain inactive, and we solve the MIP problem as shown in Section 5.2 with the CPLEX solver, but without the inactive variables in column generation. Therefore, the CPLEX solver solves the MIP problem with a reduced number of variables. The CPLEX solver is chosen since it is more suitable for solving our MIP problem (see experiments shown in Chapter 6). Note that the default settings of the CPLEX and Gurobi solvers are considered in our tests, since parameter tuning for 16 instances would just overfit. In order to compare the different combinations of solvers, the same initial solution is used for different tests for each instance, and is generated by our driver-by-driver heuristic.

Instance	Solvers	Act.var.	Gap	Reduced	CPU(CG)	CPU(BB)	Reduced
96-70-8	C/C	94%	0%	0	1,355	15,286	-39%
	G/C	55.9%	0%	0	641	1,833	-65%
87-70-8	C/C	91.5%	0%	0	1,050	50,656	0%
	G/C	49.7%	0%	0	1,238	8,283	-81.7%
89-70-8	C/C	97%	39.5%	-0.3	928	85,455	0%
	G/C	52.7%	13.3%	-26.5	1,045	85,337	0%
221-45-30	C/C	92%	3.4%	-39.5	2,301	84,057	0%
	G/C	56.2%	0%	-42.9	5,759	80,598	-0.1%
214-45-34	C/C	94%	4.2%	-1.6	1,485	84,876	0%
	G/C	55.2%	0%	-5.8	950	85,250	0%
211-45-34	C/C	95.1%	9.37%	-4.33	1,744	84,607	0%
	G/C	52.9%	0%	-13.7	780	84,520	0%
629-46-26	C/C	92.2%	7.4%	-3.5	11182	74938	0%
	G/C	51.7%	0%	-10.9	3,711	4,736	-90%
606-70-26	C/C	90%	42.2%	-31.9	1,726	84,078	0%
	G/C	47.2%	39%	-35.1	371	85,399	0%
607-70-26	C/C	94.5%	93.7%	-4	13,527	72,388	0%
	G/C	55.3%	53.9%	-43.8	4,406	81,521	0%

Table 7.5. Performance statistics of using the column generation (CG) approach with the CPLEX (C) and Gurobi (G) solvers after 24 hours of computation of rota scheduling. "BB" means branch-and-bound.

Tables 7.5 and 7.6 show the solutions obtained with our new approach compared with the solutions referred to in Table 6.6. The instances which can be solved within a minute in Table 6.6 are ignored, i.e. the instances 48-75-6 to 397-40-37 for rota scheduling. For the same reason, the instances 48-75-6 to 52-75-6 for integrated planning are not listed either.

Our column generation approach provides better solutions for both rota scheduling and integrated planning. For some instances up to 99% of the running time can be reduced (see last column: Reduced), while some achieve reductions of up to 76% in the gap to optimum (see 5th column: Reduced). Some of them can achieve both improvements, such as the instance 392-45-37 in Table 7.6. Some instances (such as 89-70-8), which do not get any benefit in their running time, stop due to the given running time (24 hours), but with a reduced gap to optimum.

Additionally, our experiments show that better solutions can be obtained if we choose the Gurobi solver instead of the CPLEX solver for column generation. The reason for this is that up to 40% fewer activated variables are selected at the end of column generation (see 2nd column: Act.var.) with the Gurobi solver. Our experiments show that the CPLEX and Gurobi solvers choose different solutions after the first iteration in column generation. Therefore, different reduced costs are calculated in the master problem of each iteration.

Instance	Solvers	Act. var.	Gap	Reduced	CPU(CG)	CPU(BB)	Reduced
9-238-11	C/C	17.73%	0%	0	422	1,930	-57%
	G/C	12.11%	0%	0	221	282	-90.8%
393-45-37	C/C	32.89%	0%	-1.68	3,491	146	-95.8%
	G/C	28.06%	0%	-1.68	1,197	60	-98.6%
392-45-37	C/C	27.96%	0%	-9	3,457	59	-85.7%
	G/C	24.57%	0%	-9	1,452	74	-93.8%
397-40-37	C/C	29.39%	0%	-4.86	2,441	55	-97.1%
	G/C	26.40%	0%	-4.86	1,165	137	-98.5%
96-70-8	C/C	37.28%	0%	0	11,477	26,689	-21.7%
	G/C	23.56%	0%	0	1,937	1,625	-92.6%
87-70-8	C/C	44.99%	0.37%	-12.13	16,047	70,118	0%
	G/C	24.4%	0%	-12.5	3,679	3,318	-91.9%
89-70-8	C/C	48.75%	84.4%	-2.1	20,771	65,365	0%
	G/C	22.35%	27.14%	-59.36	4,334	81,829	0%
221-45-30	C/C	39.33%	92%	9.7	27,216	58,611	0%
	G/C	21.39%	6.48%	-75.82	18,108	67,803	0%
214-45-34	C/C	36.59%	34.7%	-58.3	13,366	72,266	0%
	G/C	20.41%	30%	-63	746	85,654	0%
211-45-34	C/C	39.95%	90%	-9	19,506	66,476	0%
	G/C	22.1%	86%	-13	7,512	78,888	0%
629-46-26	C/C	-	-	-	-	-	-
606-70-26	C/C	-	-	-	-	-	-
607-70-26	C/C	-	-	-	-	-	-

Table 7.6. Performance statistics of using the column generation approach with the CPLEX (C) and Gurobi (G) solvers after 24 hours of computation of the integrated planning; a dash "-" indicates that the solver ran out of memory. "BB" means branch-and-bound.

According to comparisons between the solutions with sequential and integrated approaches in Chapter 6, the main improvements with the integrated approach are increases in the numbers of assigned duties and days. Table 7.7 shows the comparison for the instances which obtain an optimal sequential solution using the column generation approach (except for the instance 89-70-8, which has a gap of 13.3%). The results of the integrated approach are not optimal, but they already show an improvement of up to about 6% in the percentage of unassigned duties and days over the result of the sequential approach. An exception is the instance 211-45-34, whose solution with the integrated approach is not good enough within 24 hours to compete with its sequential solution (there is a gap of 86%), but the percentage of unassigned days is improved to optimum (with a 3.5% improvement).

Comparison of Different Approaches

The comparison of solutions obtained by different solution approaches for the rota scheduling problem is illustrated in Figure 7.14. The solutions solved by the CPLEX solver are located at the point (0,0). The solutions for simulated annealing (SA) and ant colony system (ACS) are obtained from Section 7.2.4. Although SA and ACS can get a solution within a short time (for example: 30 minutes), the quality of the solutions mostly can not compete with CPLEX and our column generation approach. The metaheuristics are only suitable to be applied to solve very large instances, i.e. the instance 607-70-26, for which a good solution can be obtained by the SA approach within 30 minutes. This value is better than the one obtained by the CPLEX solver; however, it is still not better than the one obtained by column generation.

	Unassigned duties(%)		Unassigned days(%)	
Instance	Seq.	Int.	Seq.	Int.
48-75-6	1.4	0.3	3.9	0
52-73-6	0.5	0	0.2	0
52-75-6	0.5	0	0.4	0
9-238-11	6.3	1.5	3	0.3
393-45-37	8.6	4.4	0.8	0
392-45-37	16.9	11.1	0.9	0
397-40-37	9	3.8	0.8	0
96-70-8	11.7	6.3	2.6	0
87-70-8	4	0.2	3.7	0
89-70-8	7.0	1.8	3.9	0
221-45-30	4.1	0	2.9	0
214-45-34	4.2	0.5	2.9	0
211-45-34	4.9	7.5	3.5	0

Table 7.7. The comparison of sequential (seq.) and integrated (int.) solutions according to unassigned duties and unassigned days in percentage terms (solved by CG).

For solving with the integrated approach, the advantage of applying SA is more obvious (see Figure 7.15). For instance, the result for the instance 211-45-34 solved by SA within two hours can compete with the one produced by the CPLEX solver after 24 hours; however, it is still not better than the result obtained by our CG after 24 hours. Moreover, SA produces solutions for the very large instances, which can not be solved by the CPLEX solver and our CG due to running out of memory.

Therefore, we extend the comparison of the sequential and integrated solutions in Table 7.7 into Table 7.8, where we compare the best obtained sequential solutions (solved by

CG) and integrated solutions (solved by SA). An improvement of almost 6% is achieved in the instance 607-70-26 in Table 7.8. Note that the solutions in this table are not optimal.

	Unassigned duties(%)		Unassigned days(%)	
Instance	Seq.	Int.	Seq.	Int.
629-46-26	0.24	0.06	0.04	0
606-70-26	0.57	0.037	0.05	0
607-70-26	6.3	0.29	0.03	0

Table 7.8. The comparison of sequential (seq.) and integrated (int.) solutions according to unassigned duties and unassigned days in percentage terms for very large instances.

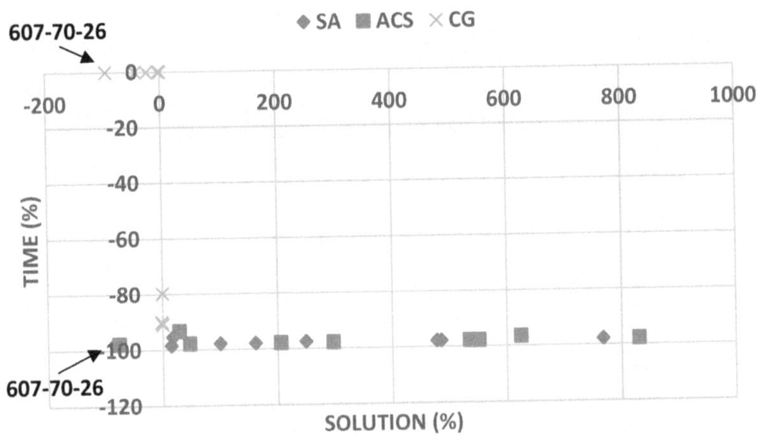

Figure 7.14. Comparison of solutions obtained by using different methods (SA, ACS and CG) with the ones solved by the CPLEX solver for the rota scheduling problem (time limit: 24 hours).

Results of Multi-Objective Simulated Annealing

Notice that a direct comparison between the approaches returning one single solution and the multi-objective approach is not possible, since the multi-objective approach provides a set of non-dominated solutions. Recall that our primary goal for this problem is to produce a set of diversified non-dominated solutions, with which the different behavior among objectives can be monitored. As a consequence, we believe that this approach can help the planner to determine his preferred weights for all objectives. More details about it will be discussed in Section 8.3.2 in relation to our decision support system. We use the same parameters as for the simulated annealing approach, shown in Section 7.2.4, in

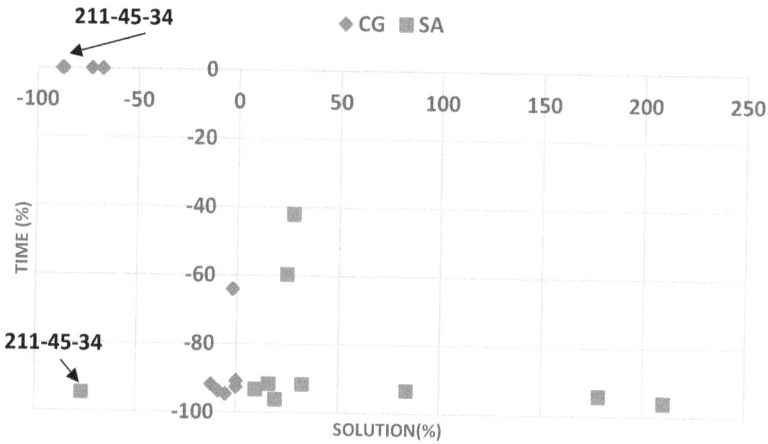

Figure 7.15. Comparison of solutions obtained by using different methods (SA and CG) with the ones solved by the CPLEX solver for the integrated problem (time limit: 24 hours).

our multi-objective approach. Moreover, the approach is terminated if the time limit of 6 hours is reached or the number of non-dominated solutions reaches 1,000.

We use a scatterplot to display the correlation between each pair of objectives and their densities (see an example in Figure 7.16 for the instance 87-70-8). The scatterplot is smoothed by using a locally weighted scatterplot smoothing method proposed by Cleveland (1979). We see a low negative correlation between the number of unassigned duties and the number of underrun days off in Figure 7.16. Some of the correlations between pairs of objectives are not obvious, since we want solutions based on weights with diverse distributions. Moreover, the range of each objective is shown. For example, the number of underrun standbys is between 0 and 40; additionally, this value has the trend to be either near 0 or between 20 and 40. Figures A.10 to A.24 show diagrams for the other instances. For the small instances, only a small set of non-dominated solutions is achieved after the time limit, therefore the correlation between each pair of objectives is not obvious. For example, in Figure A.24 the instance 9-231-9 has only one non-dominated solution after 6 hours. The reason for this is that such small instances either rarely violate many soft constraints, or do not consider many of them (for example, the instances 392-45-37, 393-45-37, and 397-40-37).

In order to see the performance of multi-objective simulated annealing, the improved Strength Pareto Evolutionary Algorithm (SPEA2) was developed, as proposed by Zitzler et al. (2001). The reason for selecting this approach is based on the analyse performed by Jones et al. (2002), which concluded that genetic algorithms were mostly adopted for the multi-objective problem, since they can naturally produce multiple solutions. The basic idea of this approach is to use the dominance criterion for fitness calculation and selection of solutions. Moreover, non-dominated solutions, which are stored in an external archive, are independent of the current population. We adopted an implementation similar to the one shown in Zitzler et al. (2001); additionally, a normalization as shown in (7.24) was applied. The set of non-dominated solutions for this approach is illustrated in Figure 7.17 for the same instance 87-70-8. However, However, the quality of the solutions provided by SPEA2 can not compete with the quality of those provided by multi-objective simulated annealing, although they provide more obvious correlations between pairs of objectives. Firstly, a longer running time is required for the SPEA2 approach, since the huge difference between the old and new solutions requires time for updating all values of all meta-information as well as the objectives for the new solution. Secondly, the SPEA2 approach produces distinctly worse values for many criteria, such as the number of unassigned duties, the number of moved days off, and maximal overtime among all drivers. According to Purshouse & Fleming (2003), all multi-objective optimization algorithms that use Pareto-ranking as a fundamental selection method will not perform efficiently on multi-objective problems with four or more objectives.

7.7. Summary

The goal of this chapter was to implement different heuristics, including metaheuristics and column generation, that obtained good solutions for those instances, which can not be solved by the standard solvers optimally within 24 hours. The standard solvers were suitable for the small instances. Different metaheuristics were implemented for the rota scheduling problem. Due to the experiments shown in Section 7.2.4, SA was the best choice among them. Therefore, SA was chosen to solve the integrated CCR and NCCR problems. Next, we have implemented the novel column generation approach for both problems.

The results reported in the previous section indicated that medium-sized and large problems can be solved by using column generation. Furthermore, the integrated approach disclosed significant improvement compared with the sequential approach; in particular, more duties were assigned in the integrated approach. This reduced the additional personnel costs. Moreover, the implemented SA can compete with our column generation approach for very large instances in the integrated problem, which can not be solved by column generation due to memory limitations.

Additionally, instead of providing one solution based on given weights of objectives, a multi-objective simulated annealing approach was implemented to provide a set of non-dominated solutions. Based on the given solutions, the planner can choose one of them to determine his/her preferred weights of objectives. A decision support system is needed to help the planner to determine them. Finally, based on the results in Chapter 6 and Section 7.6, it can be stated that different solution approaches are suitable for different problem sizes. An intelligent choice among those solution approaches is required; this will be discussed in the next chapter.

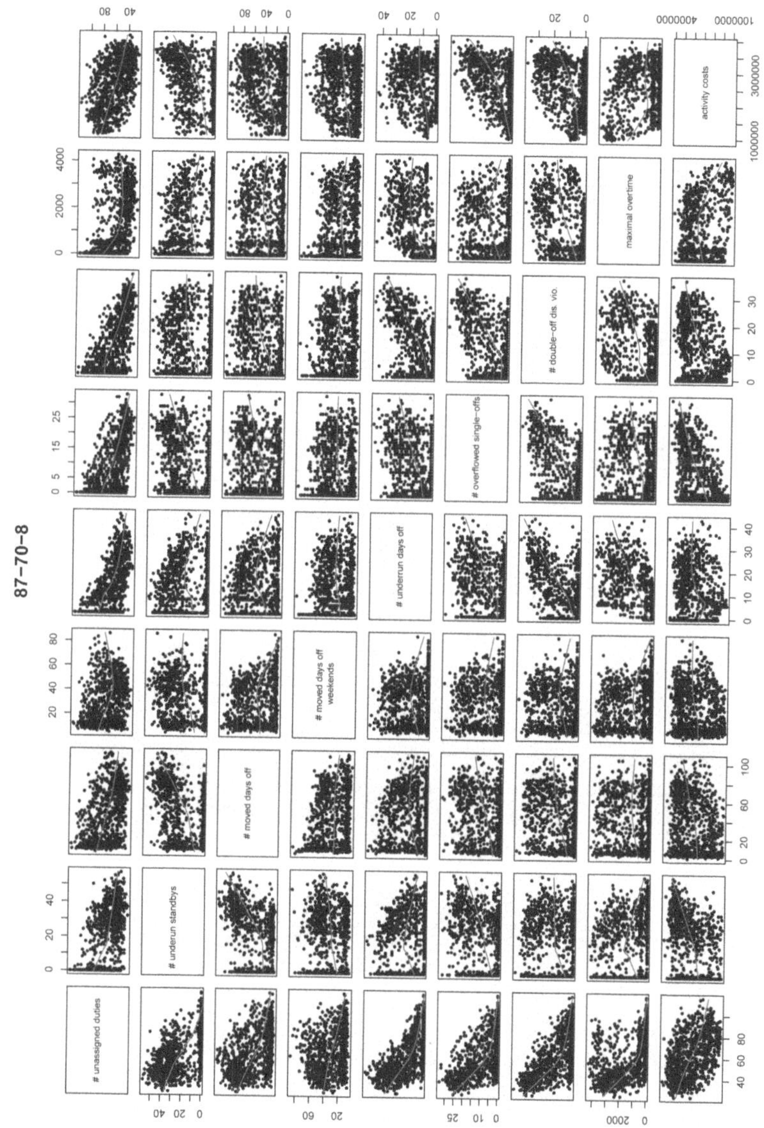

Figure 7.16. Scatterplot of the results for the instance 87-70-8 solved by multi-objective simulated annealing.

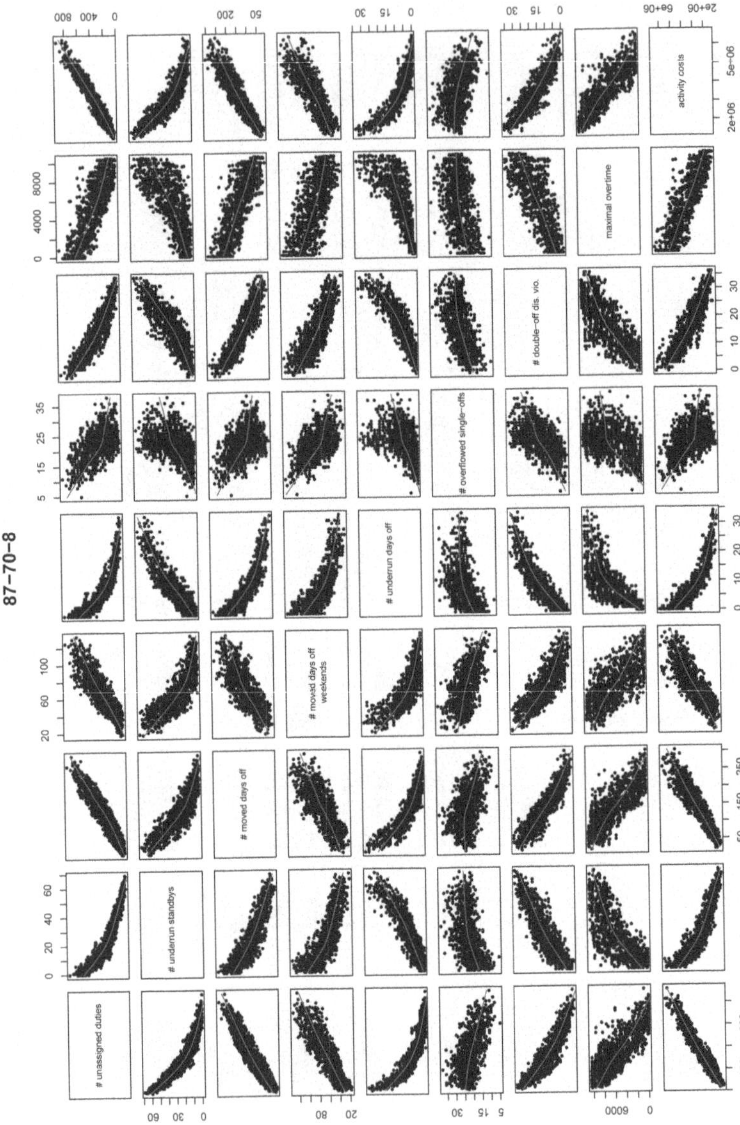

Figure 7.17. Scatterplot of the results for the instance 87-70-8 solved by SPEA2.

Part III.

Decision Support System

8. Web-Based Decision Support System for Crew Rostering

In this chapter, we begin with the reasons for the necessity of applying a web-based DSS for crew rostering in Section 8.1. In Section 8.2 we give a description of all of the functionalities of our web-based DSS. This is followed by an architecture of a model-solver integration framework in Section 8.3, which also describes model and solver agents. Finally, we give a brief summary concerning the proposed web-based DSS in Section 8.4.

8.1. Purpose of the Web-Based DSS

Due to the complex problem structure and the substantial amount of data, human planners need to put a lot of effort into the generation of rosters. Moreover, the schedules generated by a manual process may have many drawbacks, such as infeasible schedules or the lack of consideration of certain types of information.

As described in Section 2.2, the crew rostering problem considers the planning process for generating feasible and satisfactory rosters for bus drivers in public transport. *Feasible rosters* can be achieved by holding complex rules and regulations during the assignment. Moreover, such rules and regulations might differ from one bus company to another. Therefore, there is a demand for a flexible DSS to capture variant constraints and objectives. Additionally, *satisfactory rosters* are hard to obtain, since the interests of both the management and the drivers are considered in crew rostering. The interests of the management include, for example, the maximization of assigned duties, while the interests of drivers are concerned with getting desired and fairly distributed jobs. Thus, the crew rostering problem is a multi-objective problem, and the objectives might conflict with each other, such as maximizing the number of assigned duties and minimizing overtimes for drivers. A single optimal solution across all objectives does not exist. Consequently, a compromise solution should be found according to the preferences of the decision maker. It is often difficult to get an *a priori* specification of preferences since it is not clear in the beginning which specific objective values are achievable. It is very difficult to create rosters manually to keep both parties satisfied. A DSS is required to help planners to navigate to a most preferred solution. As documented in literature (see Section 3.4), there is an apparent lack of such a DSS in public bus transit that can handle variant constraints and objectives, as well as considering the interests of both the management and the drivers.

Traditionally, a DSS is supported by a specified operating system (OS), and has to be installed in a specified location. Due to the rapid development of web technologies, it is possible to deliver computerized decision support into a distributed environment, which supports, for example, remote data access. The users on the client side can use a web browser to access the DSS and to generate data at various geographical locations, using distributed data processing, i.e. independent of specific OS and hardware platforms (e.g. mobile phone, PC, or laptop). The installation of software can be avoided; instead, users without technical expertise can easily access the DSS using a browser and a user-friendly interface. Moreover, the web platform is unified. Therefore, the web-based DSS is considered as an extension of the traditional DSS to a global environment. We develop our DSS as a user-friendly web-based DSS, partly for the reason mentioned above, i.e. users can access the system anywhere. For example, a driver can access his schedule and receive changes on his way to work. Also, the bus companies need support in formulating problems, and assistance in selecting a suitable solver. The bus companies, especially small and medium-sized, should not need to pay for licenses for the solvers, which might not be suitable for their problems. Instead, a service is provided by the computer-based DSS. Our web-based DSS can be reached from the website `http://mydutyplan.de/`.

8.2. Functionality of the Web-Based DSS

There are different classifications for a DSS: for example, at the technical level described in Power (1997), and at the conceptual level shown in Power (2002). Marakas (2003) defines the typical components of a DSS: the users, the user interface, the data management system (including components for gathering, storing and organizing the data that will be useful for the decision making), the model management system (providing variable models for the analytical capabilities in DSS), and the knowledge engine (which recognizes the problem, generates solutions, and provides functions related to the management of the solving process).

We propose the structure and functionality of a web-based DSS as illustrated in Figure 8.1, which shows its structure scheme and the functionality of each component. Our DSS system is divided into two parts: the client side and server side. The client side includes users and a web browser interface, while the server side consists of a web server, DSS server, and database server. Compared with the components of the DSS described in Marakas (2003), the user interface is replaced with the web browser interface in our web-based DSS. Additionally, the data management is performed on a database server. Moreover, the DSS server provides the model management functionalities (in "formulation") and the knowledge engine (in "solution approach"). The components of our DSS and their functionalities are described below.

The users The users of the DSS are the controllers, planners, managers and drivers. The functions of each group of people are described as follows:

- Figure 8.2a illustrates all of the functions of a *planner*; here we assume a planner to be an administrator. Therefore, he or she has access to all functions, such as viewing statistics for managers. The *Controller* and planner usually belong to the same group of people. However, the controller is responsible for the recovery process for repairing disrupted rosters (see Figure 8.2b), while the planner is responsible for the planning process for generating rosters. This thesis concentrates on the planning process for the crew rostering problem, therefore only a simple function is provided for the controller in our DSS, i.e. sending SMS messages to drivers to notify them

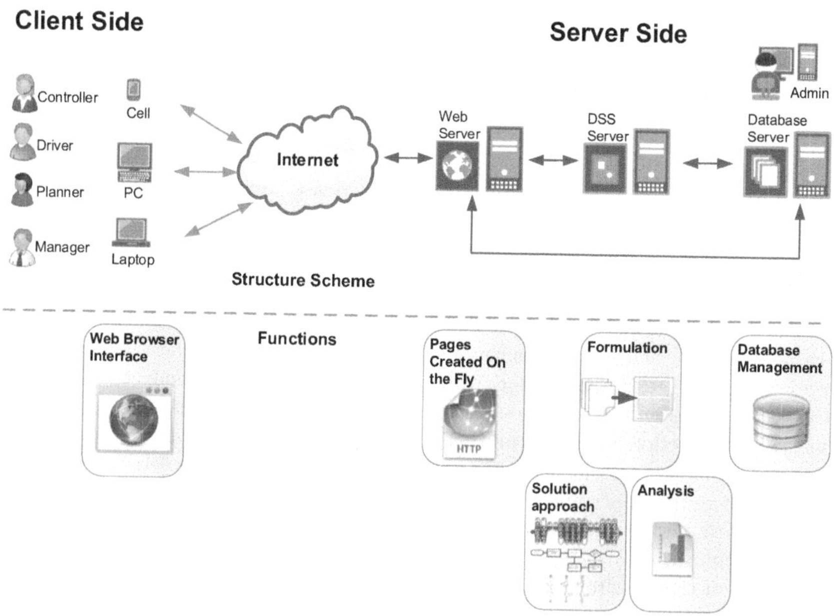

Figure 8.1. Structure scheme of the web-based DSS and the functions of each component.

of changes. Moreover, the planner can register new drivers (see Figure 8.2c), who receive information about accessing the website via email. Additionally, the planner can modify the information about a driver (see Figure 8.2d). After the planner has uploaded the verified data for the generation process (Figure 8.2e), he/she can provide the parameters that will help the solver agent to choose a suitable solver, but this is optional. Moreover, the planner can choose to receive a message via email and/or SMS if a solution is available (see Figure 8.2f). The detailed solutions are shown including the result details, the selected solver(s), and the resulting plans for all drivers (see Figure 8.2g). If the solution is not satisfactory, the planner can restart the optimization with different parameter settings. As long as the solution is accepted, the solution analysis is stored in the database.

- The *manager* can access the database to get some analyzed data for supporting decisions, such as evaluating the costs of proposed rule changes or evaluating drivers' satisfaction (see Figure 8.3).

- The *driver* can provide his/her preferences, including a desired day off or a working shift on a particular day; or a combination of jobs, such as similar jobs within one working week, in the next planning period (see Figure 8.4a). After the solutions have been accepted by the planner, the drivers can access their plans, and download them to their own calendars as shown in Figure 8.4b.

Web browser interface The users on the client side can access the DSS simply by using a web browser. Different users have different website designs based on their available functions and different user permissions (see Figures 8.2, 8.3, and 8.4). The websites were built entirely using HTML5, CSS3 and JavaScript (using the jQuery JavaScript library).

Web server Web services provide the web-based user interface, written in the C# language using the Microsoft ASP.NET MVC4 (2014) (Active Server Pages.NET Model View Control 4) framework; this enables people to easily access other servers from remote locations.

Database server This component provides for the transferring of data between the web server and DSS server. The input data from planners and drivers are analyzed and gathered in the database server. Those data include activities, driver information, and rules and regulations (see Section 2.2.1). Recall that activities include duties, standbys, days off, and others. Driver information includes not only the drivers' qualification details (for example: vehicle types) and work-accounts, but also their stated preferences. The planner can access the database to modify the data, add new data, and upload modified data. Data that are ready for optimization are gathered into a .csv or .dat file. A specification of the format can be found at the website `http://dsor.de/crewrostering`. The solutions and analysis provided by the DSS server are stored on the database server. All historical solutions are categorized according to different problem types/sizes, to support the decision making by a model agent and a solver agent, which will be described in the next subsection. To create, configure, and use databases on the web for our web-based DSS, we chose to use the data management services of Windows Azure described in Calder et al. (2011) (Microsoft's cloud application platform), which uses Microsoft SQL Server technology. Therefore, we only need to focus on our DSS services, since the processing of replication, encryption, patch management, and backups will be taken from the data management services of Windows Azure. The maintenance cost is reduced while manageability and scalability are increased by running SQL Server databases in the cloud.

DSS server The planner can start the optimization as long as the input data are complete and verified. The optimization process occurs on our DSS server, providing the mathematical formulation, solution approaches and results analysis. The mathematical formulation involves the generation of a model based on the rules and regulations provided by the bus company and drivers' preferences, and the problem type (such as CCR or NCCR). A model agent is provided to support the model formulation. Details of this can be found in the next subsection. The generated model is in the form acceptable to a MIP, a column generation or a metaheuristic solver. The intelligent selection of a solver is based on a solver agent. Details about the process of model-solver integration are described in next subsection. The evaluation of results is stored on the database server.

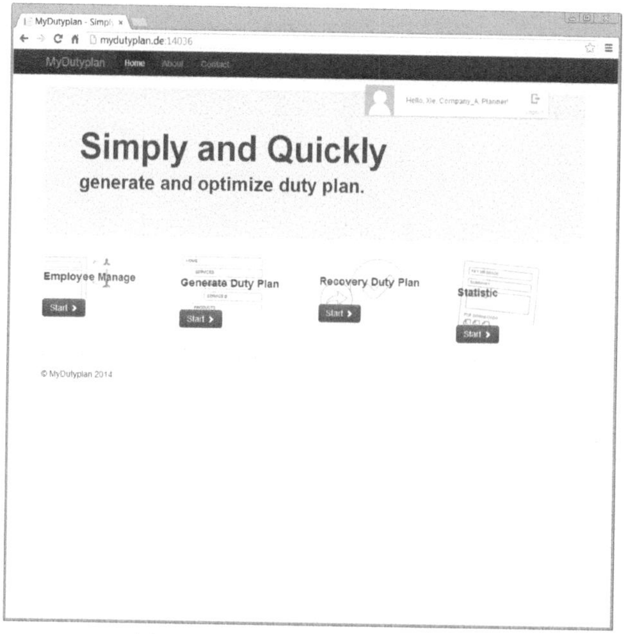

(a) The overview page for the planner.

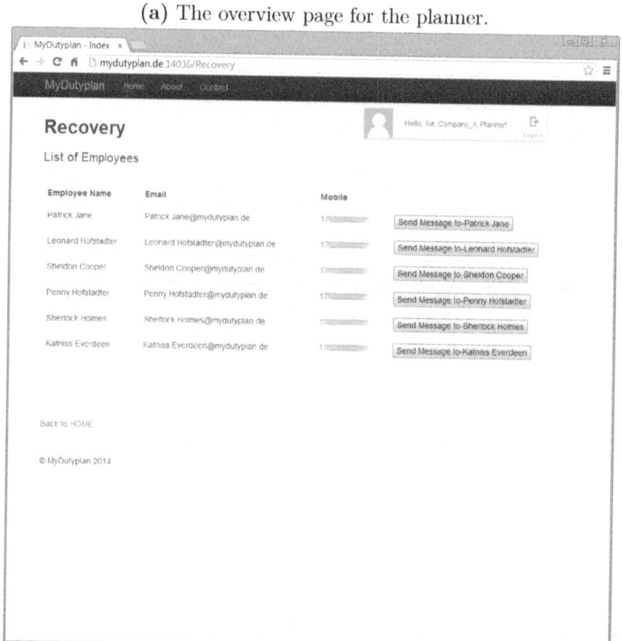

(b) The page for recovery on an operational day.

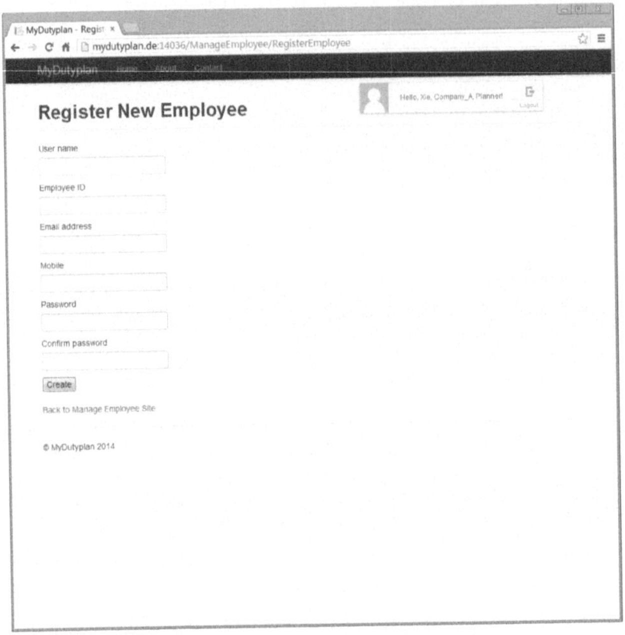

(c) The page for registration of a new employee.

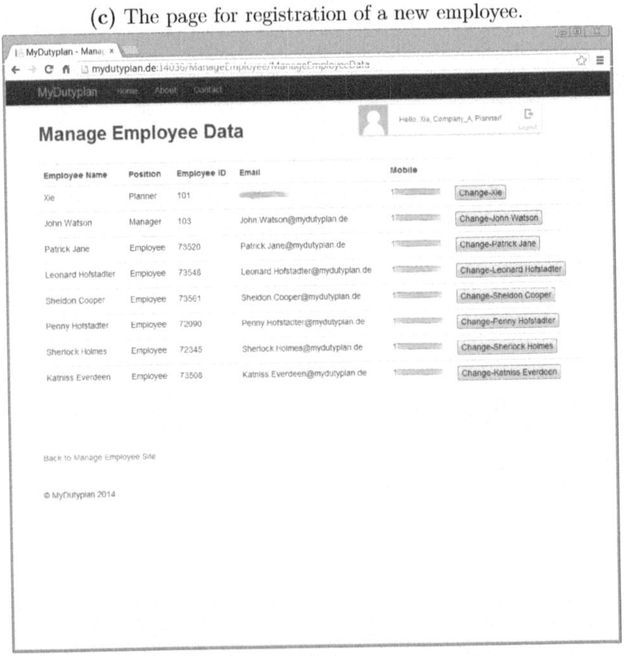

(d) The page for managing all employee data.

(e) The page for uploading the data file for the generation of rosters.

(f) The page with the options for the generation process.

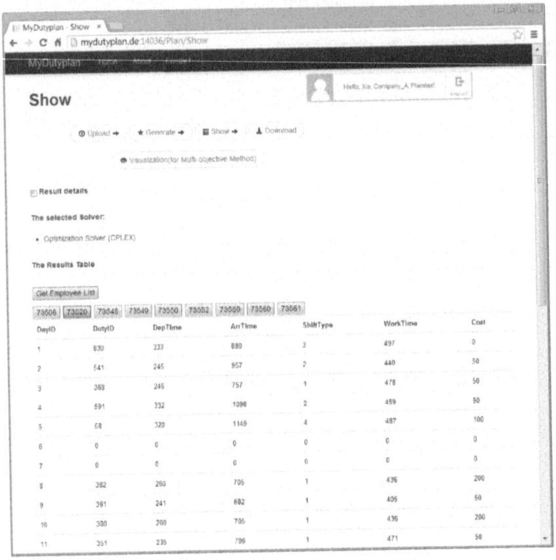

(g) The results page, including the plans for all drivers and additional result information such as the selected solver.

Figure 8.2. The website for the planner and the corresponding functions.

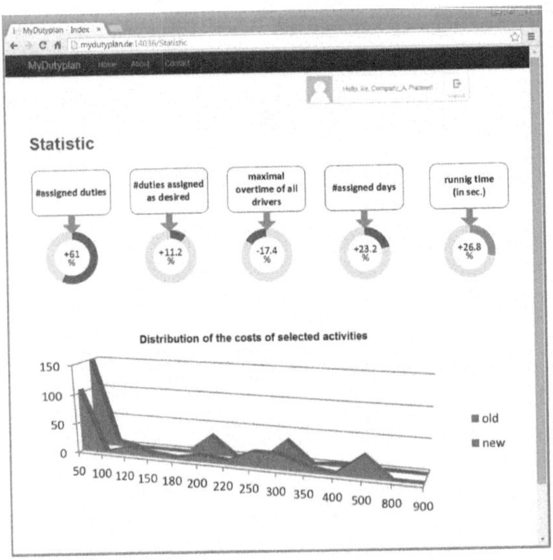

Figure 8.3. The website for the manager and the corresponding functions.

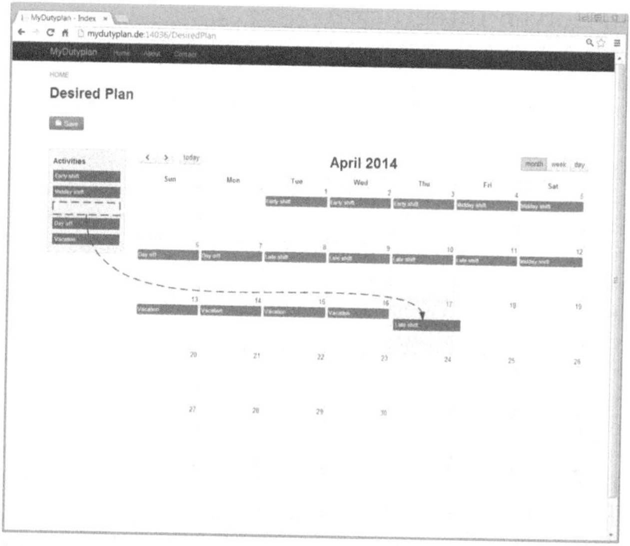

(a) The page for a driver to enter his/her desires for the next period.

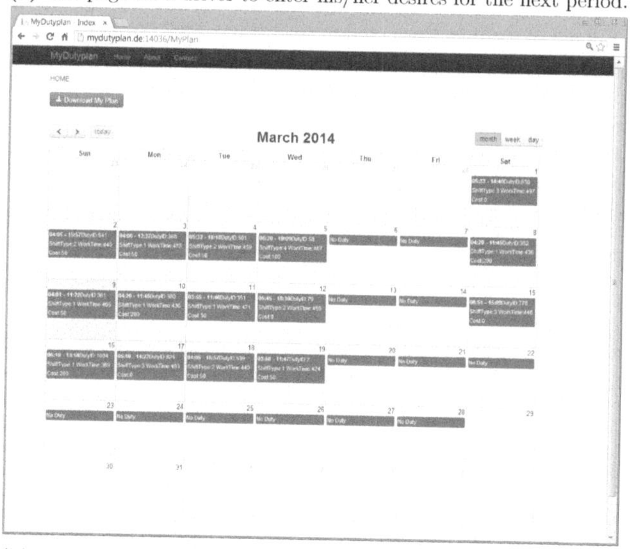

(b) The page for a driver, showing his/her plan in calendar format for the current period.

Figure 8.4. The website for a driver and the corresponding functions.

8.3. Model-Solver Integration

The architecture of a model-solver integration framework in our optimization process is shown in Figure 8.5, which is based on the idea described by Lee & Huh (2006) for autonomous and intelligent model solution. The planner firstly defines the problem (such as rules) and the requirements for the solver (such as the running time). Model and solver agents are intelligent agents, consisting of computer software for supporting the automated selection of a suitable model and solver. The choices of agents are based on the historical data in the database, which are described in Section 6.1. Figure 8.6 shows a sequence diagram to describe how a planner obtains a solution. First of all, the planner sends a request for a model to the model agent based on the given information, including rules and drivers' preferences, whilst he or she also sends a request for a solver to the solver agent, with details such as running time or gap to optimum. Based on the planner's request, the model agent checks the rules and recognizes the problem type (such as CCR or NCCR), which sometimes also depends on the historical data, such as whether the (similar) plan was formulated as sequential or integrated planning. When all preparations are complete, the model is generated. In order to solve this model, the solver agent chooses a solver, based on the data about the model and the planner's request. The selected solver solves the model, and the results with analyses, are stored as historical data.

The model-solver integration framework is implemented in the C# programming language, making full use of its object-oriented nature. Figure 8.7 illustrates an overview of the implementation. The rules checker identifies the rules while the problem-type recognizer identifies the problem type. The link between the problem-type recognizer and network generator corresponds to the generation of a problem-specified network. Constraints corresponding to the rules and to the network are generated by the model generator. As long as the model is generated, the solver type is chosen in the solver-type recognizer. Also, the corresponding solver will be selected to run the model.

8.3.1. Model Agent

The model agent is responsible for checking rules, determining the problem type, and generating the network, which are requirements for the formulation of a model.

Rules Checker

As mentioned before, the working regulations often differ from one bus company to another. The most-used working regulations are described in Section 2.2.1. Three types of rules can be defined as constraints, i.e. horizontal, vertical, and quality rules. Moreover, one bus company might enforce the rules more strictly than another. A simple example is shown below.

Example 4. A company rule states that there must be at least one double-off within D days. Bus company A wants to hold to this rule, while bus company B allows it to be slightly violated. Therefore, for company A, the rule is formulated as a set of hard

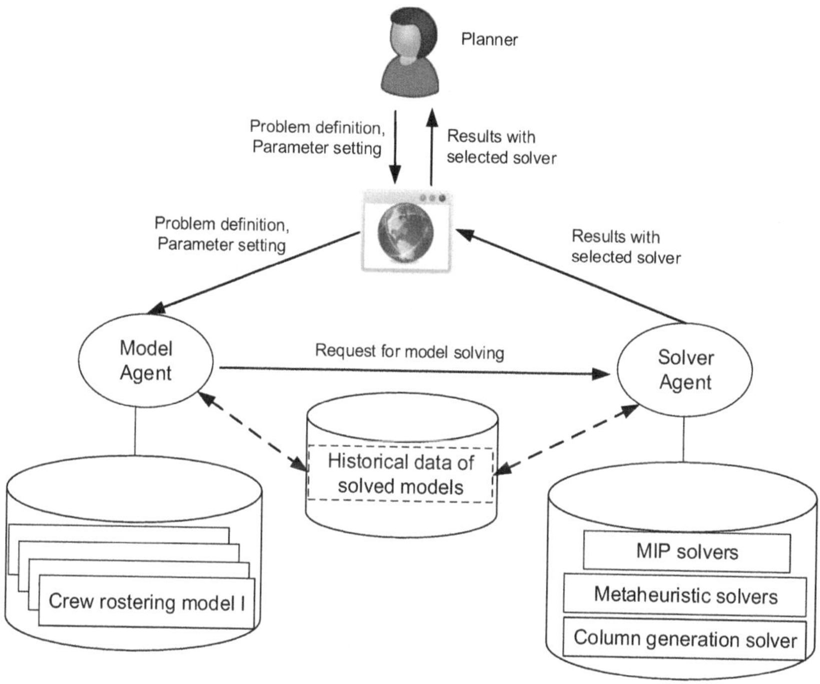

Figure 8.5. Architecture of a model-solver integration framework.

constraints (see constraints (8.1)) in the mathematical model, while for company B it is formulated as a set of soft constraints (see objective (8.2) and constraints (5.11)).

$$\sum_{t'=t}^{t+D} \sum_{e \in \mathcal{A}_{m,t',d}} x_e^a \geq 1 \qquad \forall m \in \mathcal{M}, d \in \mathcal{D}_{df}, t \in \{1, \ldots, T_m - D\} \tag{8.1}$$

$$\min \sum_{m \in \mathcal{M}} C^d \cdot \delta_m \tag{8.2}$$

$$\sum_{t'=t}^{t+D} \sum_{e \in \mathcal{A}_{m,t',d}} x_e^a \geq 1 - \delta_m \qquad \forall m \in \mathcal{M}, d \in \mathcal{D}_{df}, t \in \{1, \ldots, T_m - D\} \tag{5.11}$$

Based on the data provided by a model agent, which activates or deactivates some restrictions, a customized crew rostering model is generated. The planners' requirements

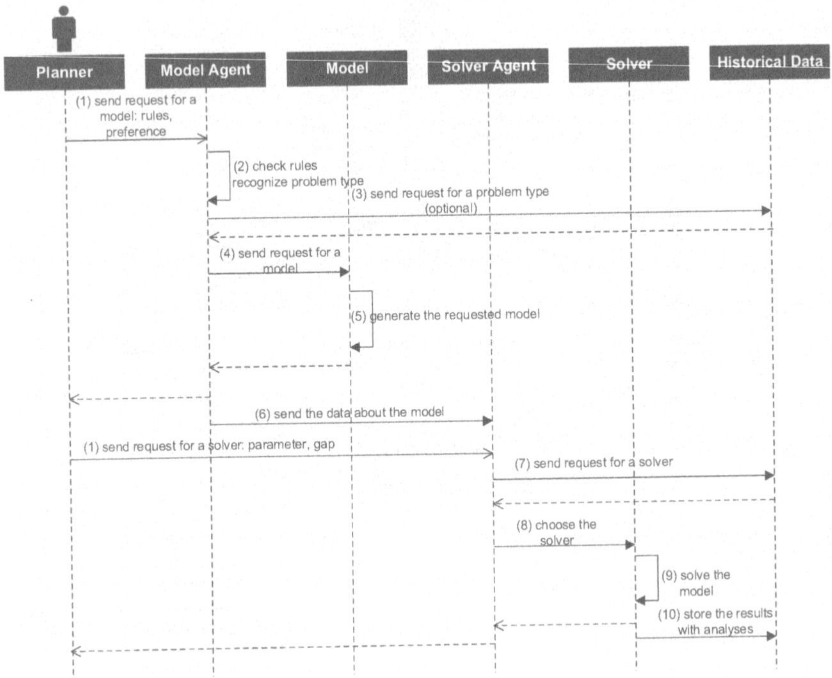

Figure 8.6. Process of getting a required solution for the planner.

can include labor rules and drivers' preferences, such as holding the limit on the maximum number of consecutive working days, and trying to provide an even workload for all drivers.

Problem-Type Recognizer

The possible problem types are listed below. Their descriptions of them are shown in Chapters 5 and 7. A recognizer is developed to identify the problem types, some of which can be recognized by the given information. Figure 8.8 shows the input information for different problem types.

- Cyclic crew rostering (CCR) can be recognized by its feature, i.e. restricted capacities of activities based on days of the week.

- Non-cyclic crew rostering (NCCR) can be recognized by its feature, i.e. restricted capacities of activities based on calendar dates.

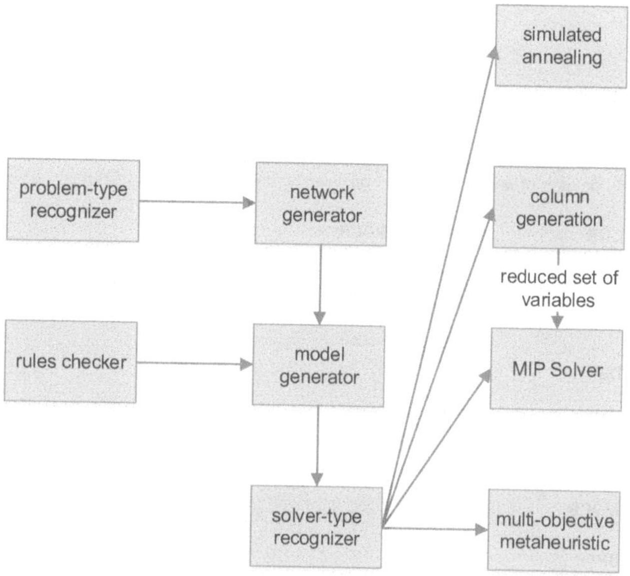

Figure 8.7. Abstract implementation of the model-solver integration framework.

- Multi-objective crew rostering (MOCR) is provided to identify the desired weight of each objective for the planner. If the weights of objectives are not provided as input, then the multi-objective approach is required.

- Rota scheduling (RS) is identified by having no duties as input.

- Duty sequencing (DS) is identified by the duties and rotas provided; these rotas specify the distributions of assigned shifts and other activities.

- Sequential planning (SP) and Integrated planning (IP) share the same input information. The choice will be left to the agent solver. Although the results of integrated planning show better solutions compared with the ones solved by sequential planning as shown in Section 6.3, a sequential approach might be preferred in some cases, where using the integrated approach is too time-consuming, or is unsolvable due to limited running time or memory.

Combinations of different problem types are possible, such as CCR and DS, or NCCR and IP. Details of this can be found in Chapters 5 and 7.

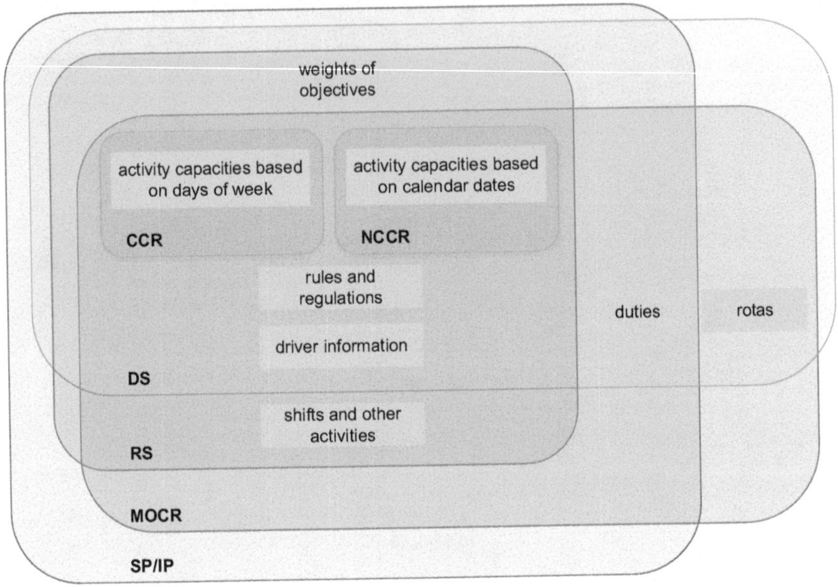

Figure 8.8. Input information for different problem types.

Network Generator

Once the problem type has been identified, the network for the corresponding problem is generated. The slight differences between generating networks for CCR and for NCCR, as well as for sequential planning and for integrated planning, are shown in Section 5.1.

8.3.2. Solver Agent

As described earlier, the planner can send the parameter values, such as running time or gap to optimum, to the solver agent. Based on those parameters, the solver agent can choose a suitable solver for the generated model. The solvers available include an MIP solver, such as the CPLEX and Gurobi solvers as shown in Chapter 5; a metaheuristic (MH) solver as shown in Sections 7.2 and 7.3; a column generation (CG) solver as described in Sections 7.4.1 and 7.4.2; and a multi-objective metaheuristic (MOMH) solver as described in Section 7.5. Figure 8.9 shows the possible solver types for each problem type; for example, DS can be solved using the MIP solvers within short running times.

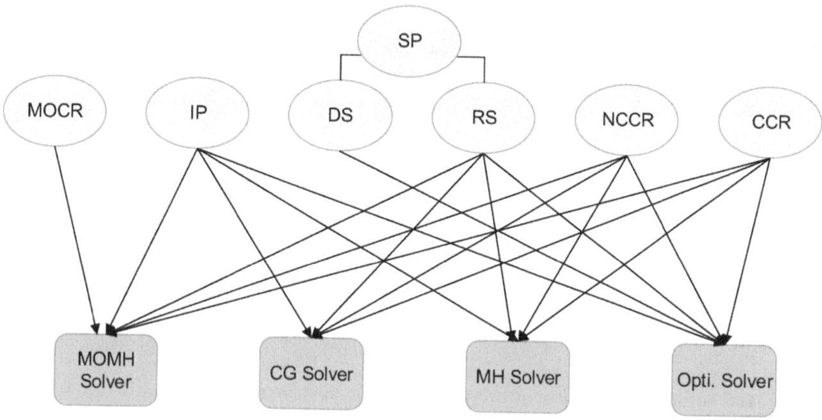

Figure 8.9. The possible solver types for each problem type.

Optimization Solver

The optimization solvers used in our DSS refer to commercial MIP solvers, such as the CPLEX and Gurobi solvers. Such solvers are suitable for small and medium-sized problems. The experiments with real-world instances are shown in Sections 6.2 and 6.3. The values of (Bin; Cols; Rows; NZs) indicate the difficulty of the crew rostering problem. Due to our experiments, MIP solvers are suitable for the instances with values lower than (200,000; 200,000; 150,000; 500,000) for rota scheduling, and the instances with values lower than (150,000; 150,000; 1,000,000; 1,000,000) for integrated planning.

Column Generation Solver

Recall that, as shown in Figure 8.10, in the process of column generation the crew rostering problem is divided into two sub-problems, i.e. the restricted master problem and the pricing problem. In the restricted master problem, a master problem is solved with limited variables for activities to get their reduced costs. Based on these reduced costs, the pricing problem is solved in parallel for each driver to generate new variables for activities with negative reduced costs. Then the master problem restarts with new variables being entered, until no new variables for activities can be found. Details of our column generation models for CCR and NCCR, and for the sequential and integrated approaches, are shown in Sections 7.4.1 and 7.4.2.

Column generation is proved to be the best solver for problems of these sizes, which the MIP solvers cannot solve optimally within 24 hours. However, in the case of solving very large instances (for example, 629-46-26, 606-70-26, and 607-70-26) with integrated

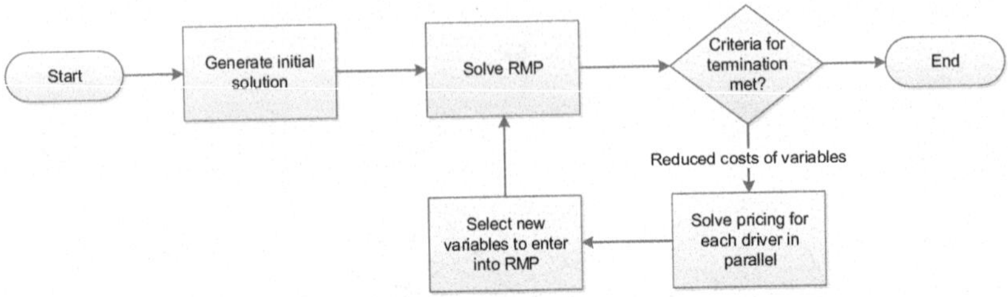

Figure 8.10. Illustration of the process of the column generation approach.

planning, the column generation approach is unable to solve them optimally due to running out of memory. More details are shown in Section 7.6.

Metaheuristic Solver

Three metaheuristic solvers have been implemented in this work, i.e. simulated annealing, ant colony optimization, and tabu search. The simulated annealing approach is proved to be more suitable than tabu search and ant colony optimization for our problem. Their running times are short (within two hours), however, the quality of their results cannot compete with the quality of those obtained using the MIP solvers and, especially, the column generation solver. Therefore, it is worth using simulated annealing to solve the very large instances with integrated planning, which the column generation solver is unable to solve.

Multi-Objective Metaheuristic Solver

A multi-objective metaheuristic solver is chosen to assist the human planner to see the differences in behavior between different specific objective values. Figure 8.11 illustrates an example solved by multi-objective simulated annealing. The planner can improve or worsen one objective to see relationship between this objective and the others, and the actual solution is marked in blue. After the planner chooses a solution, he/she can save it. The weight of each objective can easily be calculated based on the following equation:

$$w_1 * f_1 = w_2 * f_2 = ... = w_n * f_n \tag{8.3}$$

where w_i is defined as a variable that indicates the weight of the objective f_i, $\forall i \in \{1, ..., n\}$. If f_i is equal to 0, then let w_i be $\max\{f_i : i = 1, ..., n\}$. After determining the weights, we can solve this problem with only one objective using different solvers described in previous subsections. As an example, we assume that the planner accepts the marked solution in Figure 8.11. Table 8.1 shows the result achieved with the selected weights when using the CPLEX solver. This result is similar to, and even better than, the result shown in Figure 8.11. Figures A.25 to A.39 show similar visualizations for the other instances.

Information	
Selected activity costs	216,780
# underrun days off	48
# overflowed single-offs	0
# unassigned duties	4
# double-off distance violations	0
# underrun standbys	0
# used moved days off	0
# used moved days off on weekends	0
Maximal overtime (in hours)	4,876

Table 8.1. The solution for rota scheduling for the instance 48-75-6 (CPLEX solver).

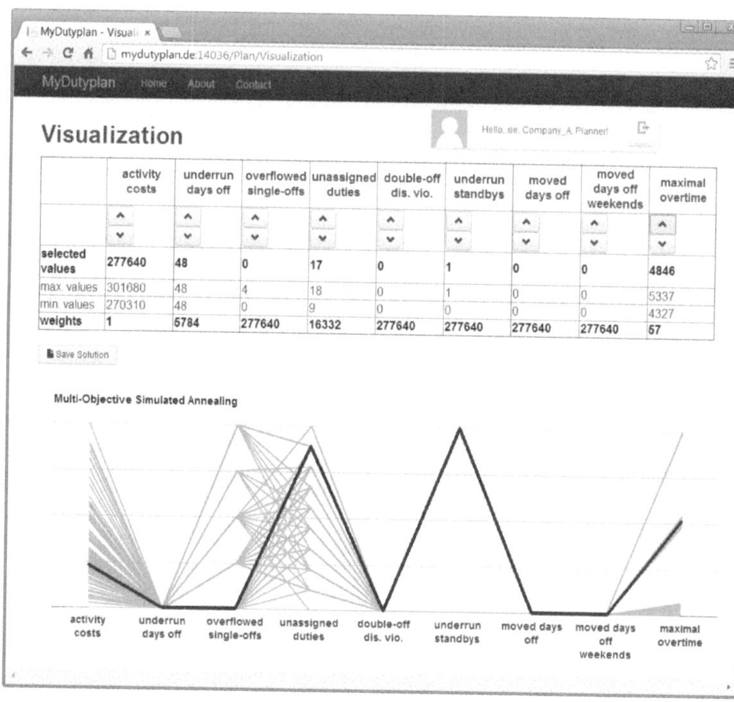

Figure 8.11. The set of non-dominated solutions for the instance 48-75-6 solved by multi-objective simulated annealing.

8.4. Summary

In this chapter, we have proposed a web-based DSS to cover the planning process for the crew rostering problem in public bus transit. We developed a model-solver integration framework for the crew rostering problem in which a model agent identified the problem, generated the dedicated network model, and provided the interface to a solver agent, while the solver agent intelligently chose the most suitable solver, such as an optimization, a column generation or a metaheuristic solver. Moreover, we have suggested a multi-objective method to assist the human planner to determine the preferred weights of different objectives. Our system had the flexibility to cope with different rules and regulations among different bus companies. A customized model, and a corresponding solution approach for each problem, were provided. Moreover, some functions were provided to support other users in this DSS, i.e. managers, drivers, and controllers.

9. Conclusion & Outlook

This thesis investigates the crew rostering problem in public bus transit. In previous chapters, we have studied this particular problem, various solution approaches, and a web-based decision support system. In this chapter we conclude the thesis by highlighting the contributions that it makes and providing some potential directions for future research.

9.1. Summary

In Chapter 2 we introduced the cyclic and non-cyclic crew rostering problems in public bus transit, the necessary background for combinatorial optimization problems, and solution approaches. Moreover, in Chapter 3 we reviewed models and solution techniques that are used in literature for sequential and integrated cyclic and non-cyclic crew rostering problems, especially their widely used application in the airline sector. Chapter 4 concluded with the required work and scope of the thesis.

The main contribution made by this thesis with regard to integrated cyclic and non-cyclic crew rostering problems was described in Chapter 5. More specifically, we proposed the first multicommodity network flow models for both cyclic and non-cyclic crew rostering problems in the literature. We extended the network design proposed by Cappanera & Gallo (2004) for solving the aircrew rostering problem. During the last couple of years there has been an increasing amount of attention on solving the crew rostering problem within one step in public bus transit, but with less consideration of drivers' preferences. We developed our network models with consideration for the preferences of both the companies and the drivers. In Chapter 6 our computational study involved 16 real-world instances from six different bus companies in Germany, which included up to about 37,000 activities to be assigned to 607 drivers in 70 days. To the best of our knowledge, instances with this size and complexity have not been tackled before. The exact optimization is suitable for small instances when using the integrated approach, as these can be solved optimally within one minute. Significantly more running time was required to solve medium-sized and large instances. Very large instances were unsolvable due to running out of memory.

In order to cope with the larger real-world instances used in previous chapters, different heuristic approaches have been implemented (see Chapter 7). Our implemented column generation was suitable for medium-sized and large instances, which can be solved optimally within two hours, thereby saving at least 90% in running time compared with the exact approach. Some large instances can be solved by our column generation within 24 hours. Those results were still not optimal, but the gaps to optimum were 60% smaller compared with the exact approach. However, very large instances can not be solved by column generation due to memory shortages (discussed in Chapter 7.6); instead, the simulated annealing approach was proved to be suitable for solving this class of instances compared with our implemented ant colony and tabu search algorithms, and good solutions can be obtained within two hours. Regardless of which approach was applied, the integrated approach was proved to produce significant savings compared with the sequential approach, i.e. up to 6% more assigned duties and up to 4% more assigned days, as well as more duties assigned as desired (based on drivers' preferences).

The crew rostering problem in this thesis is a multi-objective problem. We applied different approaches for solving it with one objective problem using the sum of weighted objectives in previous chapters. The weights were provided by the bus companies. A multi-objective simulated annealing approach was developed to provide a set of non-dominated solutions, which would support the human planner in determining the preferred weights.

Due to the complexity of the crew rostering problem, different approaches are suitable for different classes of instances. Moreover, the rules and regulations differ from one bus company to another, due to factors such as deregulation. Therefore, the prototype of a web-based decision support system was presented in Chapter 8, in which all solution methods presented earlier were incorporated with the model and solver agents. The human planner in a bus company can therefore obtain the required rosters using a dedicated model and solution approach selected by model and solver agents, respectively. Furthermore, the decision support system provided some simple functions for drivers, managers, and controllers.

As mentioned in Chapter 4, we stated two research goals. In short, our objectives were: (1) to develop models and techniques for the integrated approach for both cyclic and non-cyclic crew rostering problems in public bus transit that make it possible to tackle large real-world instances; (2) to develop a web-based decision support system to support different requirements and reduce the required human effort. From our perspective, these goals have been achieved. In Chapters 5, 6, and 7, we presented results according to the first goal. We obtained promising results concerning the effectiveness of our methods for large problem instances. With respect to our second goal, we proposed a web-based decision support system with a model-solver integration framework in Chapter 8.

9.2. Theoretical Implications

As mentioned before in this chapter, the main theoretical implications of this thesis are the development of novel multicommodity network models for solving integrated cyclic and non-cyclic crew rostering problems, and the application of different efficient solution approaches, including column generation and simulated annealing, for solving large real-world problems. We obtained promising results concerning the effectiveness of our methods for large problem instances. Moreover, the integrated approach was proved to outperform the sequential approach. Additionally, a multi-objective simulated annealing approach was developed to provide a set of non-dominated solutions, from which a preferred solution is chosen by the human planner. Based on that solution, the weights of objectives can easily be determined. Finally, we would like to make some suggestions for future research in the field of crew rostering. The real-world instances we gathered to evaluate the goals of this thesis were published at the web page `http://dsor.de/crewrostering`, which can serve as a starting point.

As shown in Sections 6.3 and 7.6, the optimal solutions for the integrated problem still contain some unassigned duties. As mentioned before, one reason for this is the sequential approach used for the crew scheduling and rostering problems, i.e. we use the duties generated in the crew scheduling problem as input for the crew rostering problem. This is one of the drawbacks of this sequential approach. Therefore, there is a need to study the (iterative) integration of both problems.

Another reason for the unassigned duties is the shortage of drivers; therefore, the planning of additional (part-time) drivers is required in the optimization process for the crew rostering problem in further research.

The generated rosters for the crew rostering problem can easily be disrupted on the day of operations, because of absences of drivers and other disruptions. In this thesis, we assume the number of standbys is given in advance. Stochastic optimization with standbys is required when solving the crew rostering problem, in order to produce robust rosters. The first attempt at solving a two-stage stochastic rota scheduling problem was shown in Xie et al. (2012b). In the future, more research about stochastic optimization in the integrated approach is required.

Still, many types of disruptions can not be considered in the planning process, such as incidents, variations in traffic conditions, and vehicle breakdowns, so recovery methods are required for all problems in the operational planning process. Because there are many diverse types of disruptions and different goals, our decision support system should be extended to integrate diverse solution approaches for different problems, and a manual solution process of human controllers. Moreover, these solutions should be generated quickly, since there is no time to wait in a disrupted situation.

Moreover, the models we developed are based on the rules and regulations that apply in German bus companies. Our network model needs to be extended in the future to adopt new rules that will apply to these companies, and to companies in other countries and regions.

9.3. Practical Implications

A web-based decision support system, such as the one whose development is, reported in this thesis holds several important practical implications for bus companies.

First, a model-solver framework was developed to support the planners' job. Our mathematical models and solution approaches were embedded in the framework, which can solve the problem automatically according to the planners' requirements, such as the given running time. The planners do not need to make the decisions about which mathematical model and solution approach should be chosen, and do not even need to know the details of the optimization.

Secondly, some functions are provided to the drivers, managers, and controllers. Drivers are able to submit their preferences online and download their schedules. Some simple functions are developed for managers and controllers; for example, a manager can see some statistics about the generated schedules, while a controller can send messages to drivers about changes on the day of operations.

However, our prototype does not support all of the needs of a bus company, such as recovery methods on the day of operations. It is difficult for controllers to find alternative crew rosters in a short period of time, without incurring substantial additional costs and causing major disturbance to further operations. Therefore, practical research could also be devoted to developing a web-based decision support system to assist them and propose suitable solutions.

Bibliography

Ahuja, R., Magnanti, T., & Orlin, J. (1993). *Network flows: theory, algorithms, and applications.* Prentice Hall, United States.

Ansótegui, C., Sellmann, M., & Tierney, K. (2009). A gender-based genetic algorithm for the automatic configuration of algorithms. In *Principles and Practice of Constraint Programming — CP 2009* (pp. 142–157). Springer.

ASP.NET MVC4 (2014). Microsoft ASP.NET. `http://www.asp.net/mvc/mvc4`. Last retrieved 03.04.2014.

Barnhart, C., Johnson, E., Nemhauser, G., Savelsbergh, M., & Vance, P. (1998). Branch-and-price: Column generation for solving huge integer programs. *Operations Research, 46*, 316–329.

Barnhart, C., & Laporte, G. (2006). *Handbooks in Operations Research & Management Science* Volume 14. Elsevier.

Bengtsson, L., Galia, R., Gustafsson, T., Hjorring, C., & Kohl, N. (2007). Railway crew pairing optimization. In *Algorithmic Methods for Railway Optimization* (pp. 126–144). Springer.

Bhargava, H. K., King, A. S., & McQuay, D. S. (1995a). Decisionnet: An architecture for modeling and decision support over the World Wide Web. In *Proceedings of the Third International Society for Decision Support Systems Conference* (pp. 541–550). Volume 2.

Bhargava, H. K., Krishnan, R., & Kaplan, D. (1995b). On generalized access to a WWW-based network of decision support services. In *Proceedings of 3rd International Conference on DSS, Hong Kong* (pp. 22–23).

Bhargava, H. K., Power, D. J., & Sun, D. (2007). Progress in web-based decision support technologies. *Decision Support Systems, 43*, 1083–1095.

Bianco, L., Bielli, M., Mingozzi, A., Ricciardelli, S., & Spadoni, M. (1992). A heuristic procedure for the crew rostering problem. *European Journal of Operational Research, 58*, 272–283.

Bodin, L., Golden, B., Assad, A., & Ball, M. (1983). Routing and scheduling of vehicles and crews: the state of the art. *Computers & Operations Research, 10*, 63–211.

Booth, N. L., Everman, E. J., Kuo, I. L., Sprague, L., & Murphy, L. (2011). A web-based decision support system for assessing regional water-quality conditions and management actions. *JAWRA Journal of the American Water Resources Association, 47*, 1136–1150.

Burke, E., & Kendall, G. (2005). *Search Methodologies: Introductory Tutorials in Optimization and Decision Support Techniques.* Springer.

Burke, E. K., & Silva, J. L. (2005). The design of memetic algorithms for scheduling and timetabling problems. In N. Krasnogor, W. Hart, & J. Smith (Eds.), *Recent Advances in Memetic Algorithms, Studies in Fuzziness and Soft Computing* (pp. 289–311). Springer, Berlin & Heidelberg Volume 166.

Calder, B., Wang, J., Ogus, A., Nilakantan, N., Skjolsvold, A., McKelvie, S., Xu, Y. K., Srivastav, S., Wu, J. S., Simitci, H. et al. (2011). Windows azure storage: a highly available cloud storage service with strong consistency. In *Proceedings of the Twenty-Third ACM Symposium on Operating Systems Principles* (pp. 143–157). ACM.

Cappanera, P., & Gallo, G. (2004). A multicommodity flow approach to the crew rostering problem. *Operations Research*, *52*, 583–596.

Caprara, A., Fischetti, M., Guida, P., Toth, P., & Vigo, D. (1999). Solution of large-scale railway crew planning problems: The Italian experience. In *Computer-Aided Transit Scheduling* (pp. 1–18). Springer.

Caprara, A., Fischetti, M., Toth, P., Vigo, D., & Guida, P. (1997). Algorithms for railway crew management. *Mathematical Programming*, *79*, 125–141.

Caprara, A., Focacci, F., Lamma, E., Mello, P., Milano, M., Toth, P., & Vigo, D. (1998a). Integrating constraint logic programming and operations research techniques for the crew rostering problem. *Software: Practice Experience*, *28*, 49–76.

Caprara, A., Kroon, L., Monaci, M., Peeters, M., & Toth, P. (2006). Passenger railway optimization. *Handbooks in Operations Research and Management Science*, *14*, 129–187.

Caprara, A., Monaci, M., & Toth, P. (2001). A global method for crew planning in railway applications. In *Computer-Aided Scheduling of Public Transport* (pp. 17–36). Springer, Berlin Heidelberg.

Caprara, A., Toth, P., Vigo, D., & Fischetti, M. (1998b). Modeling and solving the crew rostering problem. *Operations Research*, *46*, 820–830.

Carraresi, P., & Gallo, G. (1984). A multi-level bottleneck assignment approach to the bus drivers' rostering problem. *European Journal of Operational Research*, *16*, 163–173.

Catanas, F., & Paixão, J. (1995). A new approach for the crew rostering problem. In J. Daduna, I. Branco, & J. Paixao (Eds.), *Computer-Aided Transit Scheduling* (pp. 267–277). Springer, Berlin & Heidelberg Volume 430 of *Lecture Notes in Economics and Mathematical Systems*.

Černý, V. (1985). Thermodynamical approach to the traveling salesman problem: An efficient simulation algorithm. *Journal of Optimization Theory and Applications*, *45*, 41–51.

Chew, K. (1991). Cyclic schedule for apron services. *Journal of the Operational Research Society*, (pp. 1061–1069).

Cleveland, W. S. (1979). Robust locally weighted regression and smoothing scatterplots. *Journal of the American Statistical Association*, *74*, 829–836.

Constantino, A. A., de Mendonca Neto, C. F. X., & Novaes, A. G. (2006). Crew rostering problem with distribution of workload based on preferences. *Annals of Operations Research*, . In press.

Dantzig, G. B., Orden, A., & Wolfe, P. (1955). The generalized simplex method for minimizing a linear form under linear inequality restraints. *Pacific Journal of Mathematics*, *5*, 183–195.

Day, P., & Ryan, D. (1997). Flight attendant rostering for short-haul airline operations. *Operations Research*, *45*, 649–661.

De Pont, G. (2006). *Personalized Crew Rostering at Netherlands Railways*. Master's thesis University of Tilburg.

Deb, K. (2001). *Multi-objective Optimization using Evolutionary Algorithms*. John Wiley & Sons, Chichester.

Desaulniers, G., & Hickman, M. (2007). Public transit. *Handbooks in Operations Research and Management Science*, *14*, 69–128.

Desrochers, M., & Soumis, F. (1989). A column generation approach to the urban transit crew scheduling problem. *Transportation Science*, *23*, 1–13.

Desrosiers, J., Lasry, A., McInnis, D., Solomon, M. M., & Soumis, F. (2000). Air transat uses altitude to manage its aircraft routing, crew pairing, and work assignment. *Interfaces*, *30*, 41–53.

Dorigo, M. (1992). *Optimization, Learning and Natural Algorithms*. Ph.D. thesis Dipartimento di Elettronica, Politecnio di Milano, Italy.

Dorigo, M., & Gambardella, L. (1997). Ant colony system: A cooperative learning approach to the traveling salesman problem. *IEEE Transactions on Evolutionary Computation*, *1*, 53–66.

Dorigo, M., Maniezzo, V., & Colorni, A. (1996). Ant system: optimization by a colony of cooperating agents. *IEEE Transactions on Systems, Man, and Cybernetics, Part B: Cybernetics*, *26*, 29–41.

Dorigo, M., & Stützle, T. (2010). Ant colony optimization: overview and recent advances. In *Handbook of Metaheuristics* (pp. 227–263). Springer.

Ehrgott, M. (2005). *Multicriteria Optimization* Volume 2. Springer.

El Moudani, W., Cosenza, C. A. N., de Coligny, M., & Mora-Camino, F. (2001). A bi-criterion approach for the airlines crew rostering problem. In *Evolutionary Multi-Criterion Optimization* (pp. 486–500). Springer.

Emden-Weinert, T., Kotas, H., & Speer, U. (2000). *DISSY — A driver scheduling system for public transport*. Technical Report VSS GmbH and Bremer Straßenbahn AG, Bremen, Germany.

Ernst, A., Jiang, H., Krishnamoorthy, M., Owens, B., & Sier, D. (2004). An annotated bibliography of personnel scheduling and rostering. *Annals of Operations Research*, *127*, 21–144.

Ernst, A., Krishnamoorthy, M., & Dowling, D. (1998). Train crew rostering using simulated annealing. In *Proceedings of International Conference on Optimization Techniques and Applications* (pp. 859–866). Perth.

Fahle, T., Junker, U., Karisch, S., Kohl, N., Sellmann, M., & Vaaben, B. (2002). Constraint programming based column generation for crew assignment. *Journal of Heuristics*, *8*, 59–81.

Ferreira, J. V., & Guimarães, R. C. (1995). A travelling salesman model for the sequencing of duties in bus crew rotas. *Journal of the Operational Research Society*, (pp. 415–426).

Freling, R., Lentink, R., & Wagelmans, A. (2004). A decision support system for crew planning in passenger transportation using a flexible branch-and-price algorithm. *Annals of Operations Research*, *127*, 203–222.

Gamache, M., & Soumis, F. (1998). A method for optimally solving the rostering problem. *OR in Airline Industry*, (pp. 124–157).

Gamache, M., Soumis, F., Marquis, G., & Desrosiers, J. (1999). A column generation approach for large-scale aircrew rostering problems. *Operations Research*, *47*, 247–263.

Garey, M., & Johnson, D. (1979). *Computers and Intractability: A Guide to the Theory of NP-Completeness*. W. H. Freeman and Company.

Glover, F. (1986). Future paths for integer programming and links to artificial intelligence. *Computers & Operations Research*, *13*, 533–549.

Glover, F. (1989). Tabu search - part I. *ORSA Journal on Computing*, *1*, 190–206.

Glover, F. (1990a). Tabu search - part II. *ORSA Journal on Computing*, *2*, 4–32.

Glover, F. (1990b). Tabu search: A tutorial. *Interfaces*, *20*, 74–94.

Glover, F., & Laguna, M. (1997). *Tabu Search* Volume 22. Springer.

Gorry, G. A., & Morton, M. S. S. (1971). *A framework for management information systems* Volume 13. Massachusetts Institute of Technology.

Guo, Y. (2005). *Decision Support Systems for Airline Crew Recovery*. Ph.D. thesis University of Paderborn.

Guo, Y., Mellouli, T., Suhl, L., & Thiel, M. (2006). A partially integrated airline crew scheduling approach with time-dependent crew capacities and multiple home bases. *European Journal of Operational Research*, *171*, 1169–1181.

Gurobi Optimization (2014). Gurobi Optimizer 5.5.0. Gurobi: `http://www.gurobi.com/`. Last retrieved 02.03.2014.

Handler, G. Y., & Zang, I. (1980). A dual algorithm for the constrained shortest path problem. *Networks*, *10*, 293–309.

Hanne, T., Dornberger, R., & Frey, L. (2009). Multiobjective and preference-based decision support for rail crew rostering. In *IEEE Congress on Evolutionary Computation CEC'09* (pp. 990–996).

Hao, G., Lai, K., & Tan, M. (2004). A neural network application in personnel scheduling. *Annals of Operations Research*, *128*, 65–90.

Hartog, A., Huisman, D., Abbink, E., & Kroon, L. (2009). Decision support for crew rostering at NS. *Public Transport*, *1*, 121–133.

IBM Corporation (2014). IBM ILOG CPLEX Optimizer 12.2. IBM: `http://www-01.ibm.com/software/integration/optimization/cplex-optimizer/`. Last retrieved 02.03.2014.

Irnich, S., & Desaulniers, G. (2005). Shortest path problems with resource constraints. In G. Desaulniers, J. Desrosiers, & M. Solomon (Eds.), *Column Generation* chapter 2. (pp. 33–65). Springer, New York.

Jachnik, J. (1981). Attendance and rostering systems. In A. Wren (Ed.), *Computer Scheduling of Public Transport* (pp. 337–344). Elsevier.

Jones, D. F., Mirrazavi, S. K., & Tamiz, M. (2002). Multi-objective meta-heuristics: An overview of the current state-of-the-art. *European Journal of Operational Research*, *137*, 1–9.

Jones, V. P., Brunner, J. F., Grove, G. G., Petit, B., Tangren, G. V., & Jones, W. E. (2010). A web-based decision support system to enhance IPM programs in Washington tree fruit. *Pest Management Science*, *66*, 587–595.

Karmarkar, N. (1984). A new polynomial-time algorithm for linear programming. *Combinatorica*, *4*, 373–395.

Kirkpatrick, S., Gelatt Jr, C. D., & Vecchi, M. (1983). Optimization by simulated annealing. *Science*, *220*, 671–680.

Kohl, N., & Karisch, S. (2004). Airline crew rostering: Problem types, modeling, and optimization. *Annals of Operations Research*, *127*, 223–257.

Kohli, R., Piontek, F., Ellington, T., VanOsdol, T., Shepard, M., & Brazel, G. (2001). Managing customer relationships through e-business decision support applications: a case of hospital–physician collaboration. *Decision Support Systems*, *32*, 171–187.

Kyngäs, J., & Nurmi, K. (2011). Days-off scheduling for a bus transportation company. *International Journal of Innovative Computing and Applications*, *3*, 42–49.

Lee, C., & Chen, C. (2003). Scheduling of train drivers for Taiwan railway administration. *Journal of Eastern Asia Society of Transportation Studies*, *5*, 292–306.

Lee, K., & Huh, S. (2006). A model-solver integration framework for autonomous and intelligent model solution. *Decision Support Systems*, *42*, 926–944.

Leuthardt, H. (1998). Kostenstrukturen von Stadt-, überland-und Reisebussen. *NAHVERKEHR*, *16*, 19–23.

Lezaun, M., Pérez, G., & de la Maza, E. (2006). Crew rostering problem in a public transport company. *Journal of the Operational Research Society*, *57*, 1173–1179.

Lezaun, M., Pérez, G., & de la Maza, E. (2007). Rostering in a rail passenger carrier. *Journal of Scheduling*, *10*, 245–254.

Lučić, P., & Teodorović, D. (1999). Simulated annealing for the multi-objective aircrew rostering problem. *Transportation Research Part A: Policy and Practice*, *33*, 19–45.

Lučić, P., & Teodorović, D. (2007). Metaheuristics approach to the aircrew rostering problem. *Annals of Operations Research*, *155*, 311–338.

Maenhout, B., & Vanhoucke, M. (2010). A hybrid scatter search heuristic for personalized crew rostering in the airline industry. *European Journal of Operational Research*, *206*, 155–167.

Marakas, G. M. (2003). *Decision support systems in the 21st century* Volume 134. Prentice Hall, New Jersey.

Marriott, K., & Stuckey, P. (1998). *Programming with Constraints: an Introduction*. MIT Press.

Medard, C., & Sawhney, N. (2007). Airline crew scheduling from planning to operations. *European Journal of Operational Research*, *183*, 1013–1027.

Mesquita, M., Moz, M., Paias, A., Paixão, J., Pato, M., & Respício, A. (2011). A new model for the integrated vehicle-crew-rostering problem and a computational study on rosters. *Journal of Scheduling*, *14*, 319–334.

Metropolis, N., Rosenbluth, A., Rosenbluth, M., Teller, A., & Teller, E. (1953). Equation of state calculations by fast computing machines. *The Journal of Chemical Physics*, *21*, 1087.

Monfroglio, A. (1996). Hybrid genetic algorithms for a rostering problem. *Software: Practice and Experience*, *26*, 851–862.

Moz, M., & Pato, M. (2007). A genetic algorithm approach to a nurse rerostering problem. *Computers & Operations Research*, *34*, 667–691.

Moz, M., Respício, A., & Pato, M. (2009). Bi-objective evolutionary heuristics for bus driver rostering. *Public Transport*, *1*, 189–210.

Nemhauser, G., & Wolsey, L. (1988). *Integer and Combinatorial Optimization* Volume 18. Wiley, New York.

Ngai, E. W., & Wat, F. (2005). Fuzzy decision support system for risk analysis in e-commerce development. *Decision support systems*, *40*, 235–255.

Nurmi, K., Kyngäs, J., & Post, G. (2011). Driver rostering for a Finnish bus transportation company. In *IAENG Transactions on Engineering Technologies — Special Edition of the International Multiconference of Engineers and Computer Scientists 2011* (p. 15). World Scientific Volume 7.

Pedrosa, D., & Constantino, M. (2001). Days-off scheduling in public transport companies. In S. Voß, & J. Daduna (Eds.), *Computer-Aided Scheduling of Public Transport* (pp. 215–232). Springer, Berlin & Heidelberg Volume 505 of *Lecture Notes in Economics and Mathematical Systems*.

Power, D. (1997). Web-based decision support systems. *DSstar, The On-Line Executive Journal for Data-Intensive Decision Support*, *1*.

Power, D. (2002). *Decision Support Systems: Concepts and Resources for Managers*. Greenwood Publishing Group.

Power, D. J., & Kaparthi, S. (2002). Building web-based decision support systems. *Studies in Informatics and Control*, *11*, 291–302.

Prakash, J., Sinha, S., & Sahay, S. (1984). Bus transportation crews planning by goal programming. *Socio-Economic Planning Sciences*, *18*, 207–210.

Purshouse, R. C., & Fleming, P. J. (2003). Evolutionary many-objective optimisation: An exploratory analysis. In *The 2003 Congress on Evolutionary Computation (CEC 2003)* (pp. 2066–2073). IEEE Volume 3.

Randall, M., & Lewis, A. (2002). A parallel implementation of ant colony optimization. *Journal of Parallel and Distributed Computing*, *62*, 1421–1432.

Respício, A., Moz, M., & Pato, M. (2007). *A Memetic Algorithm for a Bi-objective Bus Driver Rostering Problem*. Centro de Investigação Operacional, Universidade de Lisboa.

Ryan, D. (1992). The solution of massive generalized set partitioning problems in aircrew rostering. *Journal of the Operational Research Society*, (pp. 459–467).

Sellmann, M., Zervoudakis, K., Stamatopoulos, P., & Fahle, T. (2000). Integrating direct CP search and CP-based column generation for the airline crew assignment problem. In *Proceedings of the CP-AI-OR'00* (pp. 163–170).

Serafini, P. (1994). Simulated annealing for multi objective optimization problems. In *Multiple Criteria Decision Making* (pp. 283–292). Springer.

Sodhi, M. S., & Norris, S. (2004). A flexible, fast, and optimal modeling approach applied to crew rostering at London Underground. *Annals of Operations Research*, *127*, 259–281.

Steinzen, I. (2007). *Topics in Integrated Vehicle and Crew Scheduling in Public Transport*. Ph.D. thesis University of Paderborn.

Stützle, T. (1998). Parallelization strategies for ant colony optimization. In *Proceedings of the 5th International Conference on Parallel Problem Solving from Nature, PPSN V* (pp. 722–731). Springer.

Stützle, T., & Hoos, H. H. (2000). Max–min ant system. *Future Generation Computer Systems*, *16*, 889–914.

Sundarraj, R. (2004). A web-based AHP approach to standardize the process of managing service-contracts. *Decision Support Systems*, *37*, 343–365.

Tadei, R., Alfieri, C. A., Baracco, P., Della Croce, F., Rizzante, F., & Sbodio, M. (1995). A genetic algorithm for the rostering problem (faro tender). In *AIRO Annual Conference*. Ancona, Italy.

Townsend, W. (1986). An application of the assignment model to bus crew rostering. *IMA Journal of Management Mathematics*, *1*, 45–52.

Townsend, W. (1988). An approach to bus-crew roster design in London Regional Transport. *Journal of the Operational Research Society*, (pp. 543–550).

Wolsey, L. (1998). *Integer Programming*. Wiley-Interscience.

Xie, L., Kliewer, N., & Suhl, L. (2012a). Integrated driver rostering problem in public bus transit. *Procedia-Social and Behavioral Sciences*, *54*, 656–665.

Xie, L., Naumann, M., & Suhl, L. (2012b). A stochastic model for rota scheduling in public bus transport. In *Proceedings of 2nd Stochastic Modeling Techniques and Data Analysis International Conference* (pp. 785–792).

Xie, L., & Suhl, L. (2014). Cyclic and non-cyclic crew rostering problems in public bus transit. *OR Spectrum*, . doi:10.1007/s00291-014-0364-9.

Yu, C. (2004). A web-based consumer-oriented intelligent decision support system for personalized e-services. In *Proceedings of the 6th International Conference on Electronic Commerce* (pp. 429–437). ACM.

Yunes, T., Moura, A., & De Souza, C. (2005). Hybrid column generation approaches for urban transit crew management problems. *Transportation Science*, *39*, 273–288.

Zitzler, E., Laumanns, M., & Thiele, L. (2001). SPEA2: Improving the strength Pareto evolutionary algorithm.

Zuse Institute Berlin (2014). MIPLIB 2013. ZIB: http://miplib.zib.de/miplib2003/index.php. Last retrieved 02.03.2014.

A. Additional Results

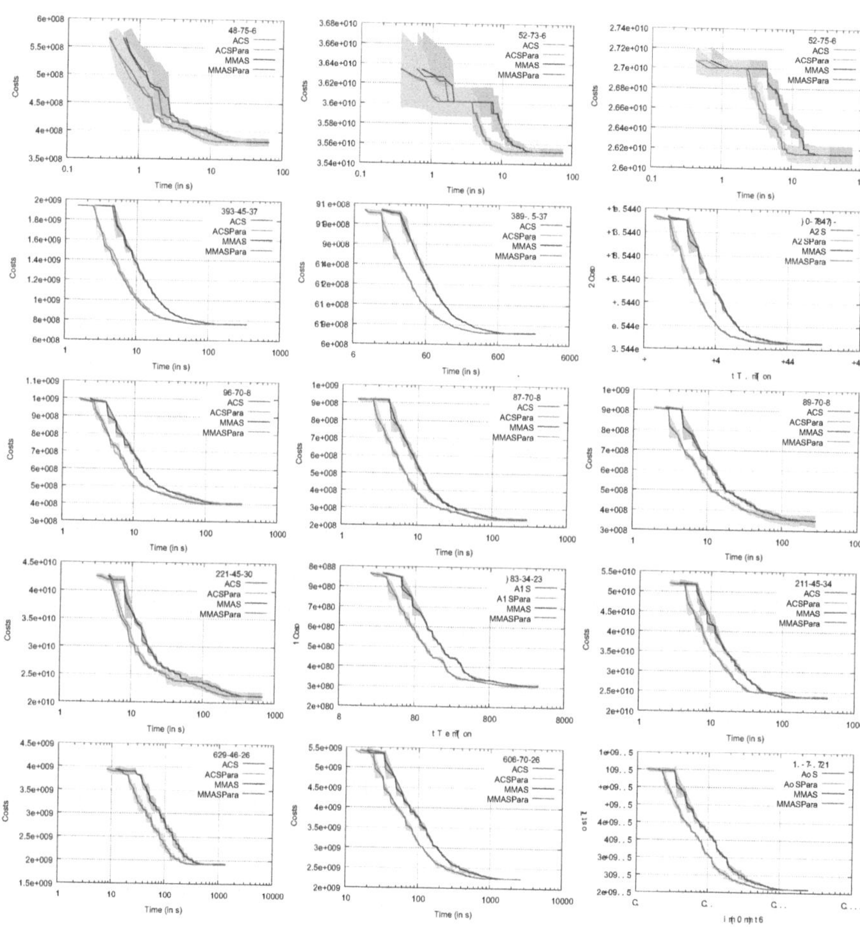

Figure A.1. Behavior of all ACO-algorithms with parallelization vs. without it for all instances (logarithmic x-scale).

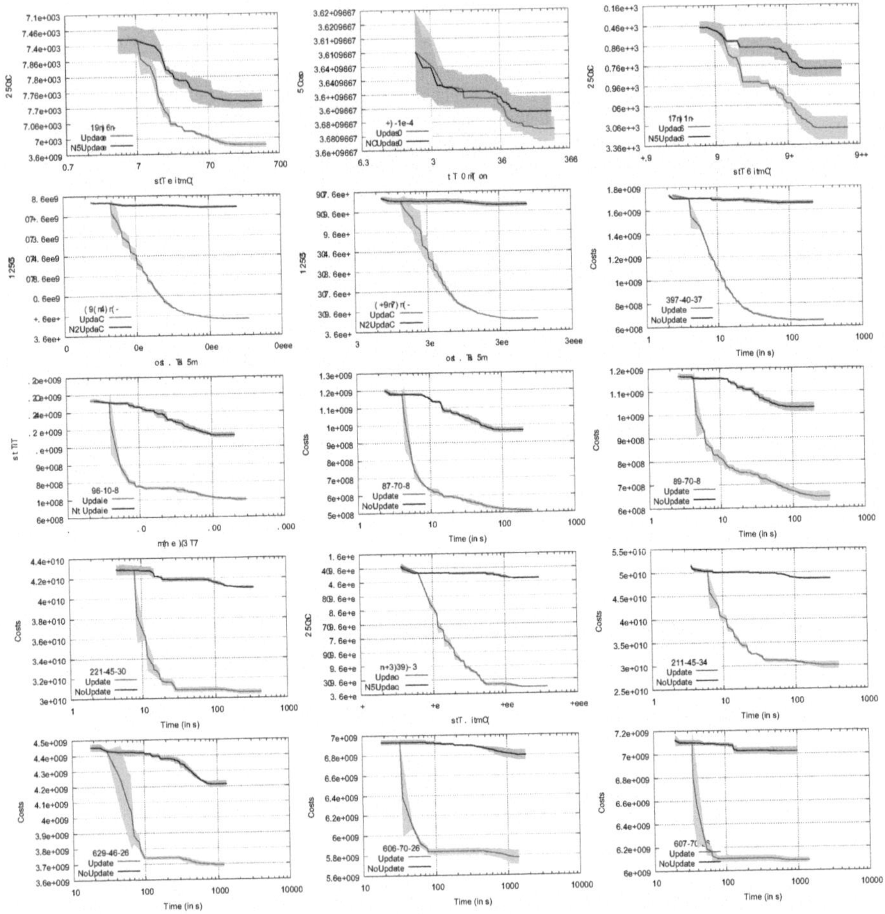

Figure A.2. Behavior of ACS with activated update of the heuristic information vs. with deactivated update for all instances (logarithmic x-scale).

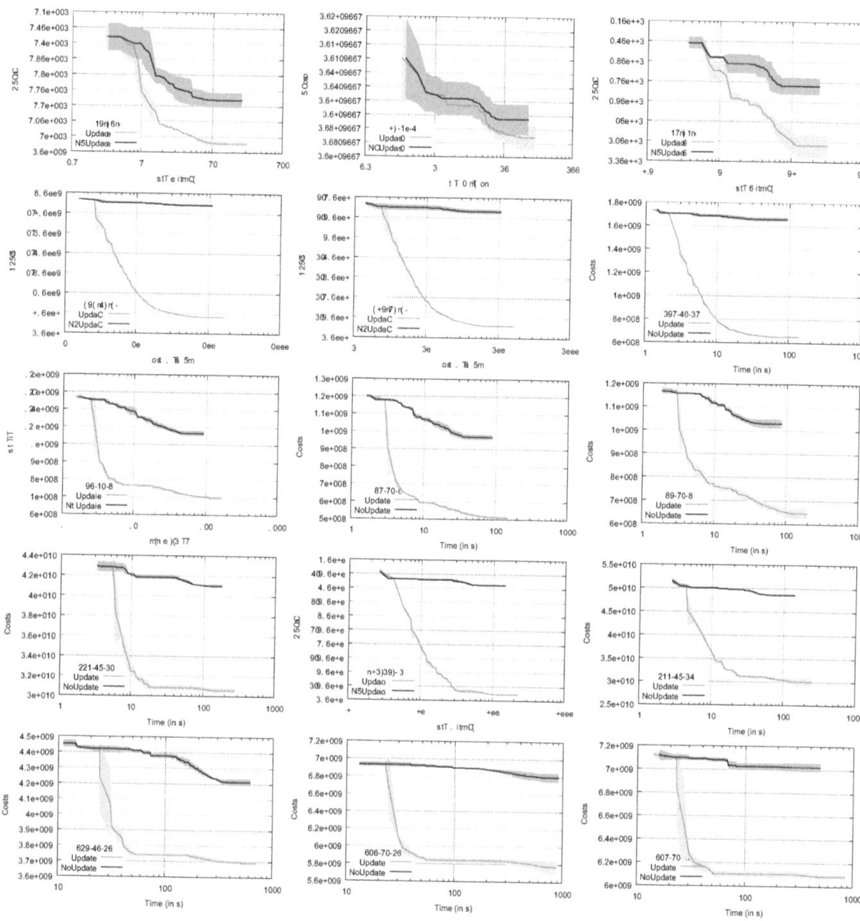

Figure A.3. Behavior of ACSPara with activated update of the heuristic information vs. with deactivated update for all instances (logarithmic x-scale).

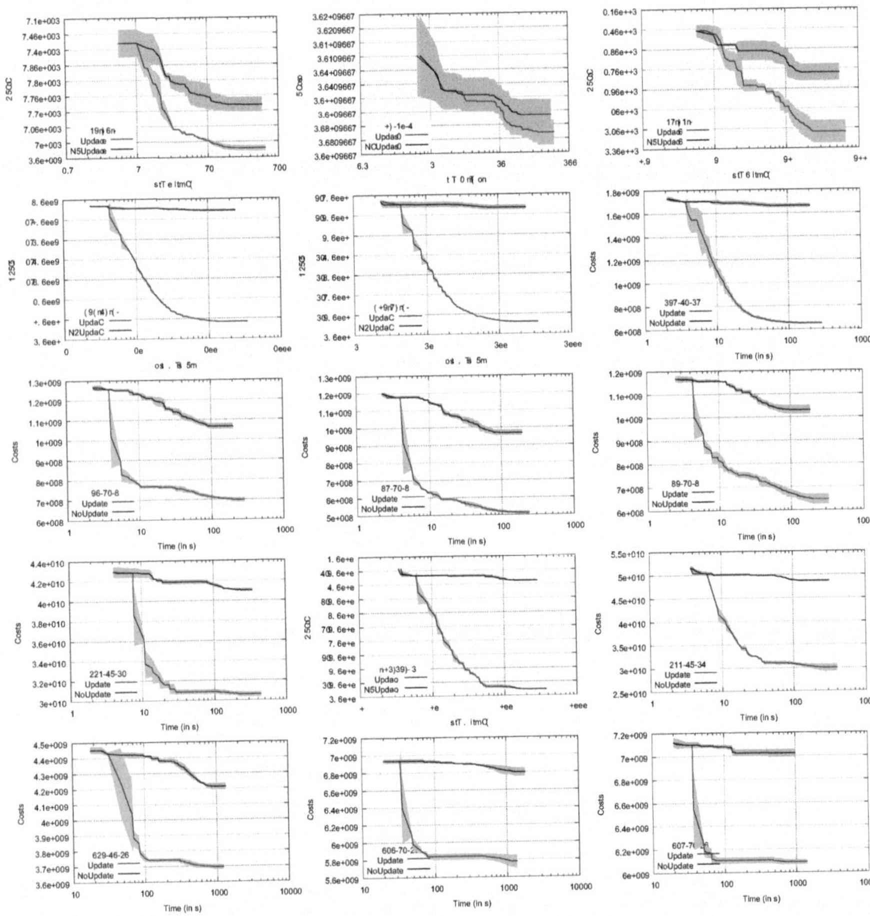

Figure A.4. Behavior of MMAS with activated update of the heuristic information vs. with deactivated update for all instances (logarithmic x-scale).

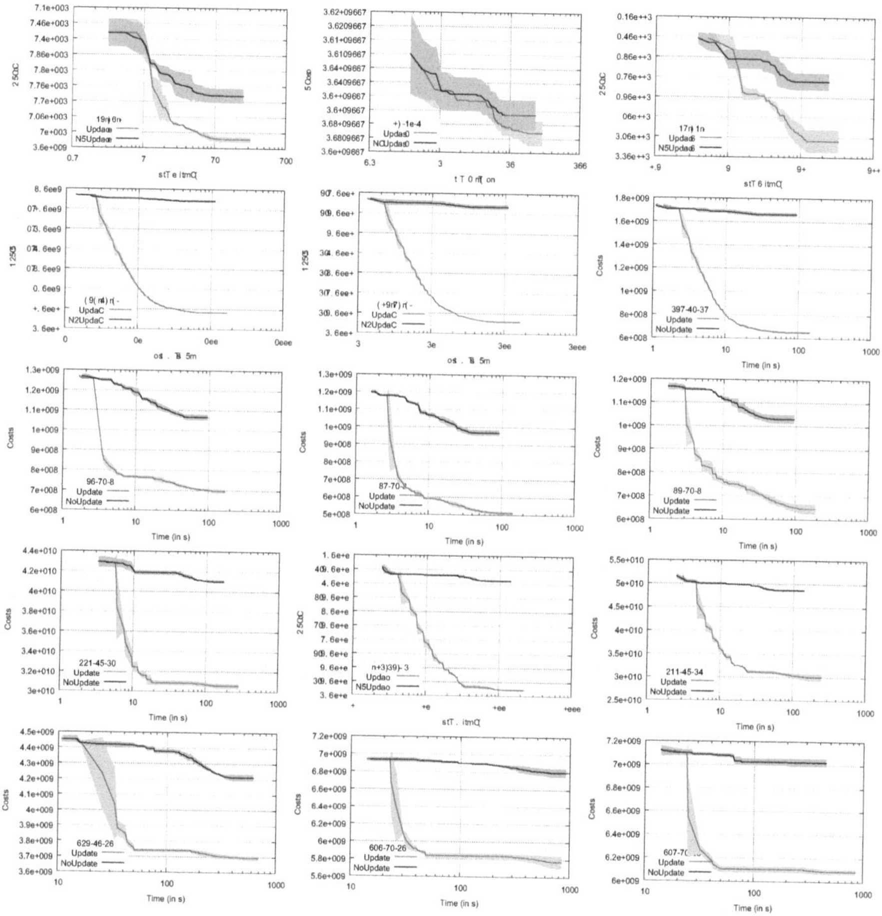

Figure A.5. Behavior of MMASPara with activated update of the heuristic information vs. with deactivated update for all instances (logarithmic x-scale).

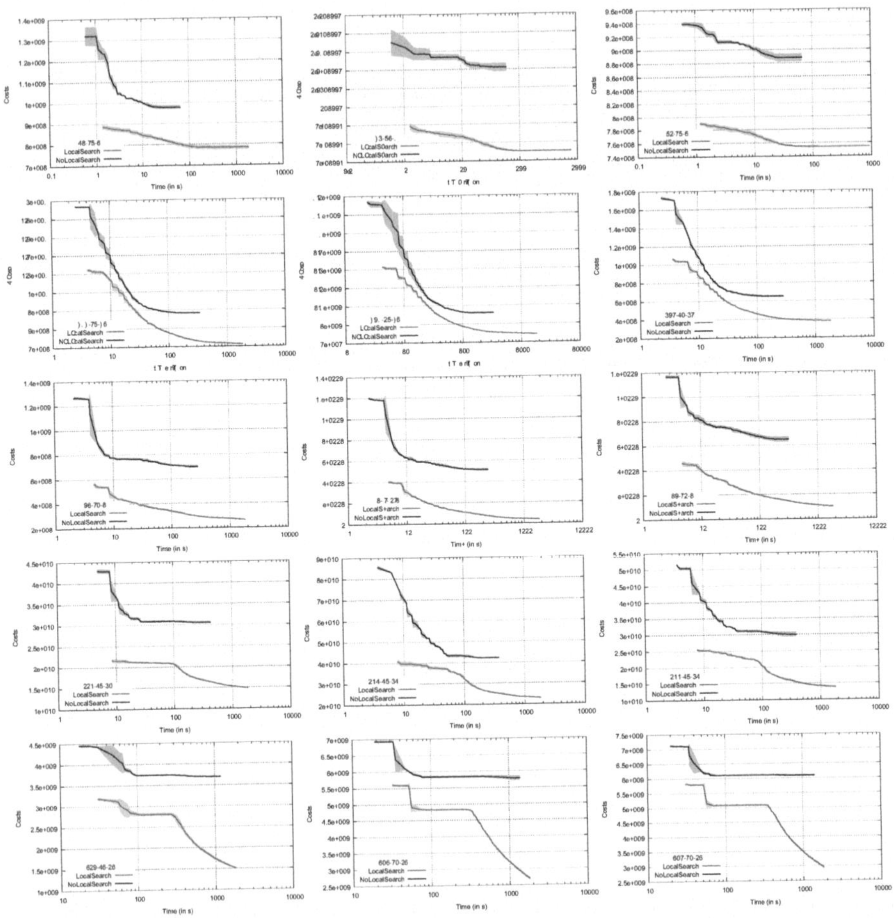

Figure A.6. Behavior of ACS with activated local search vs. with deactivated local search for all instances (logarithmic x-scale).

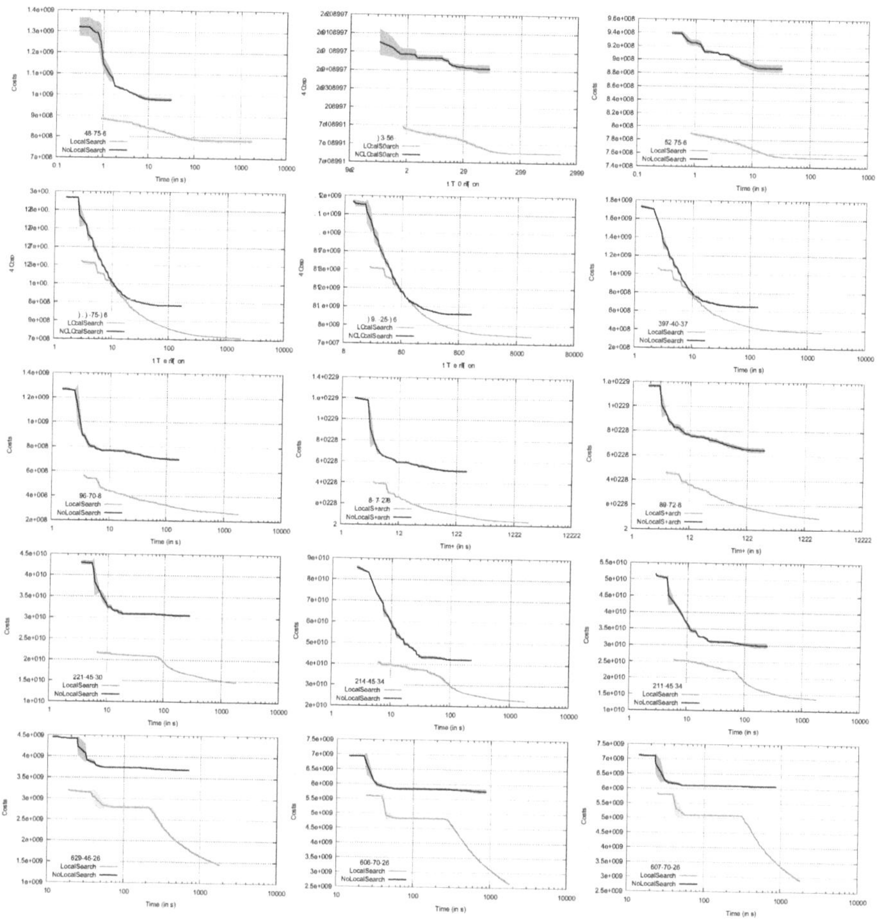

Figure A.7. Behavior of ACSPara with activated local search vs. with deactivated local search for all instances (logarithmic x-scale).

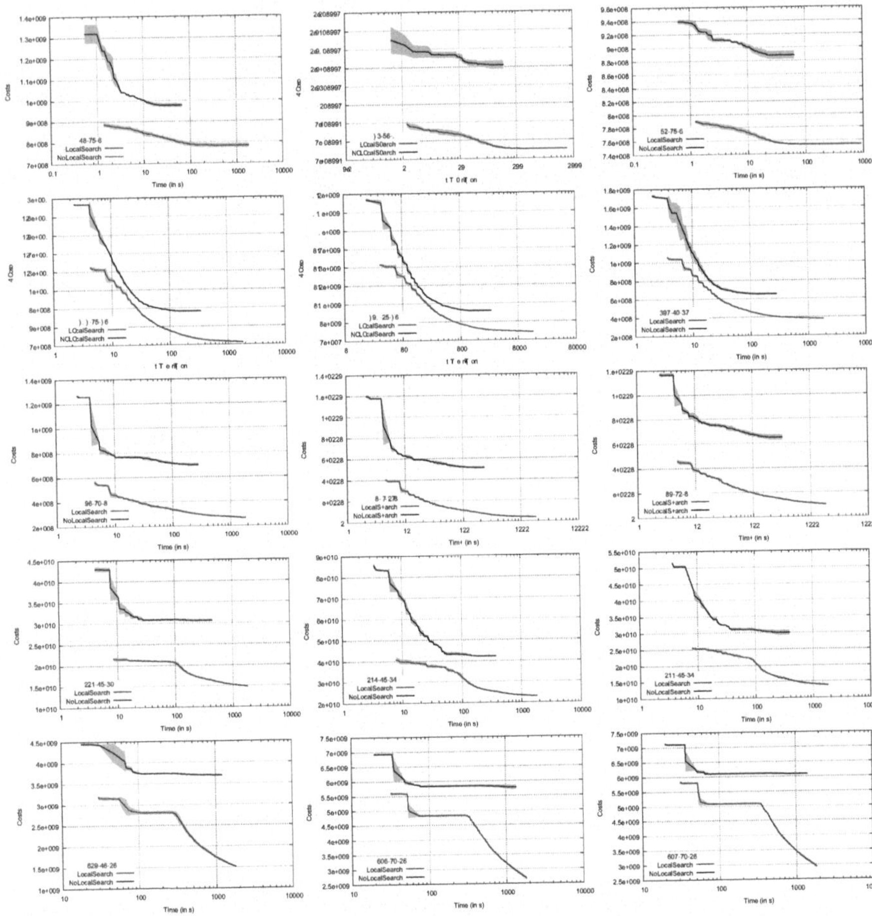

Figure A.8. Behavior of MMAS with activated local search vs. with deactivated local search for all instances (logarithmic x-scale).

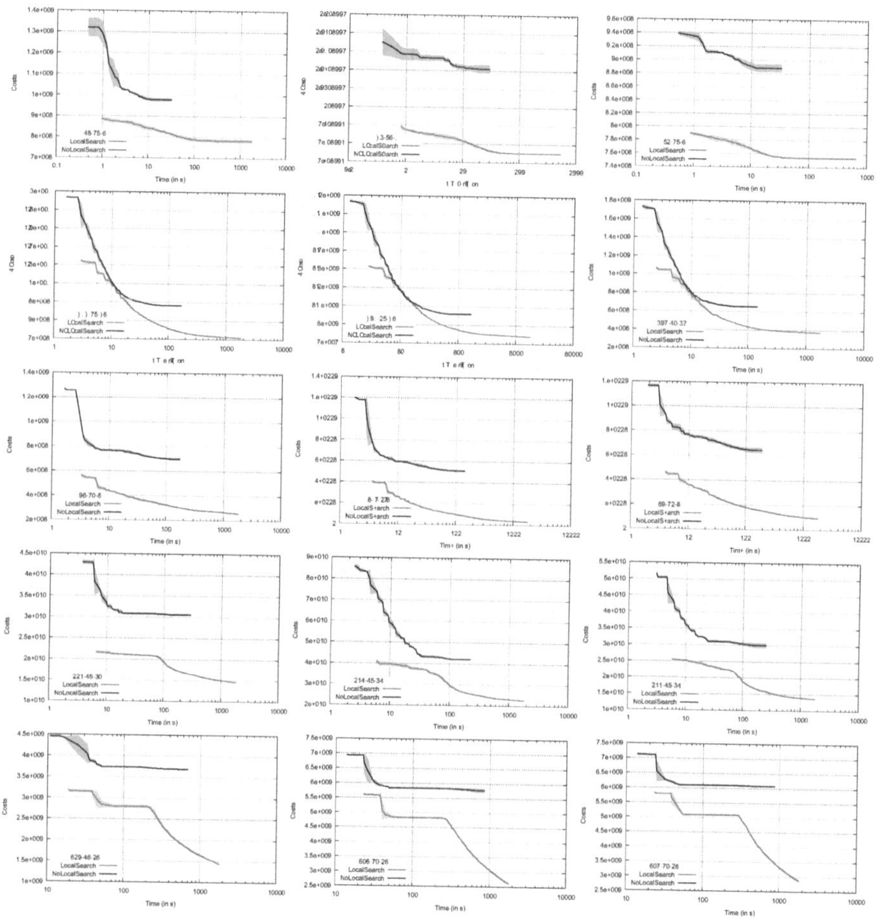

Figure A.9. Behavior of MMASPara with activated local search vs. with deactivated local search for all instances (logarithmic x-scale).

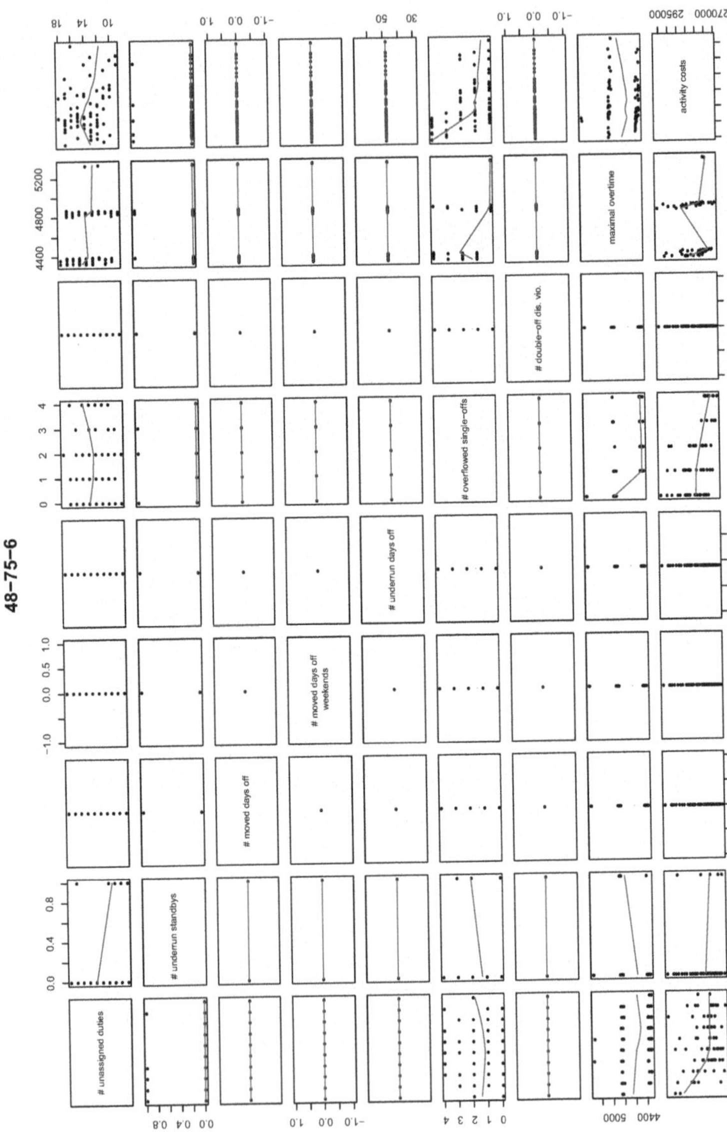

Figure A.10. Scatterplot of the results for the instance 48-75-6 solved by multi-objective simulated annealing.

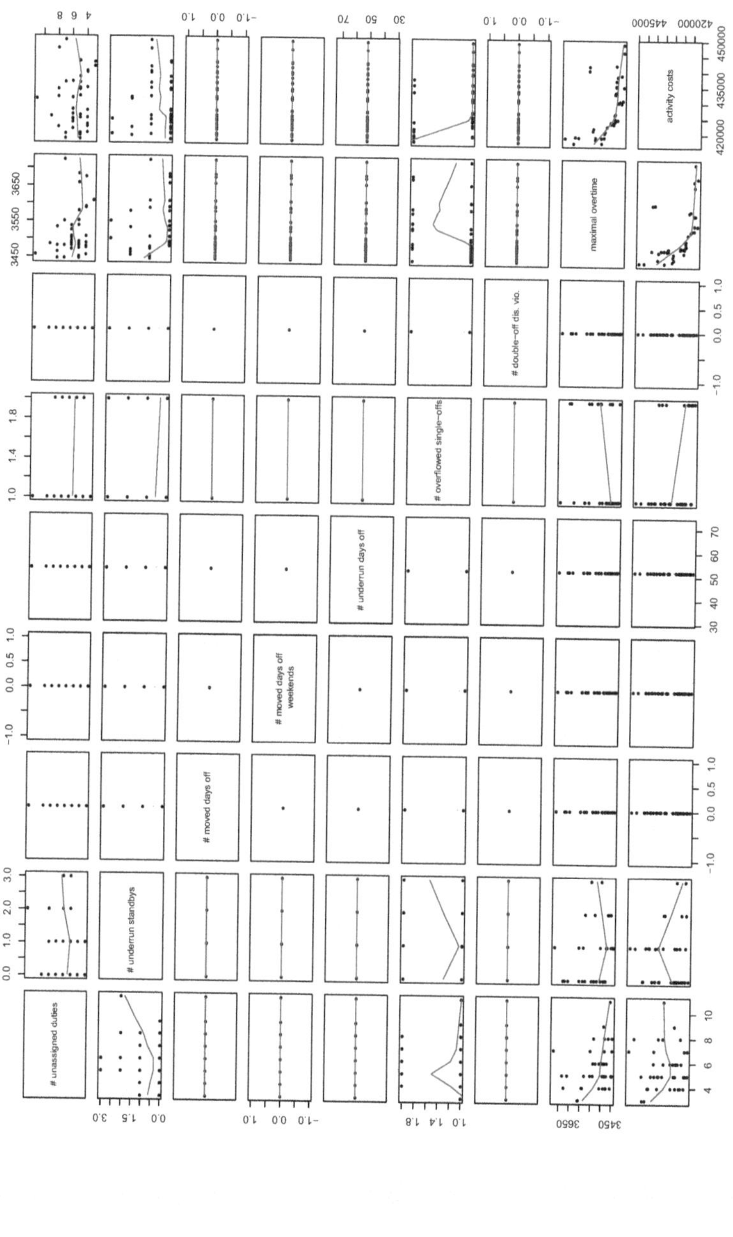

Figure A.11. Scatterplot of the results for the instance 52-73-6 solved by multi-objective simulated annealing.

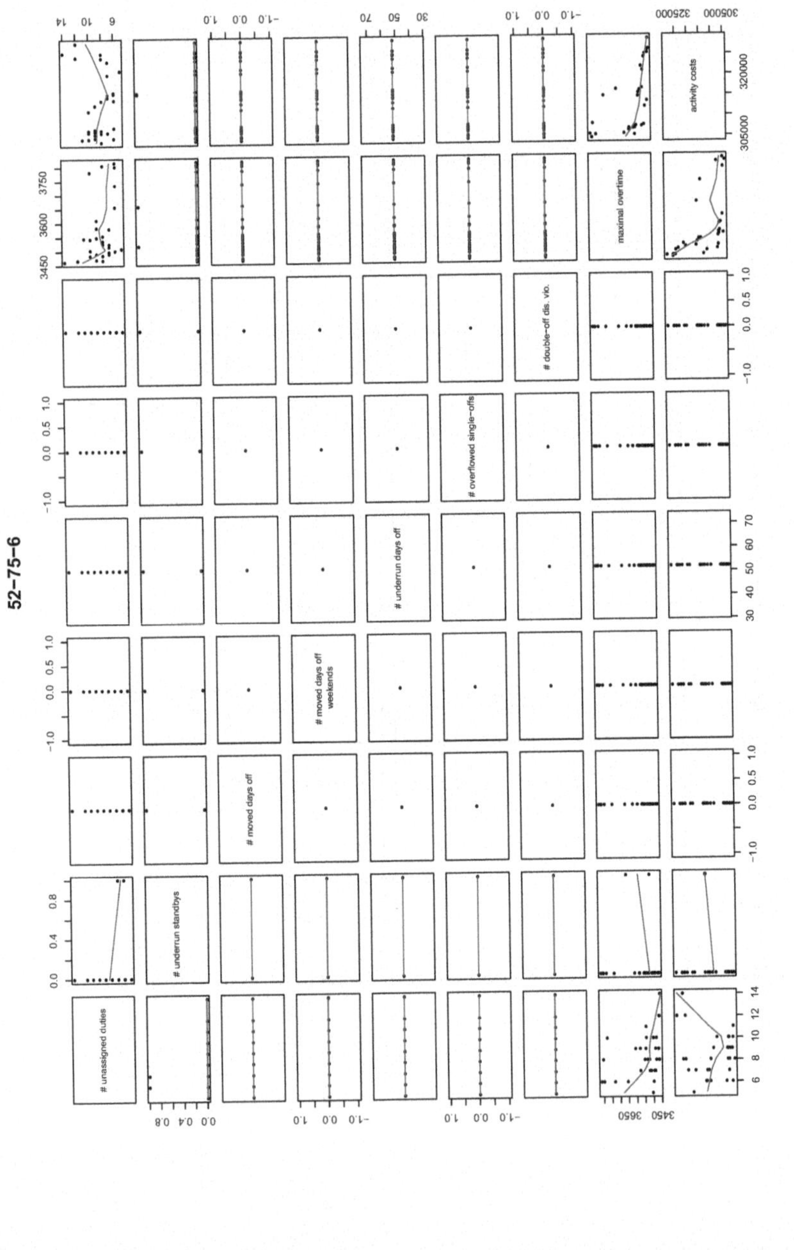

Figure A.12. Scatterplot of the results for the instance 52-75-6 solved by multi-objective simulated annealing.

Figure A.13. Scatterplot of the results for the instance 89-70-8 solved by multi-objective simulated annealing.

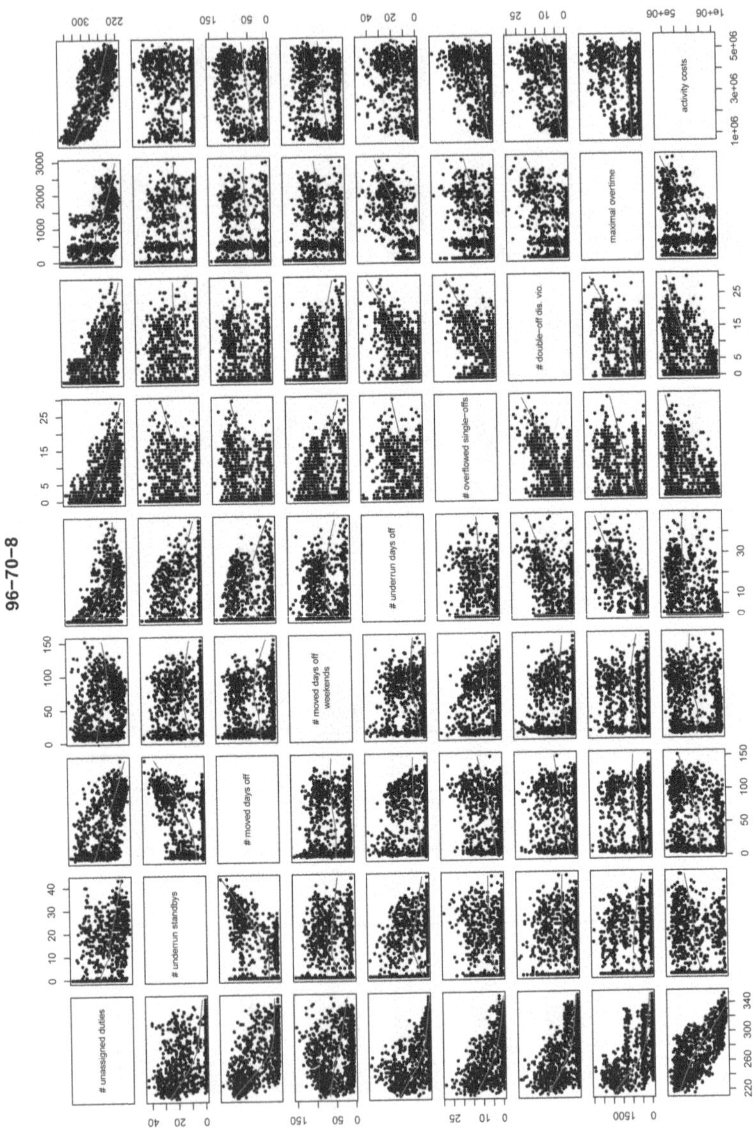

Figure A.14. Scatterplot of the results for the instance 96-70-8 solved by multi-objective simulated annealing.

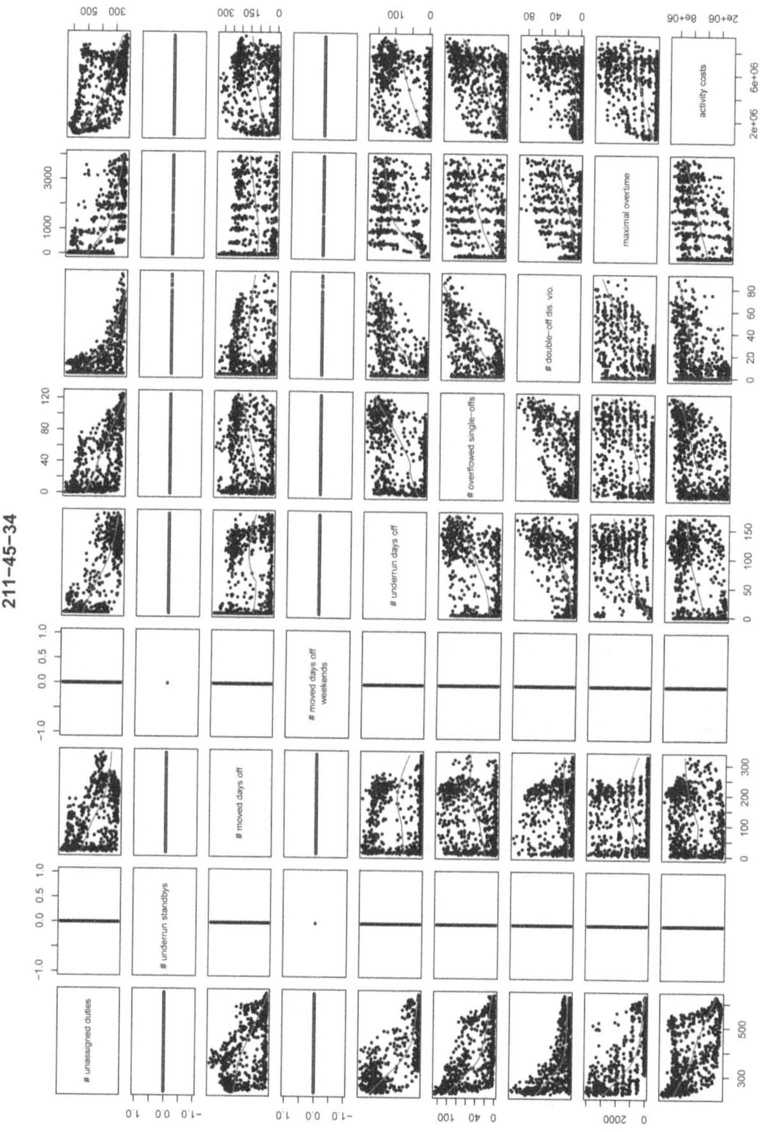

Figure A.15. Scatterplot of the results for the instance 211-45-34 solved by multi-objective simulated annealing.

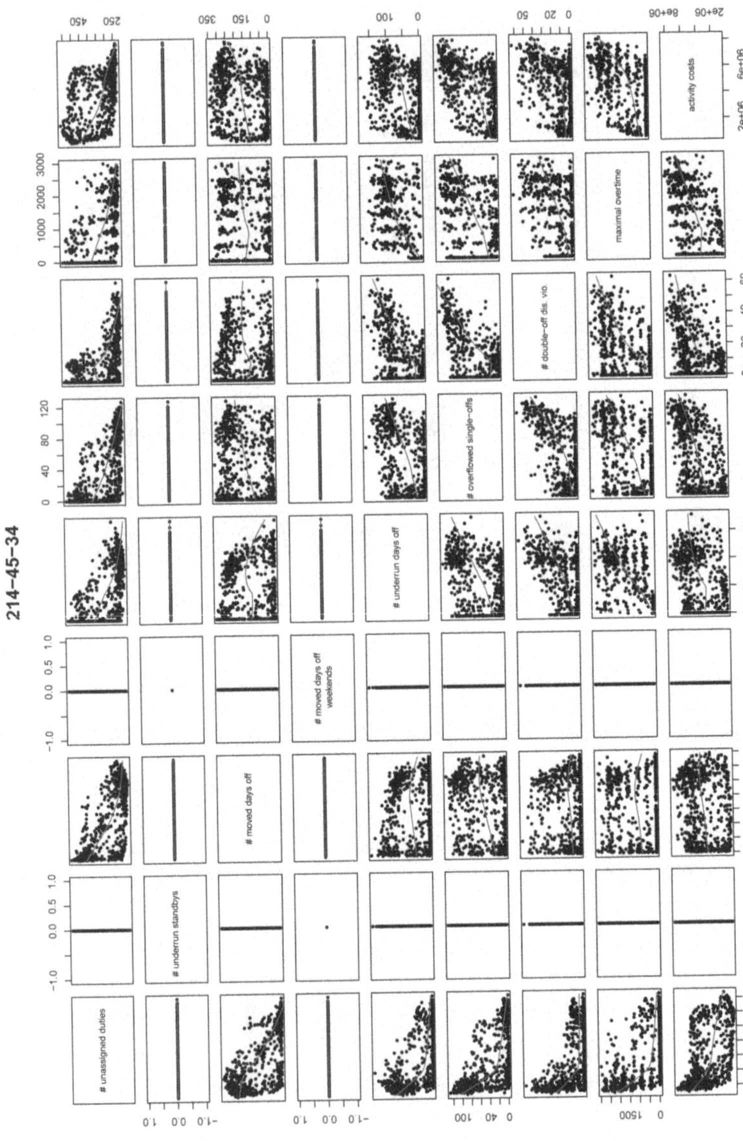

Figure A.16. Scatterplot of the results for the instance 214-45-34 solved by multi-objective simulated annealing.

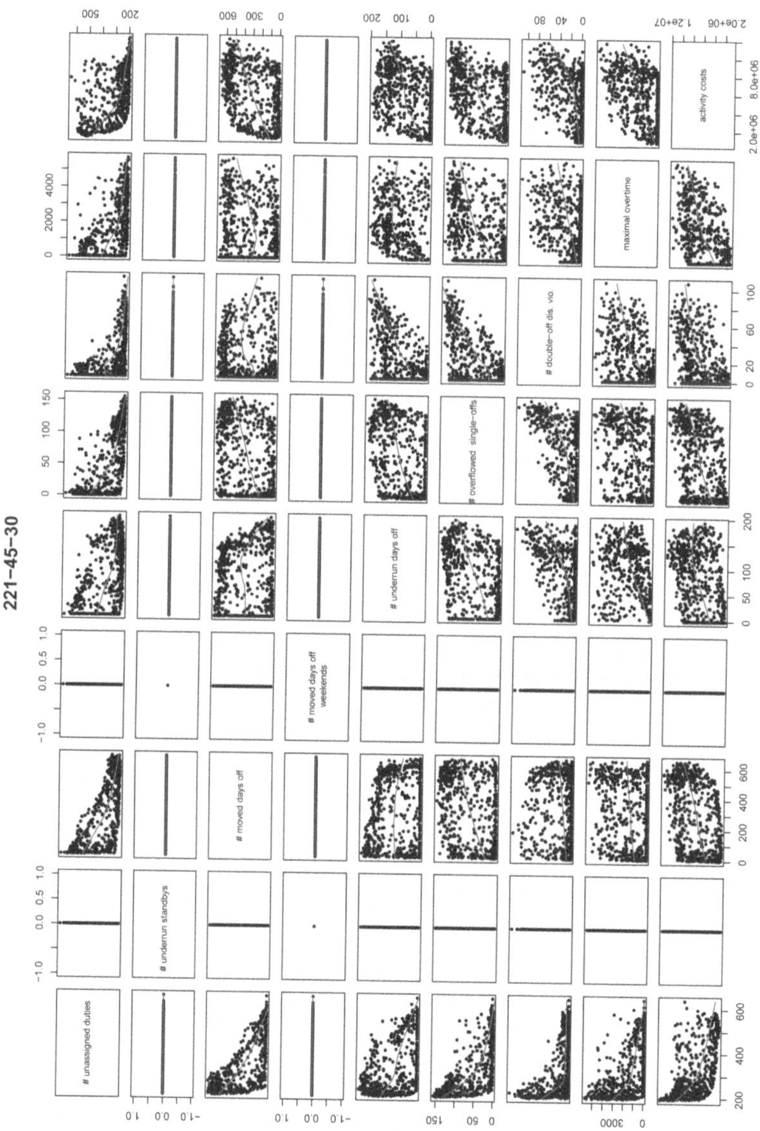

Figure A.17. Scatterplot of the results for the instance 221-45-30 solved by multi-objective simulated annealing.

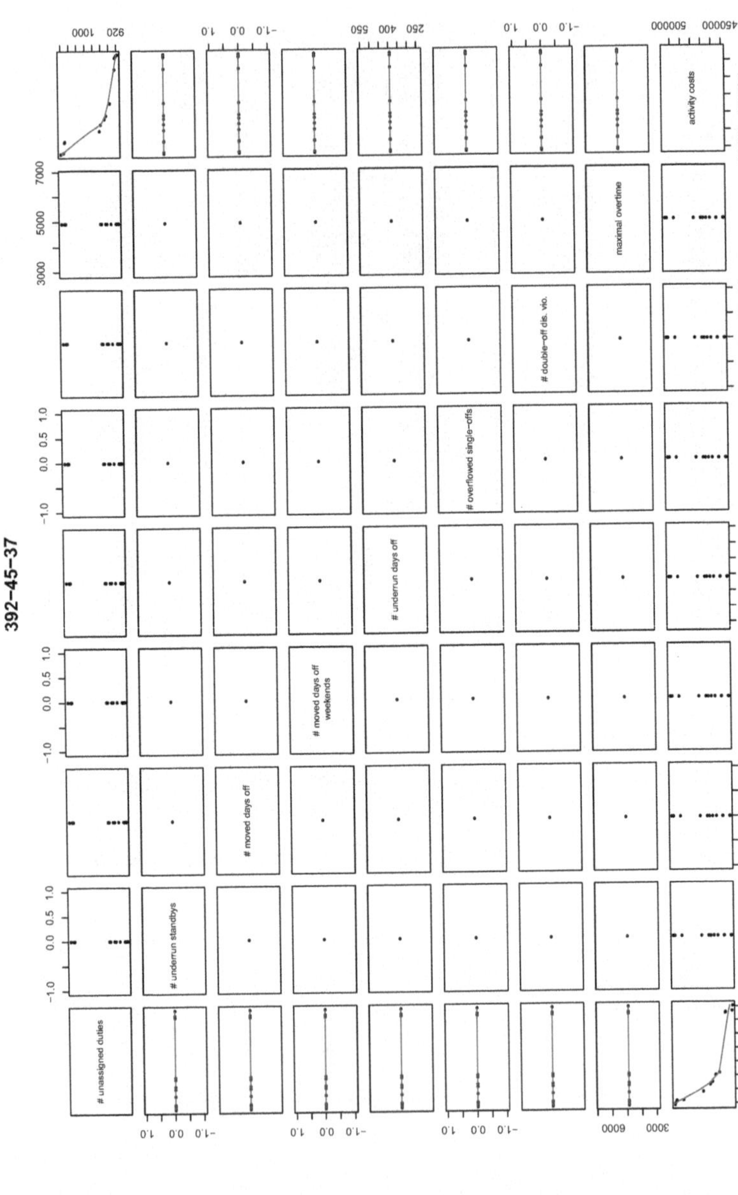

Figure A.18. Scatterplot of the results for the instance 392-45-37 solved by multi-objective simulated annealing.

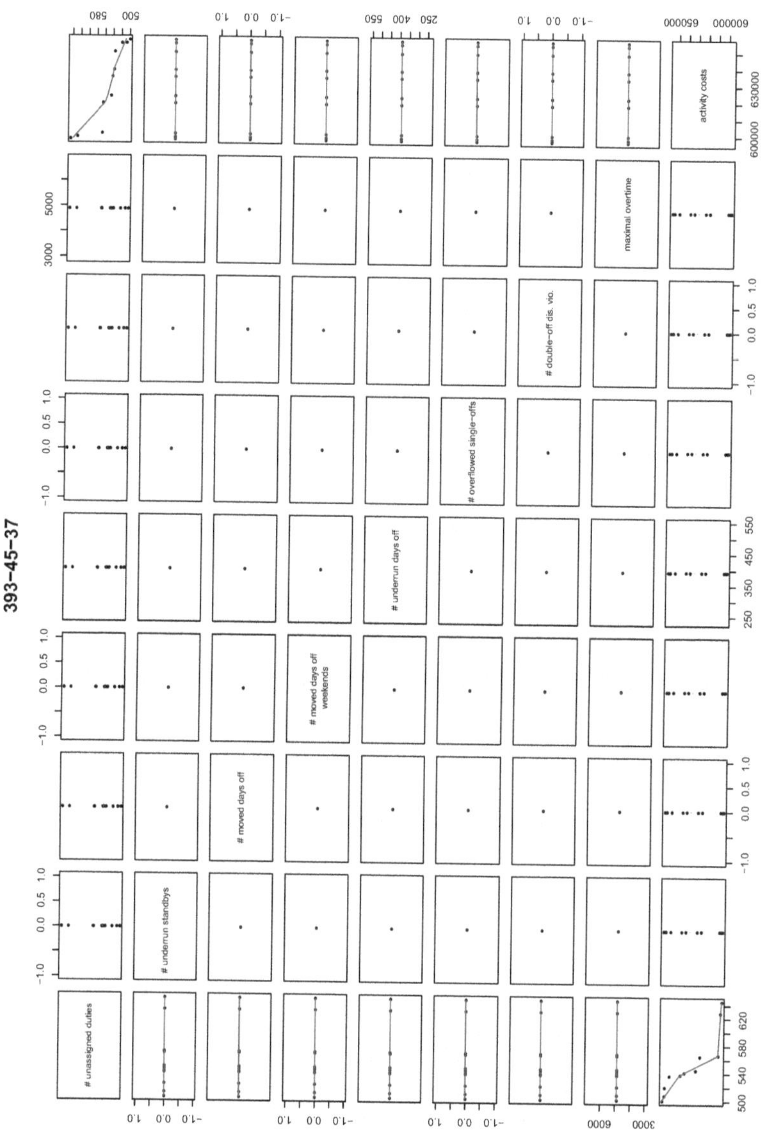

Figure A.19. Scatterplot of the results for the instance 393-45-37 solved by multi-objective simulated annealing.

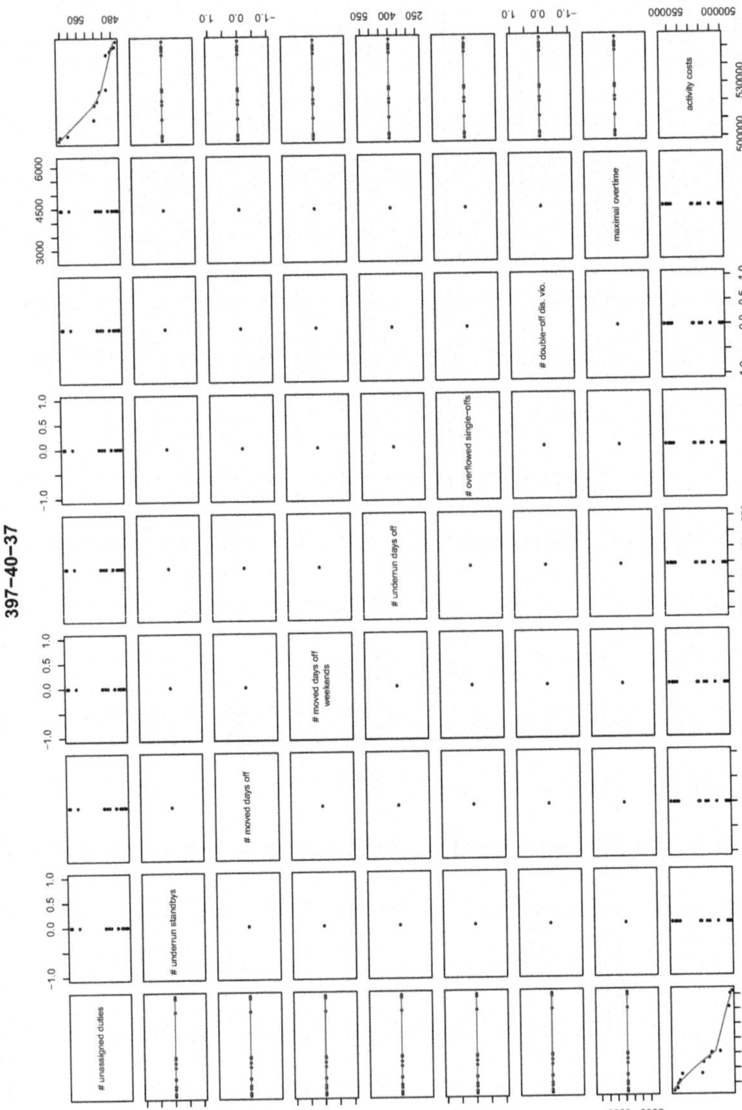

Figure A.20. Scatterplot of the results for the instance 397-40-37 solved by multi-objective simulated annealing.

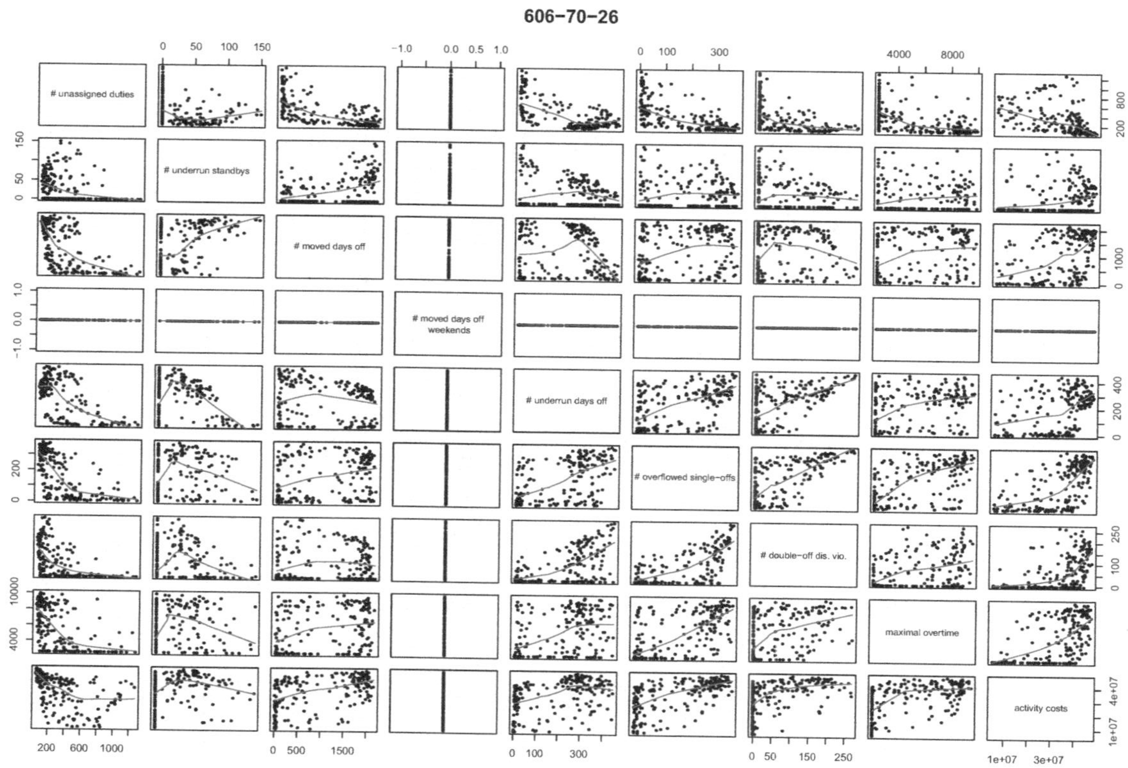

Figure A.21. Scatterplot of the results for the instance 606-70-26 solved by multi-objective simulated annealing.

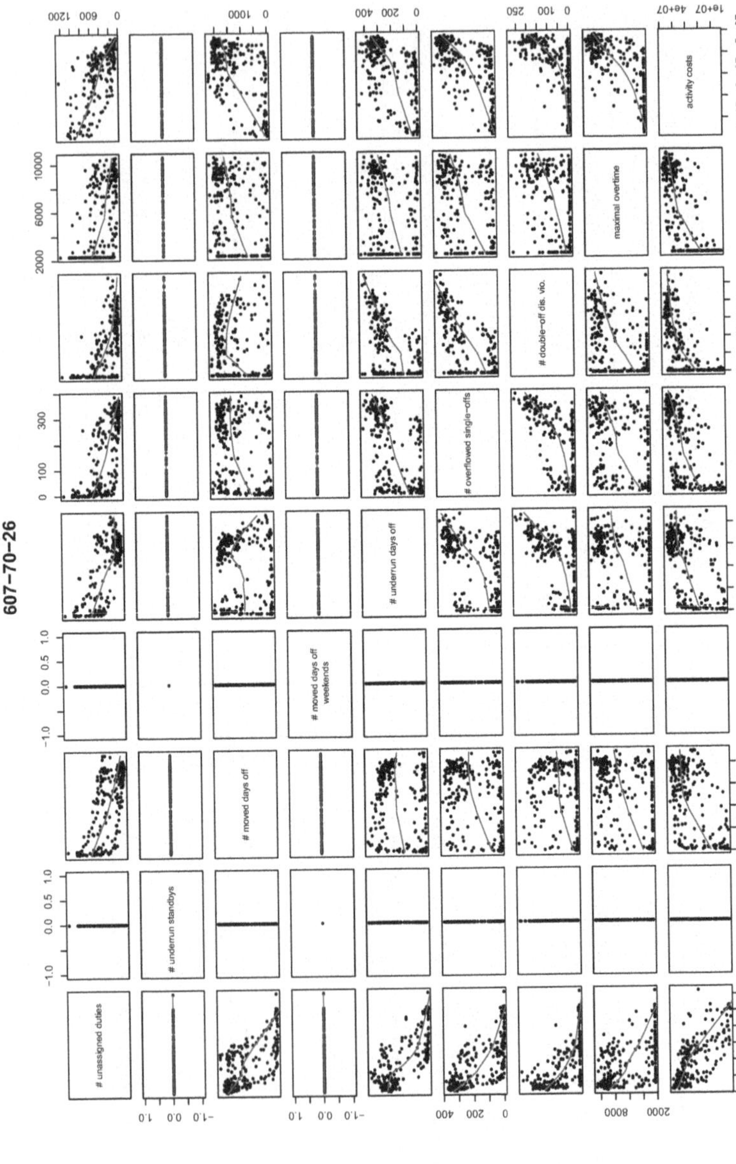

Figure A.22. Scatterplot of the results for the instance 607-70-26 solved by multi-objective simulated annealing.

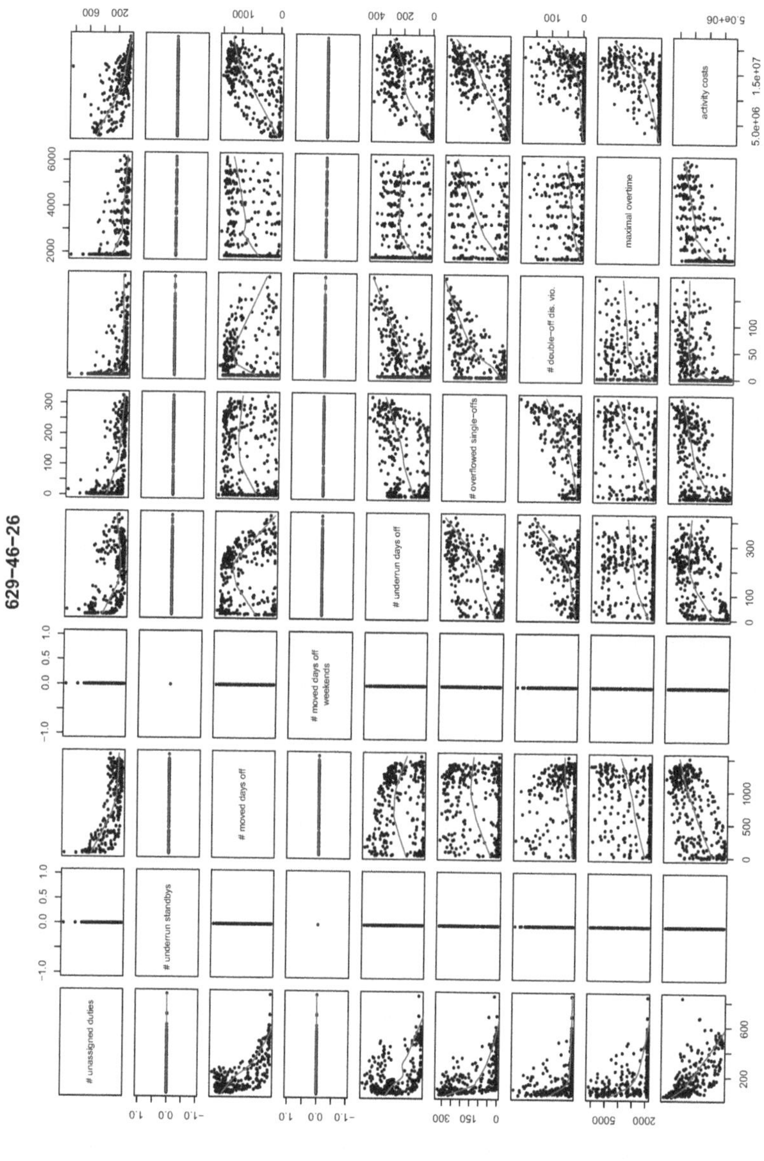

Figure A.23. Scatterplot of the results for the instance 629-46-26 solved by multi-objective simulated annealing.

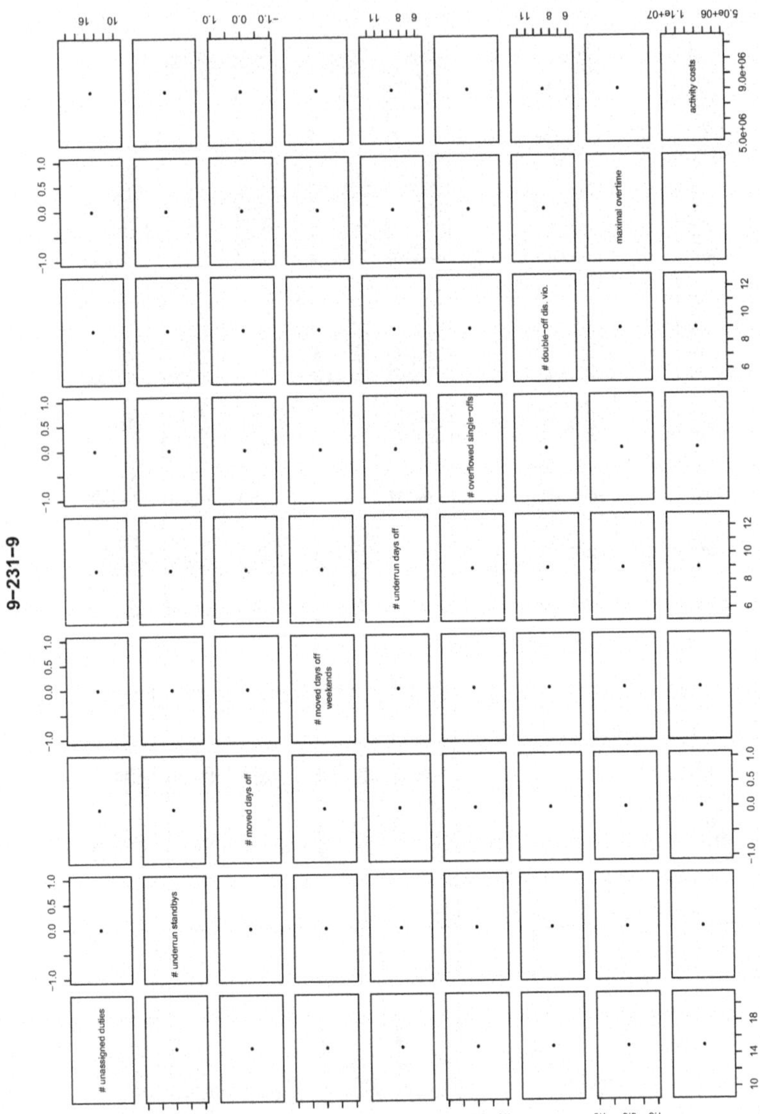

Figure A.24. Scatterplot of the results for the instance 9-231-9 solved by multi-objective simulated annealing.

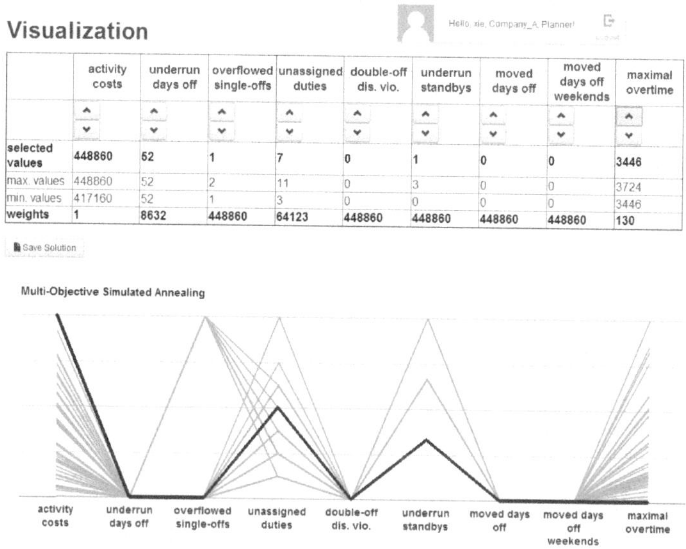

	activity costs	underrun days off	overflowed single-offs	unassigned duties	double-off dis. vio.	underrun standbys	moved days off	moved days off weekends	maximal overtime
selected values	**448860**	**52**	**1**	**7**	**0**	**1**	**0**	**0**	**3446**
max. values	448860	52	2	11	0	3	0	0	3724
min. values	417160	52	1	3	0	0	0	0	3446
weights	**1**	**8632**	**448860**	**64123**	**448860**	**448860**	**448860**	**448860**	**130**

Figure A.25. The set of non-dominated solutions for the instance 52-73-6 solved by multi-objective simulated annealing.

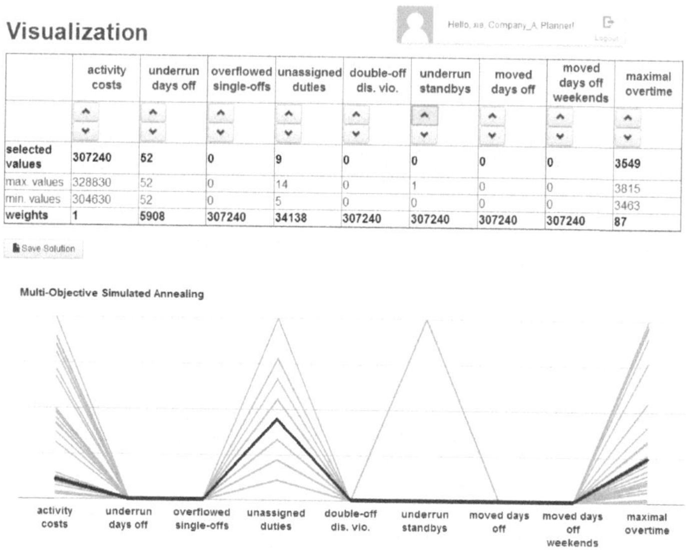

	activity costs	underrun days off	overflowed single-offs	unassigned duties	double-off dis. vio.	underrun standbys	moved days off	moved days off weekends	maximal overtime
selected values	**307240**	**52**	**0**	**9**	**0**	**0**	**0**	**0**	**3549**
max. values	328830	52	0	14	0	1	0	0	3815
min. values	304630	52	0	5	0	0	0	0	3463
weights	**1**	**5908**	**307240**	**34138**	**307240**	**307240**	**307240**	**307240**	**87**

Figure A.26. The set of non-dominated solutions for the instance 52-75-6 solved by multi-objective simulated annealing.

Visualization

	activity costs	underrun days off	overflowed single-offs	unassigned duties	double-off dis. vio.	underrun standbys	moved days off	moved days off weekends	maximal overtime
selected values	2966321	22	3	61	2	21	4	6	667
max. values	3963586	43	33	116	37	57	106	86	4258
min. values	958692	0	0	24	0	0	1	5	0
weights	1	134833	988774	48628	1483161	141253	741580	494387	4447

Save Solution

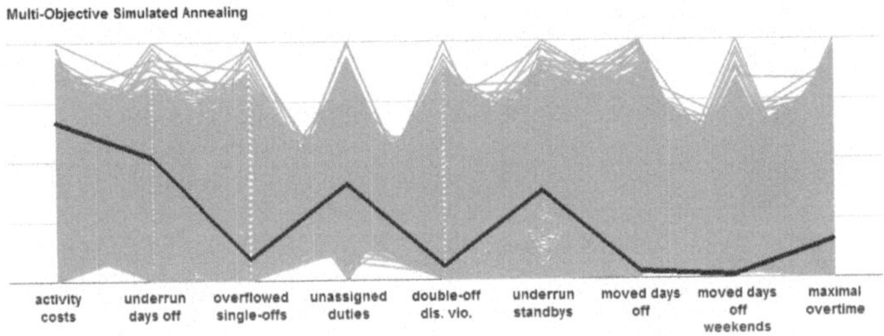

Figure A.27. The set of non-dominated solutions for the instance 87-70-8 solved by multi-objective simulated annealing.

Visualization

	activity costs	underrun days off	overflowed single-offs	unassigned duties	double-off dis. vio.	underrun standbys	moved days off	moved days off weekends	maximal overtime
selected values	5337412	41	0	74	15	0	94	45	1413
max. values	6355261	83	42	218	59	0	148	132	3370
min. values	459036	0	0	33	0	0	0	4	0
weights	1	130181	5337412	72127	355827	5337412	56781	118609	3777

Save Solution

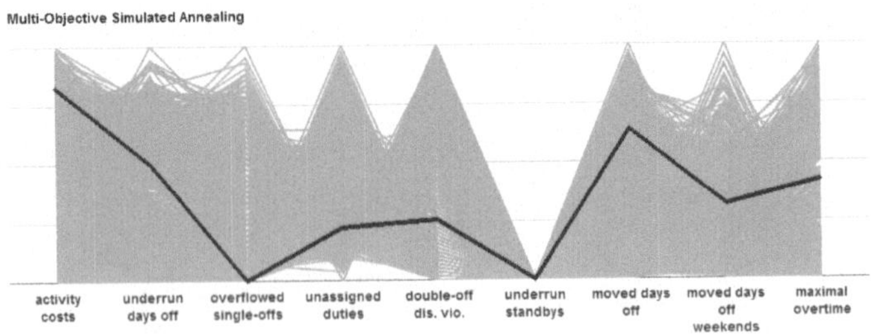

Figure A.28. The set of non-dominated solutions for the instance 89-70-8 solved by multi-objective simulated annealing.

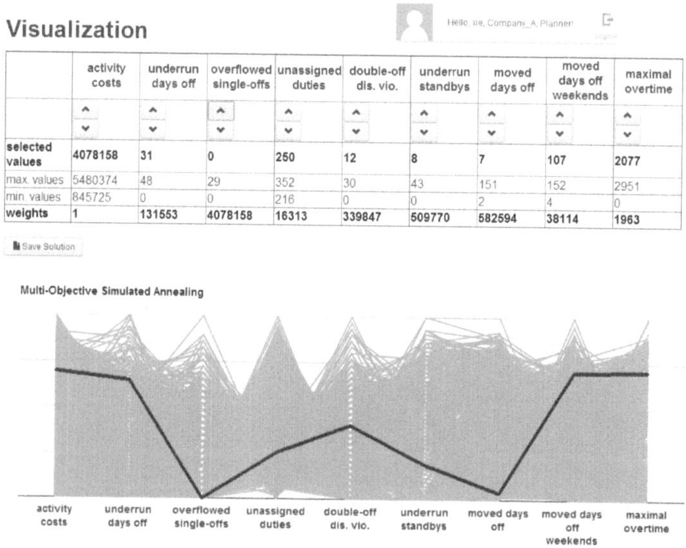

	activity costs	underrun days off	overflowed single-offs	unassigned duties	double-off dis. vio.	underrun standbys	moved days off	moved days off weekends	maximal overtime
selected values	4078158	31	0	250	12	8	7	107	2077
max. values	5480374	48	29	352	30	43	151	152	2951
min. values	845725	0	0	216	0	0	2	4	0
weights	1	131553	4078158	16313	339847	509770	582594	38114	1963

Figure A.29. The set of non-dominated solutions for the instance 96-70-8 solved by multi-objective simulated annealing.

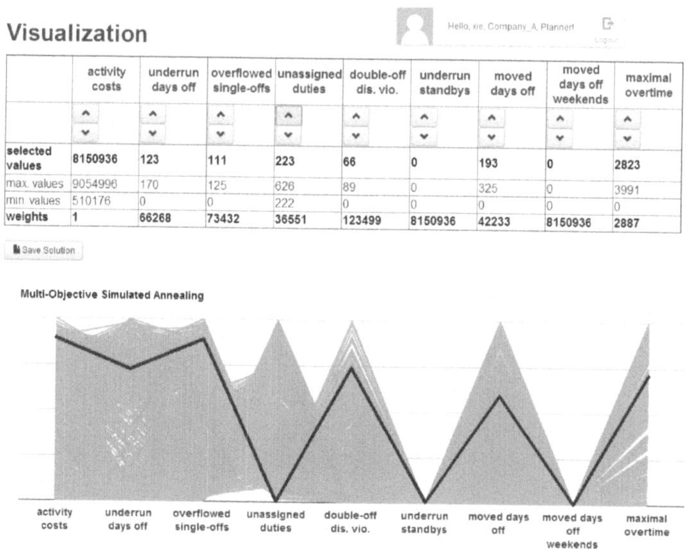

	activity costs	underrun days off	overflowed single-offs	unassigned duties	double-off dis. vio.	underrun standbys	moved days off	moved days off weekends	maximal overtime
selected values	8150936	123	111	223	66	0	193	0	2823
max. values	9054996	170	125	626	89	0	325	0	3991
min. values	510176	0	0	222	0	0	0	0	0
weights	1	66268	73432	36551	123499	8150936	42233	8150936	2887

Figure A.30. The set of non-dominated solutions for the instance 211-45-34 solved by multi-objective simulated annealing.

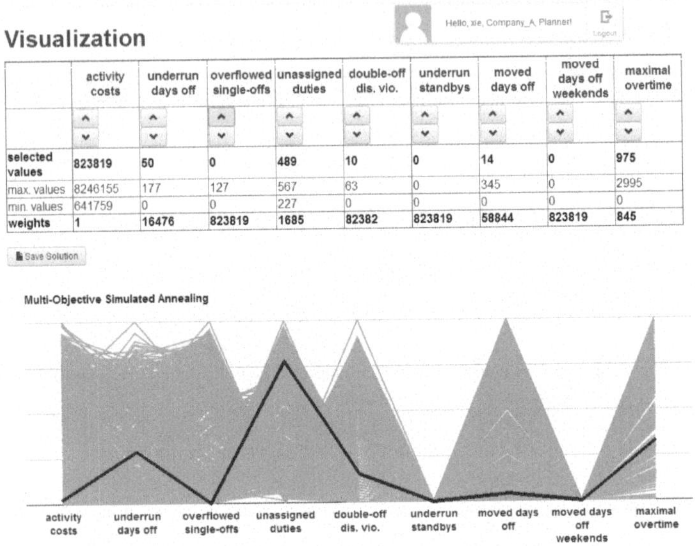

Figure A.31. The set of non-dominated solutions for the instance 214-45-34 solved by multi-objective simulated annealing.

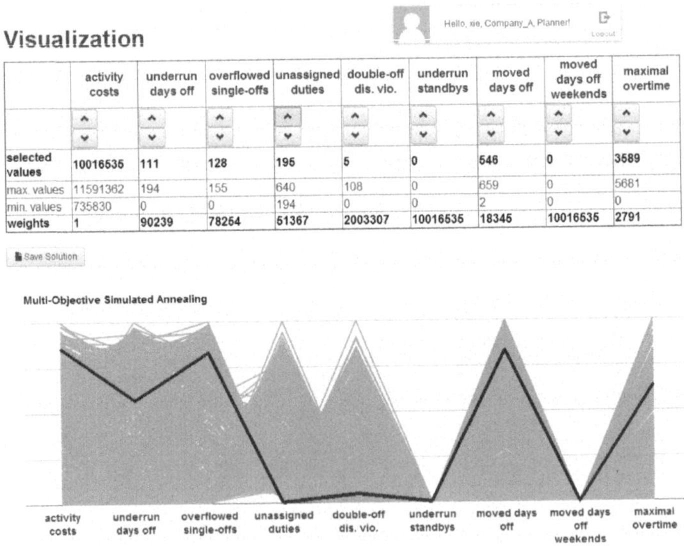

Figure A.32. The set of non-dominated solutions for the instance 221-45-34 solved by multi-objective simulated annealing.

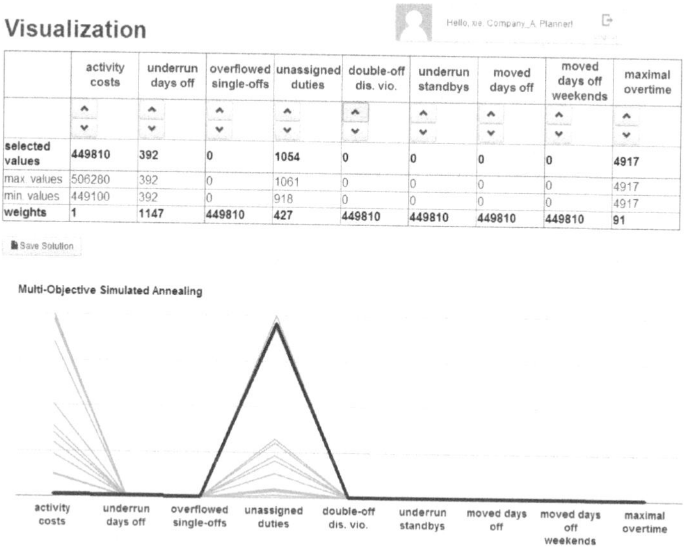

	activity costs	underrun days off	overflowed single-offs	unassigned duties	double-off dis. vio.	underrun standbys	moved days off	moved days off weekends	maximal overtime
selected values	449810	392	0	1054	0	0	0	0	4917
max. values	506280	392	0	1061	0	0	0	0	4917
min. values	449100	392	0	918	0	0	0	0	4917
weights	1	1147	449810	427	449810	449810	449810	449810	91

Figure A.33. The set of non-dominated solutions for the instance 392-45-37 solved by multi-objective simulated annealing.

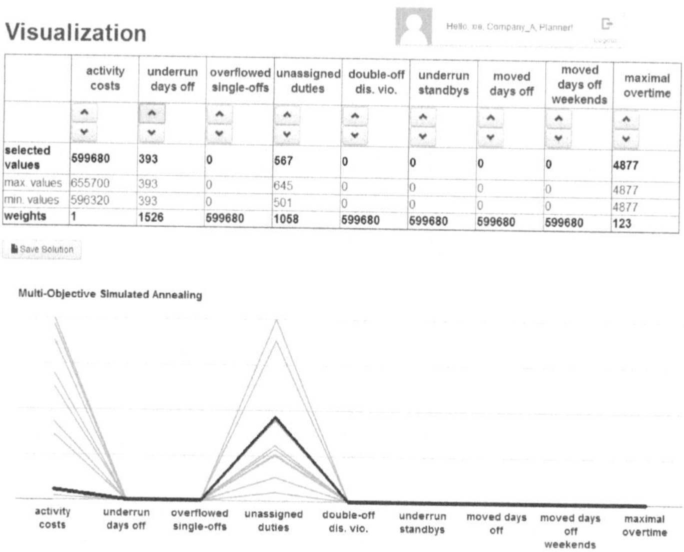

	activity costs	underrun days off	overflowed single-offs	unassigned duties	double-off dis. vio.	underrun standbys	moved days off	moved days off weekends	maximal overtime
selected values	599680	393	0	567	0	0	0	0	4877
max. values	655700	393	0	645	0	0	0	0	4877
min. values	596320	393	0	501	0	0	0	0	4877
weights	1	1526	599680	1058	599680	599680	599680	599680	123

Figure A.34. The set of non-dominated solutions for the instance 393-45-37 solved by multi-objective simulated annealing.

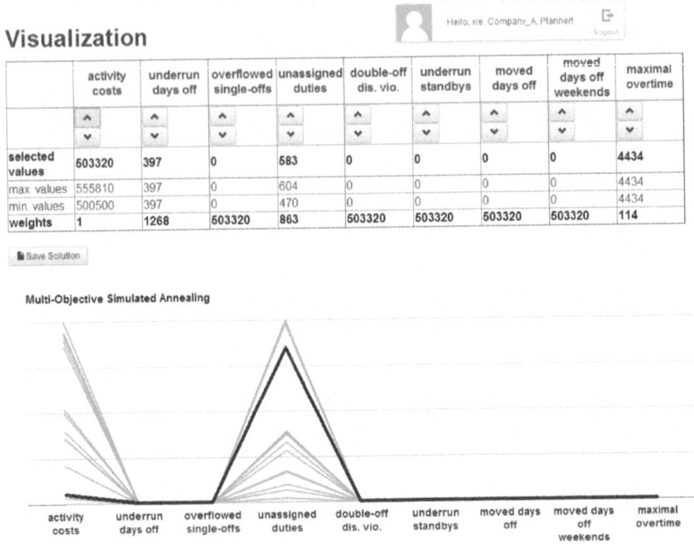

	activity costs	underrun days off	overflowed single-offs	unassigned duties	double-off dis. vio.	underrun standbys	moved days off	moved days off weekends	maximal overtime
selected values	503320	397	0	583	0	0	0	0	4434
max. values	555810	397	0	604	0	0	0	0	4434
min. values	500500	397	0	470	0	0	0	0	4434
weights	1	1268	503320	863	503320	503320	503320	503320	114

Figure A.35. The set of non-dominated solutions for the instance 397-40-37 solved by multi-objective simulated annealing.

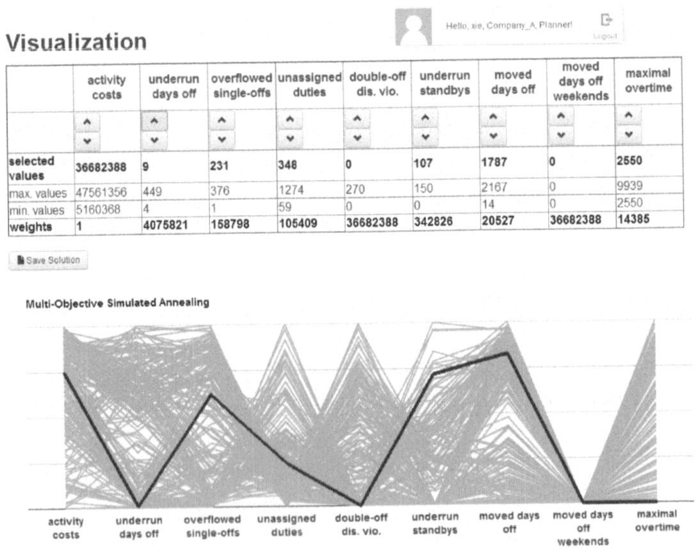

	activity costs	underrun days off	overflowed single-offs	unassigned duties	double-off dis. vio.	underrun standbys	moved days off	moved days off weekends	maximal overtime
selected values	36682388	9	231	348	0	107	1787	0	2550
max. values	47561356	449	376	1274	270	150	2167	0	9939
min. values	5160368	4	1	59	0	0	14	0	2550
weights	1	4075821	158798	105409	36682388	342826	20527	36682388	14385

Figure A.36. The set of non-dominated solutions for the instance 606-70-26 solved by multi-objective simulated annealing.

Visualization

Hello, xie, Company_A Planner!

	activity costs	underrun days off	overflowed single-offs	unassigned duties	double-off dis. vio.	underrun standbys	moved days off	moved days off weekends	maximal overtime
selected values	**30182584**	**11**	**282**	**534**	**57**	**0**	**1479**	**0**	**8162**
max. values	48811291	446	386	1248	280	0	2255	0	10578
min. values	3453559	2	0	47	0	0	15	0	2310
weights	**1**	**2743871**	**107030**	**56522**	**529519**	**30182584**	**20407**	**30182584**	**3698**

Save Solution

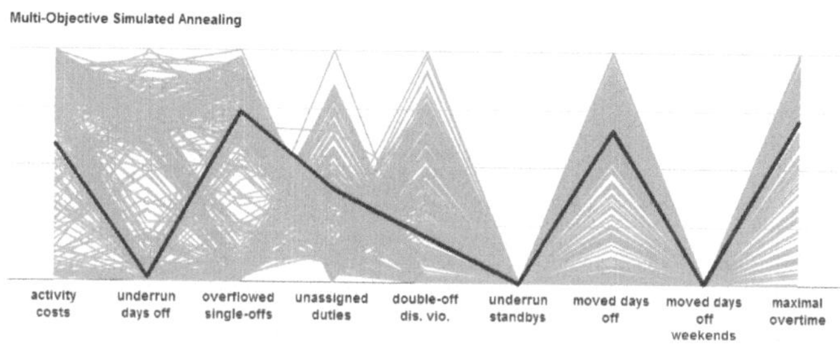

Figure A.37. The set of non-dominated solutions for the instance 607-70-26 solved by multi-objective simulated annealing.

Visualization

Hello, xie, Company_A Planner!

	activity costs	underrun days off	overflowed single-offs	unassigned duties	double-off dis. vio.	underrun standbys	moved days off	moved days off weekends	maximal overtime
selected values	**20594646**	**243**	**270**	**60**	**94**	**0**	**1338**	**0**	**3759**
max. values	21570279	410	325	837	186	0	1511	0	6170
min. values	1783868	8	2	42	0	0	2	0	1866
weights	**1**	**84752**	**76276**	**343244**	**219092**	**20594646**	**15392**	**20594646**	**5479**

Save Solution

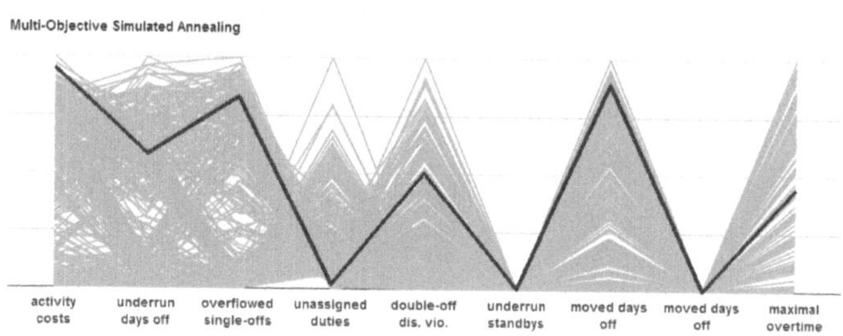

Figure A.38. The set of non-dominated solutions for the instance 629-46-26 solved by multi-objective simulated annealing.

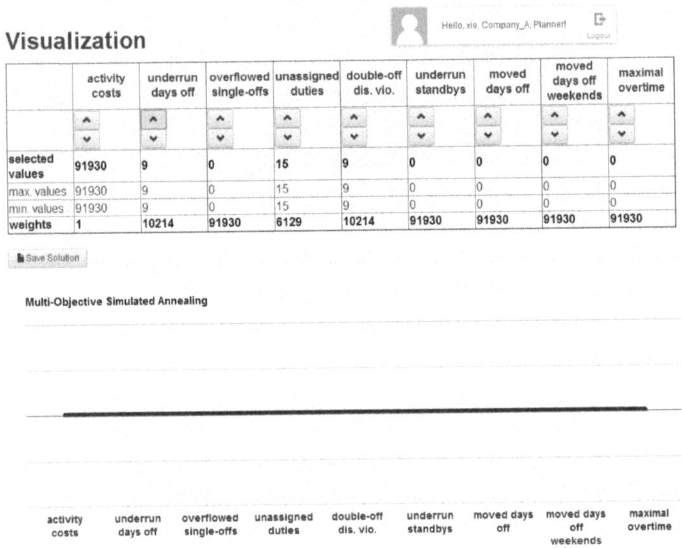

Figure A.39. The set of non-dominated solutions for the instance 9-231-9 solved by multi-objective simulated annealing.

The manufacturer's authorised representative in the EU is Springer Nature Customer Service Centre GmbH, Europaplatz 3, 69115 Heidelberg, Germany. If you have any concerns regarding our products, please contact ProductSafety@springernature.com

Printed and bound by CPI Group (UK) Ltd, Croydon, CR0 4YY
22/09/2026
02220990-0001